MEMORIA PRESS
HISTORY COLLECTION

THE BOOK OF THE ANCIENT GREEKS

Dorothy Mills

Edited by Memoria Press

www.MemoriaPress.com

THE BOOK OF THE ANCIENT GREEKS

Dorothy Mills
Edited by Memoria Press

ISBN 978-1-5477-0237-4

Cover illustration by Katie Khan

To
M. C. S. M.

PREFACE

THIS BOOK, like the first of the series, the *Book of the Ancient World,* was used in its original manuscript form by one of my history classes. It carries on the story of the way in which man has been learning how to live from the time of the coming of the Greeks to the loss of Greek independence in 146 B.C.

The spirit of a nation is expressed and its history recorded in three ways: in its political history, in its literature, and in its art. The aim of this book has been to use such parts of the political history of the Greeks, of their literature, and of their art as seem to have been the outward and visible signs of the spirit that inspired them.

It would not have been possible to write this book in this way without the kind permission of translators and publishers to use copyright translations. I gladly take this opportunity to acknowledge my debt to Professor Gilbert Murray and the Oxford University Press for the translation of the *Iphigenia in Tauris*; to Mr. A. W. Pickard, Cambridge, and the Oxford University Press for the translations from *Demosthenes*; to Mr. A. E. Zimmern and the Oxford University Press for passages from the *Greek Commonwealth*; and to the Trustees of the Jowett Fund and the Oxford University Press for translations from *Plato* and *Thucydides*; to Sir Arthur Evans for passages from an article in the *Monthly Review*; to Mr. G. S. Freeman for translations from the *Schools of Hellas* by the late Kenneth J. Freeman; to Mr. A. S. Way for a passage from the *Persians*; to Mr. A. W. Crawley for passages from the translation of the *Odyssey* by Butcher and Lang; to Mrs. Putnam for an extract from *The Lady*; to Miss Leslie White Hopkinson for her arrangement of one of the *Elegiacs of Solon*; to Messrs. Macmillan and Co. for translations from the *Iliad* by Lang, Leaf, and Myers, from *Pausanias* by Sir J. G. Frazer, from *Plato's Republic* by Davies and Vaughan, from the *Trial and Death of Socrates* by F. G. Church, from *Herodotus* by G. C. Macaulay, from *Xenophon* by H. G. Dakyns, and for various translations in *Greek Athletic Sports and Festivals* (E. N. Gardiner), *The City-State of the Greeks and Romans* (W. Warde Fowler), and *Our Hellenic Heritage* (H. R. James); to Messrs. J. M. Dent and Sons for translations from *Plutarch's Lives*; to Messrs. G. Bell and Sons for translations from *Aristophanes* by B. B. Rogers, from *Theocritus* by C. S. Calverley and from *Aristotle* by Sir F. G. Kenyon; to Messrs. George Allen and Unwin for translations from the *Homeric Hymns* by Andrew Lang; to Messrs. Edward Arnold and Co. for three poems from *Love, Worship and Death* by Sir Rennell Rodd; and to Messrs. Longmans, Green, and Co. for translations from *Select Epigrams from the Greek Anthology* by J. W. Mackail, and from *Greek History for Young Readers* by Alice Zimmern.

This book is only intended as an introduction to the history of Greek civilization, and the difficulty of my task has been to decide on what to omit. Everyone will not agree with me as to what I have taken and what I have left, but my aim will have been accomplished if the book should create a desire to know something more of the great heritage which has come to us from the Greeks.

Dorothy Mills
New York

CONTENTS

Crete & the Civilization of the Early Aegean World

The Mediterranean World

CHAPTER 1

THE MEDITERRANEAN WORLD

To THE PEOPLE of the ancient world the Mediterranean was "The Sea"; they knew almost nothing of the great ocean that lay beyond the Pillars of Hercules. A few of the more daring of the Phoenician navigators had sailed out into the Atlantic, but to the ordinary sailor from the Mediterranean lands, the ocean was an unknown region, believed to be a sea of darkness, the abode of terrible monsters and a place to be avoided. And then, as they believed the world to be flat, to sail too far would be to risk falling over the edge.

But the Mediterranean was familiar to the men of the ancient world; it was their best known highway. In those ancient times, the ocean meant separation; it cut off the known world from the mysterious unknown, but the Mediterranean did not divide; it was, on the contrary, the chief means of communication between the countries of the ancient world. For the *world* was then the coast around the sea, and first the Phoenicians and later the Greeks sailed backwards and forwards, north, south, east, and west, trading, often fighting, but always in contact with the islands and coasts. Egypt, Carthage, Athens, and Rome were empires of the Mediterranean world; and the very name *Mediterranean* indicates its position; it was the sea in the "middle of the world."

In the summer, the Mediterranean is almost like a lake, with its calm waters and its blue and sunny sky; but it is not always friendly and gentle. The Greeks said of it that it was "a lake when the gods are kind, and an ocean when they are spiteful," and the sailors who crossed it had many tales of danger to tell. The coast of the Mediterranean, especially in the North, is broken by capes and great headlands, by deep gulfs and bays; and the sea, more especially that eastern part known as the Aegean Sea, is dotted with islands, and these give rise to strong currents. These currents made serious difficulties for ancient navigators, and Strabo, one of the earliest writers of geography, in describing their troubles, says that "currents have more than one way of running through a strait." The early navigators had no maps or compass, and if they once got out of their regular course, they ran the danger of being swept along by some unknown current, or of being wrecked on some hidden rock. The result was that they preferred to sail as near the coast as was safe. This was easier, as the Mediterranean has almost no tides, and as the early ships were small and light, landing was generally a simple matter. The ships were run ashore and pulled a few feet out of the water, and then they were pushed out to sea again whenever the sailors were ready.

Adventurous spirits have always turned towards the West, and it was westwards across the Mediterranean that the civilization we have inherited slowly advanced. The early Mediterranean civilization is sometimes given the general name of Aegean, because its great centers were in the Aegean Sea and on the adjoining mainland. The largest island in the Aegean is Crete, and the form of civilization developed there is called Cretan or Minoan, from the name of one of the legendary sea-kings of Crete, while that which spread on the mainland is called Mycenaean from the great stronghold where dwelled the lords of Mycenae.

CHAPTER 2

CRETE

THE LONG NARROW ISLAND of Crete lies at what might be called the entrance to the Aegean Sea. This sea is dotted with islands which form stepping stones from the mainland of Europe to the coast of Asia Minor. Crete turns her face to these islands and her back to Egypt, and the Egyptians, who did not travel very much themselves, called the inhabitants the "Great Men of Keftiu." *Keftiu* means "*people at the back of.*" They were the men who dwelled beyond what was familiar to the Egyptians.

The Aegean world is a very beautiful one. The islands rise out of the sea like jewels sparkling in the sunshine. It is a world associated with spring, of "fresh new grass and dewey lotus, and crocus and hyacinths,"[1] a land where the gods were born, one rich in legend and myth and fairy tale, and, most wonderful of all, a world where fairy tales have come true.

In 1876 a telegram from an archaeologist flashed through the world, saying he had found the tomb of wide-ruling Agamemnon, King of Men and Tamer of Horses; and later on, in Crete, traces were found of the labyrinth where Theseus killed the Minotaur. The spade of the archaeologist brought these things into the light, and a world which had hitherto seemed dim, shadowy, and unreal suddenly came out into the sunshine.

[1] *Iliad*, XIV.

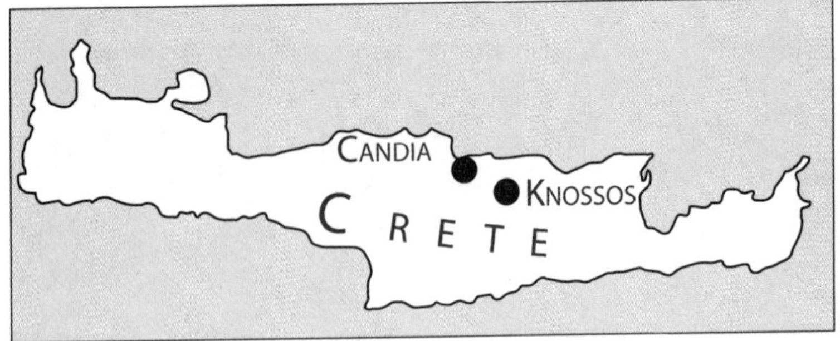

I. Legends of Crete

> There is a land called Crete in the midst of the wine-dark sea, a fair and rich land, begirded with water, and therein are many men innumerable, and ninety cities.[2]

LEGEND TELLS US that it was in this land that Zeus was born, and that a nymph fed him in a cave with honey and goat's milk. Here, too, in the same cave he was wedded, and from this marriage came Minos, the legendary hero-king of Crete. The name Minos is probably a title, like Pharaoh or Caesar, and this Minos, descendant of Zeus, is said to have become a great sea-king and tyrant. He ruled over the whole of the Aegean, and even demanded tribute from cities like Athens. But Theseus, helped by the king's daughter Ariadne, slew the Minotaur, the monster who devoured the Athenian youths and maidens, and so defeated the vengeance of the king. This Minos fully realized the importance of sea-power in the Aegean. Thucydides, the Greek historian, tells us that Minos was the first ruler who possessed a navy, and that in order to protect his increasing wealth, he did all that was in his power to clear the sea of pirates. Piracy was a recognized trade in those days, and when strange sailors landed anywhere, the inhabitants

[2] *Odyssey*, XIX.

would come down to the shore to meet them with these words: "Strangers, who are ye? Whence sail ye over the wet ways? On some trading enterprise or at adventure do ye rove, even as sea-robbers over the brine?"[3] Minos himself may have been a great pirate who subdued all the others and made them subject to him, but whether this were so or not, he was evidently not only a great sea-king; legend and tradition speak of him as a great Cretan lawgiver. Every year he was supposed to retire for a space to the cave of Zeus, where the Father of Gods and Men gave him laws for his land. It is because of the great mark left by Minos on the Aegean world that the civilization developed there is so often called Minoan, thus keeping alive forever the name of its traditional founder.

The labyrinth in which the Minotaur was slain was built by Daedalus, an Athenian. He was a very skillful artificer, and legend says that it was he who first thought of putting masts into ships and attaching sails to them. But he was jealous of the skill of his nephew and killed him, and so was forced to flee from Athens. He then came to Knossos where was the palace of Minos. There he made the labyrinth with its mysterious thousand paths, and he is also said to have "wrought in broad Knossos a dancing ground for fair-haired Ariadne."[4]

But Daedalus lost the favor of Minos, who imprisoned him with his son Icarus. The cunning of the craftsman, however, did not desert him, and Daedalus skillfully made wings for them both, and fastened them to their shoulders with wax, so that they flew away from their prison out of reach of the king's wrath. Icarus flew too near the sun, the wax melted, and he fell into the sea and was drowned; but Daedalus, we are told, reached Sicily in safety.

The Athenians believed that Theseus and Minos had really existed, for the ship in which, according to tradition, Theseus

---

[3] *Odyssey*, III.

[4] *Iliad*, XVIII.

made his voyage was preserved in Athens with great care until at least the beginning of the third century B.C. This ship went from Athens to Delos every year with special sacrifices, and one of these voyages became celebrated. Socrates, the philosopher, had been condemned to death, but the execution of the sentence was delayed for thirty days, because this ship was away, and so great was the reverence in which this voyage was held that no condemned man could be put to death during its absence. It was held that such an act would bring impurity on the city.

II. The Palaces of Crete

The first traces of history in Crete take us back to about 2500 B.C., but it was not until about a thousand years later that Crete was at the height of her prosperity and enjoying her Golden Age. Life in Crete at this time must have been happy. The Cretans built their cities without towers or fortifications; they were a mighty sea power, but they lived more for peace and work than for military or naval adventures, and having attained the overlordship of the Aegean, they devoted themselves to trade, industries, and art.

The Cretans learned a great deal from Egypt, but they never became dependent upon her as did the Phoenicians, that other seafaring race in the Mediterranean. They dwelled secure in their island kingdom, taking what they wanted from the civilization they saw in the Nile Valley; but instead of copying this, they developed and transformed it in accordance with their own spirit and independence.

The chief city in Crete was Knossos, and the great palace there was almost like a town. It was built around a large central court, out of which opened chambers, halls, and corridors. This court was evidently the center of the life of the palace. The west wing was probably devoted to business, and it was here that strangers were received. In the audience chamber was found a simple and austere seat, yet one which seizes upon the imagination, for it was said to be the seat of Minos, and is the oldest known royal throne in the world.

In the east wing lived the artisans who were employed in decorating and working on the building, for everything required in the palace was made on the spot. The walls of all the rooms were finished with smooth plaster and then painted—originally so that the paint might serve as a protection, but later because the beauty-loving Cretans liked their walls to be covered with what must have been a joy to look at, and which reminded them at every turn of the world of nature in which they took such a keen delight. The frescoes are now faded, but traces of river scenes and water, of reeds and rushes, of waving grasses, lilies, and the crocus, of birds with brilliant plumage, and of flying fish and the foaming sea can still be distinguished.

The furniture has all perished, but many household utensils have been found which show that life was by no means primitive, and the palaces were evidently built and lived in by people who understood comfort. In some ways they were quite modern, especially in the excellent drainage system they

Central courtyard of the palace at Knossos

possessed. These Cretan palaces were warmer and more full of life than those in Assyria, and they were dwelled in by a people who were young, vigorous, and artistic, and who understood the joy of the artist in creating beauty.

Near the palace was the so-called theater. The steps were so shallow that they could not have made comfortable seats, and the space for performances was too small to have been used for bull-fights, which were the chief public entertainment. The place was probably used for dancing, and it may have been that very dancing ground wrought for Ariadne.

III. Dress

The dress of the Cretan women was surprisingly modern. The frescoes on the walls, as well as small porcelain statuettes that have been found, give us a very clear idea of how the people dressed. The women had small waists, and their dresses had short sleeves, with the bodice laced in front, and wide flounced skirts often richly embroidered. Yellow, purple, and blue seem to have been the favorite colors. They wore shoes with heels and sometimes sandals. Their hair was elaborately arranged in knots, side curls, and braids, and their hats were amazingly modern.

The men, however, were not modern-looking. Their only garment was a short kilt, which was often ornamented with designs in colors, and, like the women, they had an elaborate method of hair-dressing. In general appearance the men were bronzed, slender, and agile-looking.

Some of the frescoes are so lifelike that as they were brought to light during the excavations, it almost seemed as if the spirits of the long-dead Cretans were returning to the earth. The workmen felt the spell, and Sir Arthur Evans, who excavated Knossos, has described the scene as the painting of a young Cretan was found:

Women of Crete (fresco at Knossos)

The colors were almost as brilliant as when laid down over three thousand years before. For the first time the true portraiture of a man of this mysterious Mycenaean race rises before us. There was something very impressive in this vision of brilliant youth and of male beauty, recalled after so long an interval to our upper air from what had been till yesterday a forgotten world. Even our untutored Cretan workmen felt the spell and fascination.

They, indeed, regarded the discovery of such a painting in the bosom of the earth as nothing less than marvelous, and saw in it the "icon" of a saint! The removal of the fresco required a delicate and laborious process of under-plastering, which necessitated its being watched at night, and one of the most trustworthy of our gang was told off for the purpose. Somehow or other he fell asleep, but the wrathful saint appeared to him in a dream. Waking with a start he was conscious of a mysterious presence; the animals round began to low

> and neigh, and there were visions about; in summing up his experiences the next morning, "The whole place spooks!" he said.[5]

Crete seems to have had more than the other earlier civilizations of what today is called *society*. The women were not secluded but mixed freely at court and in all social functions, and life seems to have been joyous and free from care.

IV. Religion and Literature

a. Religion

WE KNOW ALMOST NOTHING of the Cretan religion. There were no idols or images for worship and no temples. The people worshipped in their houses, and every house seems to have had a room set apart for this purpose with its shrine and altar; pillars were one of the distinguishing marks of these shrines. The chief goddess was the Mother Earth, the Source of Life, a spirit who had a good and kindly character. Sometimes she was called the Lady of the Wild Creatures, and bulls were sacrificed in her honor. Scenes representing such sacrifices are to be found on engraved gems, and the horns of the bull are frequently found set up on altars and shrines. This Earth goddess was goddess both of the air and of the Underworld: when she appears as the Goddess of the Air, she has doves as her symbol; when she appears as the Goddess of the Underworld, she has snakes.

Another sacred symbol found in connection with shrines and altars is the Axe and often a Double Axe. This seems to have been looked upon as a divine symbol representing power, for it is the axe which transforms all kinds of material into

[5] Sir Arthur Evans: in the *Monthly Review*, March, 1901.

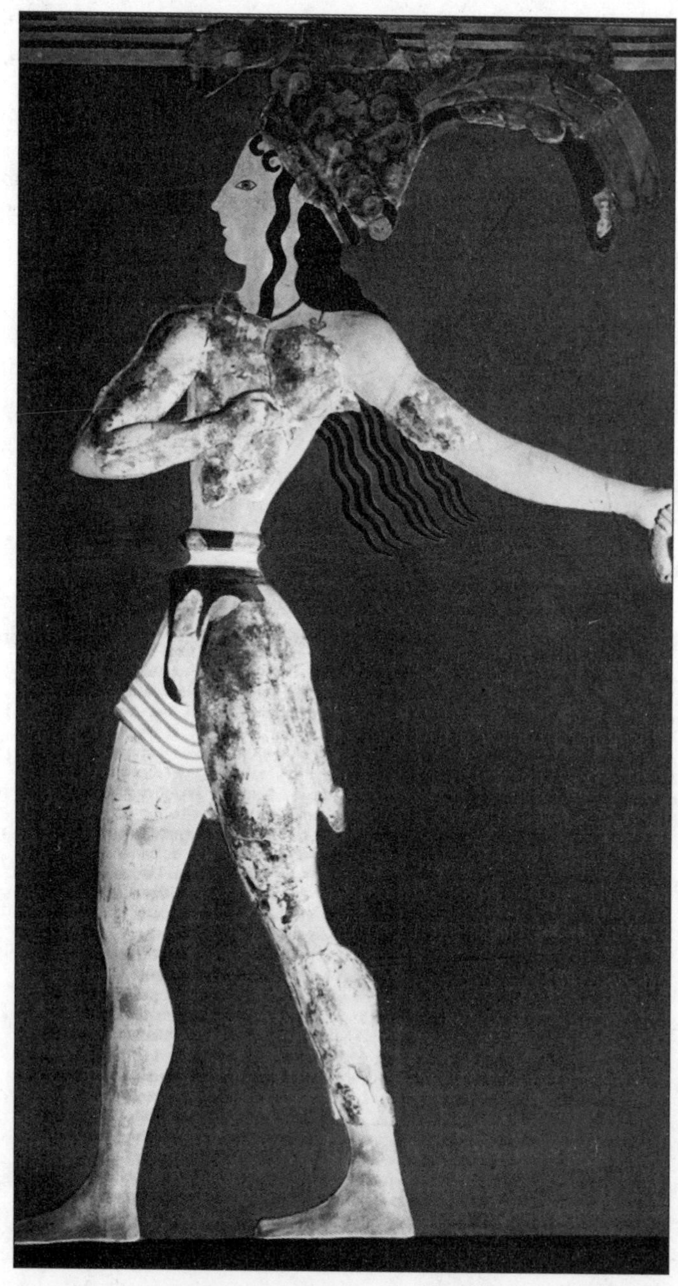

Priest-king (fresco at Knossos)

useful articles, and by means of man's toil it supplies much of what man needs. Ships could not be built without an axe, and as it was the ship which gave Crete power in the Aegean, the axe came to be looked upon as symbolizing this spirit.

These early Aegean people did not feel the need for any temples. When they worshipped in what they thought was the dwelling place of the gods, they chose lonely places, remote hilltops or caverns or the depths of a great forest. They selected for this worship some place that was apart from the daily human life and one that had never been touched by the hand of man, for they felt that it was such places that the god would choose for his dwelling. From such spots developed the idea of a temple; it was to be a building enclosed and shut out from the world, just as the forest grove had been surrounded by trees, a place apart from the life of man.

It was the custom in these early times for people to bring to the god or goddess offerings of that which was most valuable to them. The best of the flock, the finest fruit, the largest fish, the most beautiful vase were all looked upon as suitable offerings. But many people could not afford to part with the best of the firstfruits of their toil, and so it became the custom to have little images made of the animal or other offering they wished to make, and these were placed in the shrine. Such images are called *votive offerings*, and they are a source of rich material out of which the archaeologist has been able to rebuild parts of ancient life.

b. Writing and Literature

One reason why it has been so difficult to know much about the Cretan religion is because the writing has not yet been deciphered. Over sixty different signs have been recognized, but no key has yet been found by means of which the writing can be read. In the palace at Knossos a great library was found, consisting of about two thousand clay tablets. These had evidently been placed in wooden chests, carefully sealed, but at the destruction of Knossos, the fire destroyed the chests, though it actually helped to preserve the clay records. Some of these were overcharred and so became brittle and broke; but there are still quantities awaiting deciphering. The writing does not look as if it represented literature, but more as if it were devoted to lists and records. It seems strange that people dwelling in a land so rich in legend and story, and possessed of the art of writing, should not have left a literature. But in those days the songs of minstrels preserved the hero-tales in a form that was then considered permanent, for the minstrel gathered his tales together and handed them down to his successor by word of mouth in a way that we, with our careless memories, deem marvelous. This was actually considered a safer way of preserving the tales and poems than trusting them to the written form. Be that as it may, however, the writing that is there still awaits the finding of a key. But in spite of these difficulties, life in Crete can be partially reconstructed, and so it will be possible for us to spend a day in the palace of ancient Knossos.

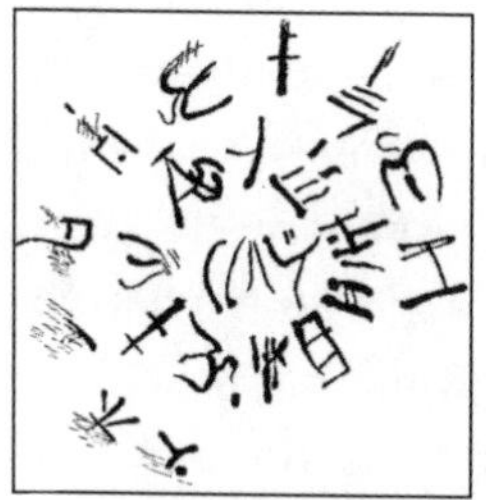

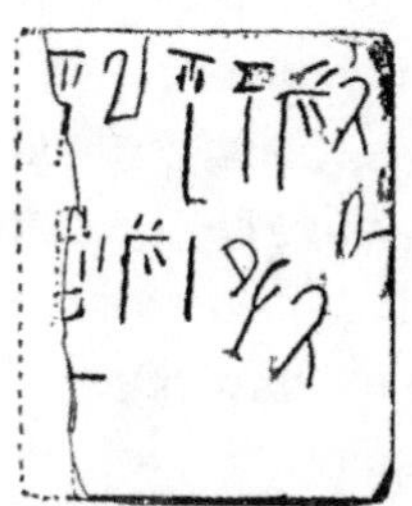

Examples of the still undeciphered script of the early Minoans of Crete

V. A Day in Crete

It is early dawn, about the year 1500 B.C. The great palace of Knossos lies quiet and still, for the inhabitants have not yet begun to stir. When they are aroused, the noise will be like the bustle of a town, for everything used in the palace is made there, from the bronze weapons used by the king when he goes out hunting to the great clay vessels in which not only wine and oil, but also other articles of food, are kept. The palace is guarded by sentries, and the first person to come out of it in the morning is an officer who goes the rounds and receives the reports of the night's watch from each sentry. He then goes into the royal storerooms, where rows of large vessels stand against the wall, and he inspects them to make sure that no robbery has taken place and also that there are no leaks, and no wine or oil lost.

By this time the sun is up and the workmen are going to the palace workshops, where some are at work on pottery, others are weaving, and others are working with metals. Some of the potters are fashioning beautiful vases, the younger workmen copying the well-known patterns, the more experienced thinking of new forms, but all of them handing over the finished vessel to the artist who paints beautiful designs on them. The weavers have been very busy of late, for today is the birthday of the princess, and great festivities are to be held in her honor, and not only the princess, but the queen and her maidens and all the ladies of the court need new and dainty robes for the functions of the day. The goldsmiths also have been hard at work, for the king has ordered exquisite jewelry as a gift for his daughter. All these workmen are now putting the finishing touches to their work, and in a few hours they will take it to the officials who will see that it is delivered to the royal apartments.

Soon all is bustling in the kitchens, for later in the day a great banquet will be held. Farmers from the countryside come with the best of their flocks, with delicious fruits and honey; fishermen from the shore have been out early and have caught fine fish. Nearly everyone who comes has brought some special dainty as a particular offering for the princess, for she is much beloved in Knossos and in all the country round about.

The morning is spent in preparation for the festivities of the afternoon. The princess is arrayed by her maidens in her new and beautiful robes; her hair is elaborately arranged, a long and tiresome process, but the time is enlivened by the merry talk of the maidens who give to their young mistress all the gossip of the palace. At length she is ready, and she goes to the great audience chamber, where the king, her father, presents to her the shining ornaments he has had made for this day. Then, sitting between her parents, she receives the good wishes of the courtiers, all of whom have brought her rich gifts.

This reception is followed by an exhibition of boxing and bull-fighting, favorite amusements of the Cretan youths; but the great excitement of the day is the wild boar hunt which follows. All the youths and younger men take part, and each hopes that he may specially distinguish himself in order that on his return he may have some trophy to present to the princess, and that she will reward him by giving him her hand in the dance that evening.

While the young men are all away at the hunt, the princess sits with her parents in the great hall or wanders with her maidens in the gardens. Great excitement prevails when the hunters return. On arriving, they hasten to the bath and anoint themselves with oil, curl their long hair, and make themselves ready for the dance. When all are ready they go out to that

> dancing place, which Daedalus had wrought in broad Knossos for Ariadne of the lovely tresses. There were youths dancing and maidens of costly wooing, their hands on one another's wrists. Fine linen the maidens had on, and the youths well-woven doublets faintly glistening with oil. Fair wreaths had the maidens, and the youths daggers of gold hanging from silver baldrics. And now they would run around with deft feet exceeding lightly, as when a potter sitting by his wheel taketh trial of it whether it run; and now anon

Luxurious boat of Crete

> they would run in lines to meet one another. And a great company stood around the lovely dance in joy; and among them a divine minstrel was making music on his lyre, and through the midst of them, as he began his strain, two tumblers whirled.[6]

The dance over, the feasting and banqueting begins. The queen and the princess with their maidens retire early to their own apartments, but the merrymaking goes on in the hall, where tales of the day's hunt are told, and old tales of other adventures are recalled by the old men, until weariness overcomes them. Then the queen sends her handmaids, who "set out bedsteads beneath the gallery, and cast fair purple blankets over them, and spread coverlets above, and thereon lay thick mantles to be a clothing over all. Then they go from the hall with torch in hand." So the youths and men lie down and go to sleep, and after the excitements of the day, "it seemed to them that rest was wonderful."[7]

VI. The Destroyers

After the glory of the Golden Age of Crete came destruction. Some tremendous disaster broke forever the power

[6] *Iliad*, XVIII.
[7] *Odyssey*, VII.

of the sea-kings. We do not know what happened, beyond the fact that Knossos was burned, but from our knowledge of the life of the time and the methods of warfare, we can make a picture of what probably took place. There may have been some terrible sea fight, in which the fleet was worsted and driven back upon the shore. Then the conquerors would march upon the town and besiege it. The inhabitants, knowing that all was at stake, would defend it to the last with the most savage fury, cheered on by the women, who knew that if the city was taken, there would be no hope for them. Their husbands and sons would be slain, the city utterly destroyed by fire, and themselves taken captive. This is what happened at Knossos. We know the fate of the city, but nothing of the conquerors. Egyptian records of this time say that "the isles were restless, disturbed among themselves," but that is all we know.

The invaders, whoever they were, and from wherever they came, do not seem to have been men of a highly civilized type, for they left untouched many works of real art, and carried off only such articles as could be turned into material wealth. These were the things they evidently valued, and the degree of civilization to which nations or individuals have attained can usually be measured by the comparative values they put on things.

And so Knossos fell, and she tasted of "the woes that come on men whose city is taken: the warriors are slain, and the city is wasted of fire, and the children and women are led captive of strangers."[8]

The old Knossos was never rebuilt, though another city grew up in the neighborhood. The site of the old palace became more and more desolate, until at length the ruins were completely hidden under a covering of earth, and the ancient power and glory of Crete became only a tradition. And so it

[8] *Iliad*, IX.

remained for long centuries until archaeologists, discovering what lay beneath those dreary-looking mounds, recalled for us that springtime of the world.

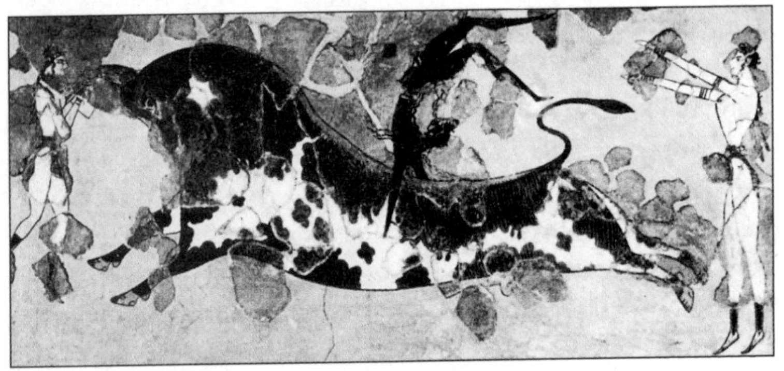

The famous Cretan sport of bull-vaulting

CHAPTER 3

THE MAINLAND

I. Troy and the First Discoveries

AN ANCIENT TRADITION told the story of how Helen, the beautiful wife of Menelaus, King of Sparta, had been carried off by Paris, son of the king of Troy, and of how the Greeks collected a mighty army under Menelaus and his brother Agamemnon, King of Argos, and sailed to Troy to bring back the lost Helen. For ten years they besieged Troy, during which time they had many adventures and many hero-deeds were performed. Glorious Hector of the glancing helm was slain by Achilles fleet of foot, and the gods and goddesses themselves came down from high Olympus and took sides, some helping the Trojans and some the Greeks. At length Troy was taken and the Greek heroes returned home, but their homeward journey was fraught with danger and they experienced many hardships. The wise Odysseus, especially, went through many strange adventures before he reached Greece again. All these tales were put together by the Greek poet Homer, and may be read in the *Iliad* and the *Odyssey*.

Until the beginning of the nineteenth century, no one had seriously thought that there was any truth in these tales. But in 1822 a boy was born in Germany who was to make the most extraordinary discoveries about these lands of legend.

Henry Schliemann was the son of a German pastor who was well versed in all these ancient legends, and as he grew up, he learned all about Troy and the old Greek tales. He lived in a romantic neighborhood; behind his father's garden was a pool, from which every midnight a maiden was said to rise, holding a silver bowl in her hand. And there were similar tales connected with the neighboring hills and forests. But there was not much money to educate the young Schliemann, and when he was fourteen years old he was taken as errand boy by a country grocer. This was not perhaps the occupation a romantic-minded youth would have chosen, but there was no help for it. One evening, there came into the shop a man who, after sitting down and asking for some refreshment, suddenly began to recite Greek poetry. The errand boy stopped his work to listen, and long afterwards he described the effect this poetry had on him:

> That evening he recited to us about a hundred lines of the poet (Homer), observing the rhythmic cadence of the verses. Although I did not understand a syllable, the melodious sound of the words made a deep impression upon me, and I wept bitter tears over my unhappy fate. Three times over did I get him to repeat to me those divine verses, rewarding his trouble with three glasses of whiskey, which I bought with the few pence that made up my whole wealth. From that moment I never ceased to pray God that by His grace I might yet have the happiness of learning Greek.

A few years later, Schliemann was taken as errand boy in a business house in Amsterdam, and he had to run on all kinds of errands and carry letters to and from the post. He says of this time:

> I never went on my errands, even in the rain, without having my book in hand and learning something by heart. I never waited at the post office without reading or repeating a passage in my mind.

Schliemann got on well, and the time came when he was able to found a business of his own. Now at last he had time to learn Greek, and he read everything written by or about the ancient Greeks on which he could lay his hands. And then came the time to which he had been looking forward all his life. He was able to free himself from his business and to sail for the Greek lands.

Schliemann believed that the tales of Troy were founded on true historic facts, but everybody laughed at this opinion, and he was often ridiculed for holding it so firmly. Now, however, he was to prove himself victorious, for he went to the place where he believed Troy had once stood and began to dig. His expectations were more than realized, for he found six cities, one of which was later conclusively proved to be the Troy of Homer! Homer had written about what was really true, and though legends and myths had been woven into his poem, the main events had really taken place, and a civilization which up to that time had, as it was thought, never existed, suddenly came out into the record of history.

Walls of Troy

II. Mycenae and Tiryns

All these discoveries sent a thrill of excitement through the world, and, of course, at first many mistakes were made. Because Troy was found to have really existed, everything found there was immediately connected with the Trojan heroes of the *Iliad*, and some things which were obviously legendary were treated as facts. Schliemann himself was not entirely free from these first exaggerations, but encouraged by what he had already discovered, he determined to find still more.

Now Pausanias, an ancient Greek traveler, had written a book about his travels, and one of the places he had visited was Mycenae, on the mainland of Greece. Here, he said, he had seen the tomb of Agamemnon, who on his return from Troy had been murdered by his wife, Clytemnestra, and hastily buried. Up to the time of Schliemann, no one had seriously believed that there had ever been such a person as Agamemnon, but the spirit of discovery was in the air, and what might not still be found! Schliemann determined that, having proved that Troy had once existed, he would find truth in still more legends; and he went to Mycenae and began to excavate. The early Greeks had not the same beliefs about the future life that the Egyptians had, but they did believe that death meant removing from the dwelling place on earth to one beneath the earth, and so the early Greek tomb was built in much the same shape as the earthly house. These Greeks did not allow man to go naked and alone into the other world; they gave to the departed to take with him all that was best and finest of his earthly possessions. They filled the tomb with everything that could add to his comfort, and if he were a king or great chief, he would be surrounded by things which would mark him out from other men and point to his great position. This being so, Schliemann thought that a king's tomb would be easily recognized; and he opened what he thought was probably the burial place of Agamemnon. What he saw swept him off his feet with excitement! Before doing anything else, he sent a telegram to the king of Greece, which was speedily published throughout the world. The telegram said: "With great joy I announce to Your Majesty that I have found the tomb of Agamemnon!"

The sensation created by this news was tremendous. That it was really the tomb of the wide-ruling King of Argos was perhaps uncertain, but it was undoubtedly the tomb of a great lord who had lived at the same time, and at his death had been buried in barbaric magnificence. Diadems, pendants, necklaces, ornaments of all kinds, goblets, plates, and vases, all of pure gold, were piled high in confusion in the tomb, and close by were other tombs also filled with untold treasure. In one grave alone, Schliemann counted 870 objects made of the purest gold. This was only the beginning of excavations at Mycenae. Later on, a great palace was uncovered, and other work at Tiryns, nearer the sea, showed that another palace had existed there.

These buildings were very unlike the palace at Knossos; the latter had no fortifications, but these were strongly fortified. They had great walls, so mighty that in ancient times the Greeks thought the walls of Tiryns had been built by demons, and Pausanias considered them even more wonderful than the pyramids. The fortress-palace of Mycenae was entered by the gate of the Lionesses, which was reached by a rather narrow road, along which only seven men could march abreast. This seems a rather mean approach to so splendid a palace, but such narrow approaches were necessary in those warlike times, for they made it more difficult for an enemy to approach the gates.

Mycenae and Tiryns are the best known today of the ancient fortress-palaces on the mainland of Greece, but at the time when they were built, there were many others. The great lords frequently chose the hilltops for their dwellings, for the sake of better security and for the protection they could then in their turn afford the surrounding country people in times of danger. Most of these fortress-palaces were in the neighborhood of the coast, for no true Greek was ever quite happy unless he were within easy reach and sight of the sea.

The Lion Gate at Mycenae

III. Life in the Homeric Age

The Homeric Age was the age of the great hero-kings and chiefs. Most of these were supposed to be descended from the gods, and they shine through the mists of the early days in Greece as splendid, gorgeous figures. Heaven was nearer to the earth in those days, and the gods came down from Olympus and mixed familiarly with man. Life was very different in this heroic age from the life of historic Greece, and it is evident from the excavations and discoveries that have been made, that it was a civilization with distinct characteristics of its own which preceded what is known as the Greece of history. It was an age when the strong man ruled by the might of his own strong arm, and piracy was quite common. Manners and customs were very primitive and simple, yet they were combined with great material splendor. Women held a high position in this society and they wore most gorgeous clothes. A Mycenaean lady, arrayed in her best, would wear a dress of soft wool exquisitely dyed or of soft shining linen, and she would glitter with golden ornaments: a diadem of gold on her head, gold pins in her hair, gold bands round her throat, gold bracelets on her arms, and her hands covered with gold rings. Schliemann says that the women he found in one of the tombs he opened were "literally laden with jewelry."

Mycenaean woman

The fortress-palaces were the chief houses, and the huts of the dependents of the king or chief would be crowded round them, but these huts have, of course, disappeared. The palaces themselves were strongly built, with courtyards and chambers opening from them. "There is building beyond building, and the court of the house is cunningly wrought with a wall and battlements, and well fenced are the folding doors; no man may hold it in disdain."[1] Excavations have proved that the Homeric palaces did indeed exist: and well fortified though they were, their gardens and vineyards and fountains must have made them very pleasant dwelling places.

> There was a gleam as it were of sun or moon through the high-roofed hall of great-hearted Alcinous. Brazen were the walls which ran this way and that from the threshold to the inmost chamber, and round them was a frieze of blue, and golden were the doors that closed in the good house. Silver were the doorposts that were set on the brazen threshold, and silver the lintel thereupon, and the hook of the door was of gold. And on either side stood golden hounds and silver, which Hephaestus had wrought by his cunning, to guard the palace of great-hearted Alcinous, being free from death and age all their days. And within were seats arrayed against the wall this way and that, from the threshold even to the inmost chamber, and thereon were spread light coverings finely woven, the handiwork of women. There the chieftains were wont to sit eating and drinking for they had continual store. Yea, and there were youths fashioned in gold, standing on firm-set bases with flaming torches in their hands, giving light through the night to the feasters in the palace. And he

[1] *Odyssey*, XVII.

> had fifty handmaids in the house, and some grind the yellow grain on the millstone, and others weave webs and turn the yarn as they sit, restless as the leaves of the tall poplar tree; and the soft olive oil drops off that linen, so closely is it woven. And without the courtyard hard by the door is a great garden, and a hedge runs round on either side. And there grow tall trees blossoming, pear trees and pomegranates, and apple trees with bright fruit, and sweet figs and olives in their bloom. The fruit of these trees never perisheth, neither faileth, winter nor summer, enduring through all the year. Evermore the West wind blowing brings some fruits to birth and ripens others. Pear upon pear waxes old, and apple on apple, yea and cluster ripens upon cluster of the grape, and fig upon fig. There, too, hath he a fruitful vineyard planted, whereof the one part is being daily dried by the heat, a sunny spot on level ground, while other grapes men are gathering, and yet others they are treading in the winepress. In the foremost row are unripe grapes that cast the blossom, and others there be that are growing black to vintaging. There, too, skirting the furthest line, are all manner of garden beds, planted trimly, that are perpetually fresh, and therein are two fountains of water, whereof one scatters his streams all about the garden, and the other runs over against it beneath the threshold of the courtyard and issues by the lofty house, and thence did the townsfolk draw water. These were the splendid gifts of the gods in the palace of Alcinous.[2]

A blue frieze just like the one described above has been found both at Mycenae and Tiryns.

---

[2] *Odyssey*, VII.

The furniture in these houses was very splendid. We read of well-wrought chairs, of fine carved chairs and of chairs inlaid with ivory and silver; of inlaid seats and polished tables; of jointed bedsteads and of a fair bedstead with inlaid work of gold and silver and ivory; of close-fitted folding doors and of doors with silver handles; and of rugs of soft wool. Rich and varied were the ornaments and vessels used: fine golden ewers and silver basins, two-handled cups, silver baskets and tripods, mixing bowls of flowered work all of silver and one that was beautifully wrought all of silver and the lips thereof finished with gold. The most famous cup of all was that of the clear-voiced orator Nestor; this had four handles on which were golden doves feeding and it stood two feet from the ground. Very skillful was all the work done in metal at this time, and the warriors went out arrayed in flashing bronze, bearing staves studded with golden nails, bronze-headed spears and silver-studded swords; their greaves were fastened with silver clasps, they wore bronze-bound helmets, glittering girdles, and belts with golden buckles. Only a god could have fashioned a wondrous shield such as Achilles bore, on which were depicted scenes from the life of the time (the description of it can be read in the *Iliad*), but the tombs at Mycenae and elsewhere have yielded weapons and treasures very similar to those used by the heroes in Homer.

IV. The Greek Migrations

It was more than a thousand years after the pyramids had been built that Crete reached her Golden Age. When Knossos was destroyed, the centers of civilization on the mainland, such as Mycenae and Tiryns, became of greater importance, and life was lived as Homer has described it. All this was the Greece of the Heroic Age, the Greece to which the Greeks of the later historical times looked back to as something that lay far behind them.

Nearly two thousand years ago the site of Mycenae was just as it had remained until the excavations of Schliemann, and in the second century A.D., a Greek poet sang of Mycenae:

> The cities of the hero-age thine eyes may seek in vain,
> Save where some wrecks of ruin still break the
> level plain.
> So once I saw Mycenae, the ill-starred, a barren height
> Too bleak for goats to pasture—the goatherds point
> the site.
> And as I passed, a graybeard said, "Here used to
> stand of old
> A city built by giants and passing rich in gold."[3]

Even to the Greeks of historical times, there was a great gap between the return of the heroes from Troy and the beginnings of their own historic Greece. That gap has not yet been entirely filled up; it is even now a more shadowy and misty period to us than the Age of the Heroes, but it was during these mysterious centuries that there were wanderings among the peoples, the restlessness and disturbance spoken of by the Egyptians. It was a dark period in the history of Greece. Wandering tribes, tall and fair men, came out from the forests of the North, over the mountains, and through the passes into Greece. Others came from the East. Some again came by sea, driven out from their island homes by invaders. There was fighting and slaying and taking of prisoners. The old civilization was broken down, but slowly something new arose in its place. There were enemies on all sides, but gradually those who were left of the conquered made terms with the conquerors; they abandoned their old language and adopted that of the newcomers, and they dwelled together, and were known

[3] Alpheus, translated by Sir Rennell Rodd in *Love, Worship and Death.*

as Greeks. The older civilizations had done their work and had perished. The time had come for the mind of man to make greater advances than he had ever before dreamed of, and in the land of Greece this period begins with the coming of the Greeks.

The Greeks

ILLYRIA
MACEDONIA
THRACIA
CHALCIDICE
EPIRUS
THESSALIA
AEGEAN SEA
ACHAEA
EUBOEA
IONIAN SEA
AETOLIA
LOCRIS
BOEOTIA
ACHAIA
ATTICA
ELIS
ARCADIA
PELOPONNESUS
MESSENIA
LACONIA
CRETA

Greece

CHAPTER 4

THE LAND OF GREECE

THE LAND TO WHICH PEOPLE belong always helps to form their character and influence their history, and the land of Greece, its mountains and plains, its sea and sky, was of great importance in making the Greeks what they were. The map shows us three parts of Greece: Northern Greece, a rugged mountainous land; then Central Greece with a fertile plain running down to more mountains; and then, across a narrow sea, the peninsula known as the Peloponnesus. One striking feature of the whole country is the nearness of every part of it to the sea. The coast is deeply indented with gulfs and bays, and the neighboring sea is dotted with islands. It is a land of sea and mountains.

The soil is not rich. About one-third of the country is mountainous and unproductive and consists of rock. Forests are found in the lower lands, but they are not like our forests; the trees are smaller and the sun penetrates even the thickest places. The trees most often found are the laurel, the oleander, and the myrtle. The forests were thicker in ancient times; they are much thinner now owing to the carelessness of peasants who, without thinking of the consequences, have wastefully cut down the trees.

The land used by the Greeks for pasture was that which was not rich enough for cultivation. Goats and sheep and pigs roamed over this land, and the bees made honey there. In ancient times there was no sugar, and honey was a necessary article of food.

The cultivated land lay in the plains. The mountains of Greece do not form long valleys, but they enclose plains, and it was here that the Greeks cultivated their corn and wine and oil, and here that their cities grew up separated from each other by the mountains. Corn, wine, and oil were absolutely necessary for life in the Mediterranean world. Every Greek city tried to produce enough corn, chiefly wheat and barley, for its inhabitants, for the difficulties and sometimes dangers were great when a city was not self-sufficient. Wine, too, was necessary, for the Greeks, though they were a temperate nation, could not do without it. Oil was even more important, for it was used for cleansing purposes, for food, and for lighting. Even today the Greeks use but little butter, and where we eat bread and butter, they eat bread and olives or bread and goat's cheese. The olive is cultivated all over Greece, but especially in Attica, where it was regarded as the gift of Athena herself. It was looking across the sea to Attica that

> In Salamis, filled with the foaming
> Of billows and murmur of bees,
> Old Telamon stayed from his roaming.
> Long ago, on a throne of the seas;
> Looking out on the hills olive-laden,
> Enchanted, where first from the earth
> The gray-gleaming fruit of the Maiden
> Athena had birth.[1]

The olive is not a large tree, and its chief beauty is in the shimmer of the leaves which glisten a silvery-gray in the sunshine. Olive trees take a long time to mature; they do not yield a full crop for sixteen years or more, and they are nearly fifty years old before they reach their fullest maturity. It is no wonder that the olive is a symbol of peace.

---

[1] Euripides: *The Trojan Women*, translated by Gilbert Murray.

Herodotus, the earliest of the Greek historians, wrote that "it was the lot of Hellas to have its seasons far more fairly tempered than other lands." The Mediterranean is a borderland, midway between the tropics and the colder North. In summer the cool winds from the North blow upon Greece, making the climate pleasant, but in winter they blow from every quarter, and, according to the poet Hesiod, were "a great trouble to mortals." Greek life was a summer life, and the ancient Greeks lived almost entirely outdoors: sailing over the sea and attending to all their affairs in the open air, from the shepherd watching his flock on the mountainside to the philosopher discussing politics in the marketplace. But the Greeks were a hardy race, and though the winter life must have been chilly and uncomfortable, life went on just the same, until the warm spring sunshine made them forget the winter cold.

What kind of people were made by these surroundings, and what was their spirit?

The hardy mountain life developed a free and independent spirit, and as the mountains cut off the dwellers in the different plains from each other, separate city-states were formed, each with its own laws and government. This separation of communities was a source of weakness to the country as a whole, but it developed the spirit of freedom and independence in the city-dweller as well as in the mountaineer. As all parts of Greece were within easy reach of the sea, the Greeks naturally became sailors. They loved the sea and were at home upon it, and this seafaring life developed the same spirit of freedom and independence.

The mild climate relieved the Greeks of many cares which come to those who live in harsher lands, and the atmosphere was clear and bracing, which stimulated clear thinking. The Greeks were the first great thinkers in the world; they were possessed of a passion for knowing the truth about all things in heaven and earth, and few people have sought truth with greater courage and clearness of mind than the Greeks.

The poor soil of their land made it necessary for them to work hard and to form habits of thrift and economy. It was not a soil that made them rich, and so they developed a spirit of self-control and moderation, and learned how to combine simple living with high thinking to a greater degree than any other nation has ever done. But if their soil was poor, they had all around them the exquisite beauty of the mountains, sea, and sky, surroundings from which they learned to love beauty in a way that has never been excelled, if, indeed, it has ever been equaled.

The spirit of a nation expresses itself and its history is recorded in various ways: in the social relations of the people both with each other and with other nations, and this is called its political history; in its language which expresses itself in its literature; and in its buildings, which is its architecture. The Greek people were lovers of freedom, truth, self-control, and beauty. It is in their political history, their literature, and their architecture that we shall see some of the outward and visible signs of the spirit that inspired them, and the land of Greece is the setting in which they played their part in the history of civilization.

CHAPTER 5

GREEK RELIGION AND THE ORACLES

THE CITY-DWELLERS in Greece lived in the plains separated from their neighbors by mountains, and this caused the development of a large number of separate communities, quite independent of each other, each having its own laws and government. But there were three things which all Greeks had in common wherever they lived: they spoke the same language, they believed in the same gods, and they celebrated together as Greeks their great national games.

The Greeks called themselves Hellenes and their land Hellas. Like the Hebrews and the Babylonians, they believed that there had been a time when men had grown so wicked that the gods determined to destroy the old race of man and create a new one. A terrible flood overwhelmed the earth, until nothing of it was left visible but the top of Mount Parnassus; and here, the old legend tells us, a refuge was found by two people, Deucalion and his wife Pyrrha, who alone had been saved on account of their righteous lives. Slowly the waters abated, until the earth was once more dry and habitable, but Deucalion and Pyrrha were alone and did not know what they should do. So they prayed to the gods and received as an answer to their prayer the strange command: "Depart, and cast behind you the bones of your mother." At first they could not understand what was meant, but at length Deucalion thought of an explanation. He said to Pyrrha, "The earth is the great mother of all; the stones are her bones, and perhaps it is these we must cast behind us." So they took up the stones that were lying about and cast them behind them, and as they did so, a strange thing happened! The stones thrown by Deucalion became men, and those thrown by Pyrrha became women, and this race of men peopled the land of Greece anew. The son of Deucalion and Pyrrha was called Hellen, and as the Greeks looked upon him as the legendary founder of their race, they called themselves and their land by his name.

These earliest Greeks had very strange ideas as to the shape of the world. They thought it was flat and circular, and that Greece lay in the very middle of it, with Mount Olympus, or as some maintained, Delphi, as the central point of the whole world. This world was believed to be cut in two by the Sea and to be entirely surrounded by the River Ocean, from which the Sea and all the rivers and lakes on the earth received their waters.

In the North of this world were supposed to live the Hyperboreans. They were the people who lived beyond the North winds, whose home was in the caverns in the mountains to the north of Greece. The Hyperboreans were a happy race of beings who knew neither disease nor old age, and who, living in a land of everlasting spring, were free from all toil and labor.

Far away in the South, on the banks of the River Ocean, lived another happy people, the Aethiopians. They were so happy and led such blissful lives that the gods sometimes used to leave their home in Olympus and go and join the Aethiopians in their feasts and banquets.

On the western edge of the earth and close to the River Ocean were the Elysian Fields, sometimes called the Fortunate Fields and the Isles of the Blessed. It was to this blissful place that mortals who were specially loved by the gods were transported without first tasting of death, and there they lived forever, set free from all the sorrows and sufferings of earth. It was a land

> Where falls not hail, or rain, or any snow,
> Nor ever wind blows loudly; but it lies
> Deep-meadow'd, happy—.

The Sun and the Moon and the Rosy-fingered Dawn were thought of as gods who rose out of the River Ocean and drove in their chariots through the air, giving light to both gods and men.

What kind of religion did the Greeks have? Now *religion* may be explained in many different ways; there have been many different religions in the world. From the earliest times men have realized that there were things in the world that they could not understand, and many people have concluded that there must be some Being greater than man, who had himself been created; and it is by what is called *religion* that men have sought to come into relationship with this Being greater than themselves.

The Egyptians in their religious beliefs had been very much occupied with the idea of the life after death, but at first the Greeks thought of this very little. The Greeks believed that proper burial was necessary for the future happiness of the soul, and want of this was looked upon as a very serious disaster, but beyond the insisting on due and fitting burial ceremonies, their thoughts were not much occupied with the future. The reason for this was probably because the Greeks found this life on earth so delightful. They were filled with the joy of being alive and were keenly interested in everything concerning life; they felt at home in the world. The gods in whom the Greeks believed were not supposed to have created the world, but they were themselves part of it, and every phase of this life that was so full of interest and adventure was represented by the personality of a god. First, it was the outside life, nature with all its mysteries, and then all the outward activities of man. Later, men found other things difficult to explain, the passions within them, love and hatred, gentleness and anger, and gradually they gave personalities to all these emotions and thought of each as inspired by a god. These gods were thought of as very near to man; men and women in the Heroic Age had claimed descent from them, and they were supposed to come down to earth and to hold frequent converse with man. The Greeks trusted their gods and looked to them for protection and assistance in all their affairs, but these gods were thought to be too human and not holy enough to be a real inspiration or to influence very much the conduct of those who believed in them.

The chief gods dwelled on Mount Olympus in Thessaly and were called the Olympians; others had dwellings on the earth, in the water, or in the Underworld. Heaven, the water, and the Underworld were each under the particular sovereignty of a great overlord amongst the gods.

> Three brethren are we [said Poseidon], Zeus and myself and Hades is the third, the ruler of the folk in the Underworld. And in three lots are all things divided, and each drew a domain of his own, and to me fell the hoary sea, to be my habitation forever, when we shook the lots; and Hades drew the murky darkness, and Zeus the wide heaven, in clear air and clouds, but the earth and high Olympus are common to all.[1]

Zeus was the greatest of the gods. He was the Father of gods and men, the lord of the lightning and of the stormcloud, whose joy was in the thunder. But he was also the lord of counsel and ruler of heaven and earth, and he was in particular the protector of all who were in any kind of need or distress, and he was the

---

[1] *Iliad*, XV.

guardian of the home. The court of every house had an altar to Zeus, the Protector of the Hearth. A great statue of Zeus stood in the temple at Olympia. It was the work of Pheidias and was considered one of the Seven Wonders of the ancient world. This statue was destroyed more than a thousand years ago by an earthquake, but a visitor to Olympia in ancient times tells us how perfectly it expressed the character of the god:

> His power and kingship are displayed by the strength and majesty of the whole image, his fatherly

Zeus

> care for men by the mildness and loving kindness in the face; the solemn austerity of the work marks the god of the city and the law—he seems like to one giving and bestowing blessings.[2]

Hera was the wife of Zeus. She was "golden-throned Hera, an immortal queen, the bride of loud-thundering Zeus, the lady renowned, whom all the Blessed throughout high Olympus honor and revere no less than Zeus whose delight is the thunder."[3]

Poseidon went to Olympus when he was summoned by Zeus, but he was the God of the Sea, and he preferred its depths as his home. His symbol was the trident, and he

Hera and Prometheus

[2] Dio Chrysostom.

[3] Homeric hymn to Hera.

was often represented as driving over the waves in a chariot drawn by foaming white horses. All sailors looked to him for protection and they sang to him: "Hail, Prince, thou Girdler of the Earth, thou dark-haired God, and with kindly heart, O blessed one, do thou befriend the mariners."[4]

Athena, the gray-eyed goddess, was the Guardian of Athens, and she stood to all the Greeks, but especially to the Athenians, as the symbol of three things: she was the Warrior Goddess, "the savior of cities who with Ares takes keep of the works of war, and of falling cities and the battle din."[5] She it was who led their armies out to war and brought them home victorious. She was Athena Polias, the Guardian of the city and the home, to whom was committed the planting and care of the olive trees and who had taught women the art of weaving

Athena

[4] Homeric hymn to Poseidon.

[5] Homeric hymn to Athena.

and given them wisdom in all fair handiwork; she was the wise goddess, rich in counsel, who inspired the Athenians with good statesmanship and showed them how to rule well and justly; and she was Athena Parthenos, the Queen whose victories were won, and who was the symbol of all that was true and beautiful and good.

Apollo, the Far Darter, the Lord of the silver bow, was the god who inspired all poetry and music. He went about playing

Apollo

upon his lyre, clad in divine garments; and at his touch the lyre gave forth sweet music. To him

> everywhere have fallen all the ranges of song, both on the mainland and among the isles: to him all the cliffs are dear, and the steep mountain crests and rivers running onward to the salt sea, and beaches sloping to the foam, and havens of the deep.

Muse

When Apollo the Far Darter "fares through the hall of Zeus, the gods tremble, yea, rise up all from their thrones as he draws near with his shining bended bow."[6] Apollo was also worshipped as Phoebus the Sun, the God of Light, and, like the sun, he was supposed to purify and illumine all things.

Following Apollo as their lord were the Muses, nine daughters of Zeus, who dwelled on Mount Parnassus. We are told that their hearts were set on song and that their souls knew no sorrow. It was the Muses and Apollo who gave to man the gift of song, and he whom they loved was held to be blessed. "It is from the Muses and far-darting Apollo that minstrels and harpers are upon the earth. Fortunate is he whomsoever the Muses love, and sweet flows his voice from his lips."[7] The Muse who inspired man with the imagination to understand history rightly was called Clio.

---

[6] Homeric hymn to Apollo.

[7] Homeric hymn to Apollo.

The huntress Artemis, the sister of Apollo, was goddess of the moon as her brother was god of the sun. She loved life in the open air and roamed over the hills and in the valleys, through the forests and by the streams. She was the

> Goddess of the loud chase, a maiden revered, the slayer of stags, the archer, very sister of Apollo of the golden blade. She, through the shadowy hills and the windy headlands rejoicing in the chase, draws her golden bow, sending forth shafts of sorrow. Then tremble the crests of the lofty mountains, and terribly the dark woodland rings with din of beasts, and the earth shudders, and the teeming sea.[8]

Artemis

[8] Homeric hymn to Artemis.

Hermes is best known to us as the messenger of the gods. When he started out to do their bidding,

> beneath his feet he bound on his fair sandals, golden, divine, that bare him over the waters of the sea and over the boundless land with the breathings of the wind. And he took up his wand, wherewith he entranceth the eyes of such men as he will, while others again he awakens out of sleep.[9]

Hermes was the protector of travelers, and he was the god who took special delight in the life of the marketplace. But there was another side to his character; he was skillful in all matters of cunning and trickery, and legend delighted in telling of his exploits. He began early. "Born in the dawn," we are told, "by midday well he harped and in the evening stole the cattle of Apollo the Far Darter."[10]

Hephaestus was the God of Fire, the divine metalworker. He was said to have first discovered the art of working iron, brass, silver, gold, and all other metals that require forging by fire. His workshop was on Mount Olympus, and here he used to do all kinds of work for the gods. Perhaps his most famous piece was the divine armor, and above all the shield he made for Achilles. Some great quarrel in which he was concerned arose in Olympus, and Zeus, in rage, threw him out of heaven. All day he fell until, as the sun was setting, he dropped upon the isle of Lemnos.

Athena and Hephaestus were always regarded as benefactors to mankind, for they taught man many useful arts.

> Sing, Muse, of Hephaestus renowned in craft, who with gray-eyed Athena taught goodly works to men on earth, even to men who before were wont to dwell in

[9] *Odyssey*, V.

[10] Homeric hymn to Hermes.

> mountain caves like beasts; but now, being instructed in craft by the renowned craftsman Hephaestus, lightly the whole year through they dwell happily in their own homes.[11]

Hestia, the Goddess of the Hearth, played an important part in the life of the Greeks. Her altar stood in every house and in every public building, and no act of any importance was ever performed until an offering of wine had been poured on her altar.

Laughter-loving, golden Aphrodite was the Goddess of Love and Beauty. She rose from the sea born in the soft white foam. "She gives sweet gifts to mortals and ever on her lovely face is a winsome smile."[12]

To the ancient Greeks, the woods, streams, hills, and rocky crags of their beautiful land were dwelled in by gods and nymphs and spirits of the wild. Chief of such spirits was Pan,

> the goat-footed, the two-horned, the lover of the din of the revel, who haunts the wooded dells with dancing nymphs that tread the crests of the steep cliffs, calling upon Pan. Lord is he of every snowy crest and mountain peak and rocky path. Hither and thither he goes, through the thick copses, sometimes being drawn to the still waters, and sometimes faring through the lofty crags he climbs the highest peaks whence the flocks are seen below; ever he ranges over the high white hills and at evening returns piping from the chase breathing sweet strains on the reeds.[13]

These were the chief gods in whom the Greeks believed. How did they worship them? The center of their worship was

---

[11] Homeric hymn to Hephaestus.

[12] Homeric hymn to Aphrodite.

[13] Homeric hymn to Pan.

the altar, but the altars were not in the temples, but outside. They were also found in houses and in the chief public buildings of the city. The temple was looked upon as the home of the god, and the temple enclosure was a very sacred place. A man accused of a crime could flee there and take refuge, and once within the temple, he was safe. It was looked upon as a very dreadful thing to remove him by force, for it was believed that to do so would bring down the wrath of the god upon those who had violated the right of sanctuary.

In the houses the altars were those sacred to Hestia, Apollo, and Zeus. The altar of Hestia stood in the chief room of the house, a libation was poured out to her before meals, and special sacrifices were offered on special occasions; always before setting out on a journey and on the return from it, and at the time of a birth or of a death in the house. The altar of Apollo stood just outside the door. Special prayers and sacrifices were offered at this altar in times of trouble, but Apollo was not forgotten in the time of joy: those who had traveled far from home stopped to worship on their return; when good news came to the house, sweet-smelling herbs were burned on his altar, and a bride took sacred fire from it to offer to Apollo in her new home.

The Greeks had no stated day every week sacred to the gods, but during the year different days were looked upon as belonging specially to particular gods. Some of these days were greater than others and were honored by public holidays. Others caused no interruption in the everyday life.

Priests were attached to the temples, but sacrifices on the altars in the city or in the home were presented by the king or chief magistrate and by the head of the household. The Greeks did not kneel when they prayed, but stood with bared heads. Their prayers were chiefly for help in their undertakings. They prayed before everything they did: before athletic contests, before performances in the theater, before the opening of the assembly. The sailor prayed before setting out to sea, the farmer before he plowed, and the whole nation before going forth to war. Pericles, the great Athenian statesman, never spoke in public without a prayer that he might "utter no unfitting word."

As time went on, the gods of Olympus seemed less near to mortal men, and they gradually became less personalities than symbols of virtues, and as such they influenced the conduct of men more than they had done before. Athena, for example, became for all Greeks the symbol of self-control, steadfast courage, and dignified restraint; Apollo of purity; and Zeus of wise counsels and righteous judgments.

A particular form of worship specially practiced by the Athenians was that known as the Sacred Mysteries, which were celebrated every autumn and lasted nine days. This worship centered around Demeter and was celebrated in her temple at Eleusis near Athens. Demeter was the Corn Goddess, and it was the story of her daughter Persephone who was carried off by Hades, Lord of the Realm of the Dead, that was commemorated in the Sacred Mysteries.

> Demeter's daughter was playing and gathering flowers, roses and crocuses and fair violets in the soft meadow, and lilies and hyacinths, and the narcissus. Wondrously bloomed the flower, a marvel for all to see, whether deathless gods or deathly men. From its root grew forth a hundred blossoms, and with its fragrant odor the wide heaven above and the whole earth laughed, and the salt wave of the sea. Then the maiden marveled and stretched forth both her hands to seize the fair plaything, but the wide earth gaped, and up rushed the Prince, the host of many guests, the son of Cronos, with his immortal horses. Against her will he seized her and drove her off weeping and right sore against her will, in his golden

> chariot, but she cried aloud, calling on the highest of gods and the best ... and the mountain peaks and the depths of the sea rang to her immortal voice.[14]

Demeter heard the cry, but could not save her daughter, and she went up and down the world seeking her. She reached Attica and was treated kindly, though the people did not at first know she was a goddess. When she had revealed herself to them, she commanded them to build her a temple at Eleusis. But still her daughter did not return to her, and the gods of Olympus took no heed of her lamenting. Then she put forth her power as Goddess of the Corn, and she caused it to stop growing over all the earth. A fearful famine followed, and Zeus tried to persuade her to relent. But she declared that "she would no more forever enter on fragrant Olympus, and no more allow the earth to bear her fruit until her eyes should behold her fair-faced daughter."[15]

At last Zeus consented to interfere, and sent Hermes to bring Persephone back to the earth. When Persephone saw the messenger, "joyously and swiftly she arose and she climbed up into the golden chariot and drove forth from the halls; neither sea, nor rivers, nor grassy glades, nor cliffs could stay the rush of the deathless horses,"[16] until they reached the temple where Demeter dwelled, who when she beheld them rushed forth to greet her daughter. But before leaving Hades, the god had given Persephone a sweet pomegranate seed to eat, a charm to prevent her wishing to dwell forever with Demeter, and it was then arranged that Persephone should dwell with Hades, the lord of the realm of the dead, for one-third of the year, and dwell for the other two-thirds with her mother and the gods of Olympus.

---

[14] Homeric hymn to Demeter.

[15] Homeric hymn to Demeter.

[16] Homeric hymn to Demeter.

This was the story around which centered the worship of the Sacred Mysteries at Eleusis. There came a time when the worship of the gods of Olympus did not satisfy the longings of the Greeks for some assurance that the soul was immortal and that there was a life after the death of the body. Demeter grew to be a symbol to the Greeks of the power of the gods to heal, save, and grant immortality. Her story became an allegory of the disappearance of the corn and fruit and flowers in the winter, and of their return in the spring, bringing with them gifts to men of hope and life. At the festival of Eleusis, a kind of mystery play on the whole legend was acted out. All those who attended the festival were required to prepare for it by a certain ritual of fasting and sacrifice, and it was believed that in the life after death all would be well with those who had taken part in the festival with pure hearts and pure hands.

The greatest religious influence in Greece was probably that of the Oracle. This was the belief that at certain shrines specially sacred to certain gods, the worshipper could receive answers to questions put to the god. In very early times, signs seen in the world of nature were held to have special meanings: the rustling of leaves in the oak tree, the flight of birds, thunder and lightning, eclipses of both the sun and moon or earthquakes.

It is easy to understand how this belief arose. A man, perplexed and troubled by some important decision he had to make, would leave the city with its bustle and noise, and go out into the country where he could think out his difficulty alone and undisturbed. Perhaps he would sit under a tree, and as he sat and thought, the rustling of the leaves in the breeze would soothe his troubled mind, and slowly his duty would become clear to him, and it would seem to him that his questions were answered. Looking up to the sky he would give thanks to Zeus for thus inspiring him with understanding. On his return home, he would speak of how he had heard the voice of Zeus speaking to him in the rustling of the leaves, and so the place would gradually become associated with Zeus, and others would go there and seek answers to their difficulties, hoping to meet with the same experience, until at last the spot would become sacred and a shrine would be built there; it would at length become known from far and near as an Oracle. Plato said of these beginnings of the Oracles that "for the men of that time, since they were not so wise as ye are nowadays, it was enough in their simplicity to listen to oak or rock, if only these told them true." Other places would in the same way become associated with other gods, until seeking answers at Oracles became a well-established custom in Greece.

The great Oracles of Zeus were at Olympia, where the answers were given from signs observed in the sacrifices offered, and at Dodona, where they were given from the sound of the rustling of the leaves in the sacred oak tree. But the greatest Oracle in all Greece was that of Apollo at Delphi. It was at Delphi that Apollo had fought with and slain the Python, and it was thought that he specially delighted to dwell there, and had himself chosen it as the place where he would make known his will.

> Here methinketh to establish a right fair temple, to be a place of oracle to men, both they that dwell in rich Peloponnesus and they of the mainland and sea-girt isles, seeking here the word of wisdom; to them all shall I speak the decree unerring, rendering oracles within my wealthy shrine.[17]

Delphi had been sacred to Apollo ever since these legendary days, and a great shrine and temple was built there in his honor.

When a Greek came to consult Apollo, he had first to offer certain sacrifices, and he always brought with him the richest gifts he could afford, which were placed in the

[17] Homeric hymn to Apollo.

treasury of the god. Then he entered the temple and placed his request in the hands of a priest, who took it into the innermost sanctuary and gave it to the prophetess, whose duty it was to present the petition to the god himself and receive the answer. In ancient times it was believed that a mysterious vapor arose in this sanctuary through a cleft in the rocky floor, and that this vapor, enveloping the prophetess, filled her with a kind of frenzy in the midst of which she uttered the words of the answer given her by Apollo. This answer was written down by the priests and often turned into verse by them, and then taken out to the inquirer. Sometimes these answers were quite plain and straightforward, such as the one which has remained true through all the ages—it was the oracle from Apollo at Delphi which said of the poet Homer: "He shall be deathless and ageless forever." But sometimes the answers were like a riddle that required much thinking over to understand, and sometimes they were so worded that they might mean either of two things, each the opposite of the other! The Oracle at Delphi was frequently consulted by the Greeks at great crises of their history, and it had great influence. It was the priests who in writing down the answer really determined its nature. They were men who were in constant touch with distant places, they had had much experience with human nature, and they were well fitted to give guidance and advice in all kinds of difficult matters. The Oracle at Delphi was thus a power in the worldly affairs of the Greeks, but it was more than that—it was also a source of moral inspiration. It encouraged all manner of civilization and the virtues of gentleness and self-control, it marked the great reformers with its approval, it upheld the sanctity of oaths, and it encouraged respect and reverence for women. On one of the temples were inscribed the sayings "Know thyself" and "Nothing in excess." It was said that these had been placed there by the ancient sages, and in later times they became famous as maxims in the teaching of the great philosophers.

The Oracle was not always right in its interpretations; it sometimes failed in seizing the highest opportunities that lay before it, but as Greek history unfolds itself before us, we can see a gradual raising of moral standards, which was due in great measure to the influence of the Oracle of Apollo at Delphi.

CHAPTER 6

THE OLYMPIC GAMES

THE GREEKS WERE BOUND together by their language, by their religion, and also by their great national games. The origin of these games is still somewhat in doubt. They probably began as some kind of religious ceremony in connection with burials, such as the Funeral Games described by Homer that were held in honor of Patroclus. But whatever may have been their origin, they were firmly established in the earliest times of historic Greece.

Greece was never free from warfare for long at a time. The very fact that the country was divided into so many small and independent states bred jealousies and hatreds, and state was often at war with state. This made it necessary that every Greek citizen should be ready at any moment to take up arms in defence of his home, and so he had to always be in good physical condition. This was brought about by regular athletic training, which was an important part of the education of every Greek. It was considered just as bad to have an ill-trained body as it was to have an ill-trained mind, and one reason why the Greeks so despised the barbarians, as they called all those who were not of the Greek race, was because the barbarian did not train his body to the same extent, and because he loved luxury so much.

All Greeks, then, received athletic training, and this training aimed at developing a beautiful body, for it was believed that to run gracefully was as important as to run swiftly. But though the Greeks loved contests and competition and strove hard for the victory, because they cared so much for grace of movement, they did not lay much stress on record-breaking; and so they kept no records of exceptional athletic feats, which prevents us from knowing details of some of their great athletic achievements.

Games were held in nearly every Greek city and were a source of great pride to the citizens. The more important festivals were those held in honor of Poseidon at Corinth, called the Isthmian Games, those at Delphi which commemorated the slaying of the Python by Apollo, called the Pythian games, and the greatest of all, held every four years at Olympia in honor of Zeus, the Olympic Games. These games were the oldest in Greece and they were at all periods the most important. The first were held, if tradition tells truly, before Greece had begun her history, and the last were held long centuries after she had ceased to be a free state. The first games in historic times were held in 776 B.C., and the interval between each festival was called an Olympiad. These Olympiads constituted the Greek calendar, which took 776 B.C. as its starting point.

This great festival at Olympia was held in August or September and lasted five days. It was a national affair, and Greeks from all over the Greek world went to Olympia to take part in it. For a whole month a truce was proclaimed throughout Greece, all warfare had to stop, and all ordinary business and pleasure gave way to the greater business of going to Olympia. The games were usually held from the eleventh to the sixteenth day of this month of truce, the days before and after being given up to the journey to and from Olympia. All roads were declared safe for these days, and great was the punishment meted out to any who dared molest the pilgrims to Olympia, for they were going to pay honor to Zeus and were considered as specially under his protection. Visitors thronged every road and came from every direction. They came from all the Peloponnesian states, from Corinth,

Athens, and Thebes. They came from the far-off Greek colonies, some from the shores of the Black Sea, looking almost like the nomads with whom they came so much in contact; some from Ionia, men clad in rich robes and of luxurious habits learned from their Oriental neighbors; others from the Western colonies, from Italy and Southern Gaul; and yet others, dark and warm-blooded men, from distant Africa. Yet all were Greeks, bound together in spite of their differences by the common ties of blood and religion. Some were rich, and were accompanied by slaves who brought everything necessary for their comfort; others were poor, who tramped the roads footsore and weary, but sustained by the thought of the joys of the festival when they reached their goal.

The gathering together of so many visitors brought all kinds of people to Olympia: merchants with rich and rare goods for sale, for a regular fair was carried on during the festival, makers of small statues hoping for orders to be placed in the temples, poets who wanted to recite their poems, musicians ready to play on their lyres to any who would listen, gymnastic trainers from all over Greece who hoped to learn some new method that would improve their own teaching, people of all and every kind. Only there were no women. The games were considered too public a festival for it to be fitting for women to be present, and the journey was too long and difficult for them to undertake. The women who lived near Olympia had a festival of their own, when they, too, raced and were awarded prizes, but it was at a different time from the great national festival.

There was no city at Olympia and but few buildings beyond the temples, so when the throng of visitors arrived, the first thing they did was to provide sleeping quarters for themselves. Certain people were allowed to sleep in some of the porticoes of the buildings connected with the temples, others had brought tents and a regular camp arose. Booths of all kinds were erected in which the merchants displayed their wares; friends and acquaintances from different parts of Greece met and talked over all that had happened to them since they last met. Many announcements, too, were made by heralds at this time; the terms of treaties between different Greek states were recited in public, for in those days of difficult communication between states, such a gathering as that at Olympia ensured that news made public then would be widely spread amongst the different states.

Ancient Olympia and the Temple of Zeus (bottom center)

Then there were visits to be made to the great temple of Zeus, and sacrifices to be offered. From the middle of the fifth century B.C. onwards, every visitor to Olympia went reverently into the temple to gaze at the great statue of Zeus. This statue was said to be so marvelously wrought that "those who enter the temple there no longer think that they are beholding the ivory of India and gold from Thrace, but the very deity translated to earth by Pheidias," and it was said that to have made such a lifelike image of the god, either Zeus must have come down from heaven and shown himself in a vision to Pheidias, or Pheidias must have gone up to heaven and beheld him there.

> The god is seated on a throne, he is made of gold and ivory, on his head is a wreath made in imitation of the sprays of olive. In his right hand he carries a Victory, also of ivory and gold; she wears a ribbon, and on her head is a wreath. In the left hand of the god is a scepter curiously wrought in all the metals; the bird perched on the scepter is an eagle. The sandals of the god are of gold, and so is his robe. On the robe are wrought figures of animals and lily flowers. The throne is adorned with gold and precious stones, also with ebony and ivory; and there are figures painted, and images wrought on it.[1]

It is said that "when the image was completed Pheidias prayed that the god would give a sign if the work were to his mind, and immediately, they say, Zeus hurled a thunderbolt into the ground."[2] "Fare ye to Olympia," said an ancient writer, "that ye may see the work of Pheidias, and account it a misfortune, each of you, if you die with this still unknown." And so gracious and full of loving-kindness was the face of the god, that

> if anyone who is heavy-laden in mind, who has drained the cup of misfortune and sorrow in life, and whom sweet sleep visits no more, were to stand before this image, he would forget all the griefs and troubles of this mortal life.[3]

But what of the competitors in the games? They had all been at Olympia for the last thirty days undergoing a final and special

---

[1] Pausanias.

[2] Pausanias.

[3] Dio Chrysostom.

training. Only men of pure Greek blood might compete, and no one who had been convicted of any crime or who was guilty of any impiety or disrespect to the gods. Each candidate had to prove that in addition to his regular athletic training, he had received special training for ten months before coming to Olympia. When they had practiced for the last time, the competitors were addressed by one of the officials in charge. He said to them:

> If you have exercised yourself in a manner worthy of the Olympic Festival, if you have been guilty of no slothful or ignoble act, go on with a good courage. You who have not so practiced, go whither you will.[4]

The names of those who were to enter for the games were then written up on a white board, and should a man withdraw after that, he was branded as a coward. As soon as the competitor was finally enrolled, a boar was offered in sacrifice to Zeus, and then he had to take a solemn oath that he was a full Greek citizen, that he had fulfilled all the conditions necessary for the games, that he would abide by the rules of the contest, and that he would play fair, and such was the spirit of honor and fairness in which the games were played, that in more than a thousand years there appear the names of only six or seven competitors who were guilty of breaking their oath.

The first day of the festival was given up to sacrifices and processions. The different states always sent official representatives to the Games, and these would make public entrance in their chariots, richly arrayed and bearing costly gifts to place in the treasury of the temple. The next three days were devoted to the actual contests.

Long before the dawn on the first of these three days, every seat in the stadium was occupied. It was situated at the foot of

[4] From E. N. Gardiner: *Greek Athletic Sports and Festivals.*

a hill, and every available spot on the slope of this hill was used by the spectators. Should anyone leave his place, even for an instant, it would be lost, and there the spectators sat the whole day through, until the sun went down. What refreshments they needed, they brought with them. The sun beat down on their bare heads, for the Games were in honor of Zeus and he was looked upon as present, and no one might enter the presence of the Father of Gods and Men with covered head. Not until the setting sun gave the signal for the end of the day's contests did they hurriedly rush off to their tents and snatch an hour or two of sleep before the coming of the dawn warned them to rise and secure their seats for the next day's spectacle.

The contests probably took place in the following order: first, there were the foot races; there were several of these varying in length from two hundred yards to three miles. The shortest race of two hundred yards was for a long time the race which brought greatest honor to the winner. Then followed the *pentathlon* which consisted of five contests: throwing the discus, throwing the spear, running, jumping, and wrestling, and the winner was required to have won three out of the five. In the *pentathlon*, in particular, great importance was attached to the gracefulness of every movement, and the jumping, discus, and spear-throwing were generally accompanied by the music of the flute. Then came what was later regarded as the greatest and most exciting race of all, the four-horse chariot race. This was a race that poets loved to describe. Homer tells us how the charioteers

> all together lifted the lash above their steeds, and smote them with the reins and called on them eagerly with words: and they forthwith sped swiftly over the plain; and beneath their breasts stood the rising dust like a cloud or whirlwind, and their manes waved on the blowing wind. And the chariots ran sometimes on

> the bounteous earth, and at other times would bound into the air. And the drivers stood in the cars, and the heart of every man beat in desire of victory, and they called every man to his horses, that flew amid their dust across the plain.[5]

The boxing and wrestling matches came last, and these were the roughest and fiercest of all the contests.

On the last day of the festival the prizes were awarded. They were very simple, but more highly valued than greater honors could have been. Each prize consisted of a wreath of olive, which had been cut from a sacred olive tree with a golden knife by a boy especially chosen for the purpose, and an old tradition required that both his parents should be alive. These wreaths used to at one time be placed on a tripod in the sight of all the people; later, a beautiful table of gold and ivory was made for them. A herald announced the name of the victor, his father's name, and the city from which he came, and then one of the judges placed the wreath on his head. This was the proudest moment of his life, and though other rewards followed on his return home, nothing ever quite equaled that glorious moment.

The last day of the festival was given up to sacrifices to Zeus, followed by banquets and feasting which lasted late into the night. Every kind of honor was shown the victors: poets wrote odes celebrating their victories, and sculptors made models for statues of them, for to every athlete who had won three victories was granted the honor of being allowed to have his statue erected in the open space outside the temple of Zeus.

The festival over, the victors, their friends, and the great throng of spectators returned to their homes. The victors were not only proud on account of their own achievements, but

---

[5] *Iliad*, XXIII.

for the glory they had brought to their city. The news of the approaching arrival of a victor was sent on ahead, and the day of his return to his native city was always honored by a public holiday. In some places it was an old custom to pull down a part of the city wall and make a special entrance, in order that he who had brought the city such glory might enter by a path never before trodden by other men. Songs of triumph were sung to greet him, and he was led to his father's house along a road strewn with flowers. Rich gifts were presented to him, and in every way he was treated as a man whom the city delighted to respect and honor. At Athens the returning victors were honored by being allowed to dine thenceforth at the public expense in the hall where the councilors and great men of the city took their meals.

Pausanias, the traveler to whom we owe descriptions of so much in ancient Greece that has now perished, visited Olympia, and he tells us that

> many a wondrous sight may be seen, and not a few tales of wonder may be heard in Greece; but there is nothing on which the blessing of God rests in so full a measure as the rites of Eleusis and the Olympic Games ...

and Pindar, the Greek poet who has most often sung of the Olympic Games, summed up the feelings of every victor in the words: "He that overcometh hath, because of the Games, a sweet tranquility throughout his life forevermore."

CHAPTER 7

The Greek City-State

Whenever men live together in communities, no matter how small they may be, some form of law has to be observed, in order to maintain order, and so that there may be justice between man and his neighbors. The form that this law takes in different places and in different communities is what is called government.

The earliest form of government in Greece was, like all primitive governments, that of the family, and the word of the head of the family was law to all those belonging to it. The land on which they lived belonged to the family as a whole, not to separate individuals, and the dead were always buried there. In time, the family claimed the land as their own, where they had lived for generations, and where their ancestors were buried.

After a time it became more convenient for families to join together and live in one community. By this means the labor of cultivating the land could be more evenly distributed, and in times of attack from enemies, larger and stronger forces could be used for defence. This grouping of families together made a *village,* and the strongest and most capable man in the village would become its chief.

In time, just as families had found it more to their advantage to group themselves together and form villages, so did the villages living in the same neighborhood find it a better thing to join together and form a still larger community, which became known as a *kingdom,* because instead of having a chief they were ruled by a king. At first the kings, like the chiefs,

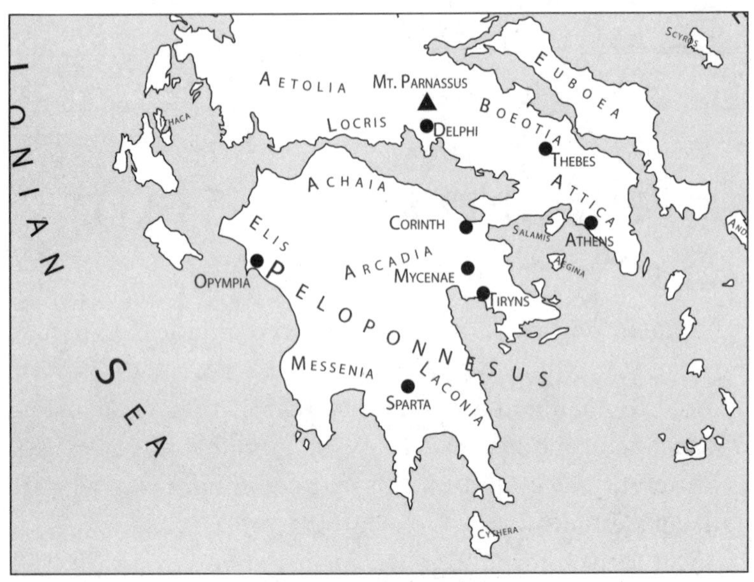

Attica and Peloponnesus

were chosen because of their ability and power. Later the office became hereditary and was handed down from father to son.

Now because the Greek communities lived in the plains, separated from each other by mountains, instead of forming one large kingdom, they formed a great many small ones. There was in ancient times no king of Greece, but Athens, Sparta, Corinth, Thebes, and countless other cities had their own independent forms of government, their own rulers, their own armies, their own ships, and except that they were all Greek and were all bound together by ties of language and religion, they were quite independent of each other. All these independent cities became known in time as city-states, for to the Greek the state meant the city; the territory immediately surrounding it was included in the state, but the city was the most important part of it.

All communities are always governed in one of three ways: either by one man, by a few men, or by many men, and the Greeks tried all these ways until they found the one that answered best to their ideals of what a city-state should be. All states did not develop in the same way, but one stands out from the others as having most nearly reached the Greek ideal. That state was Athens. Her story shall be told in its own place; in this chapter we will see what the Greeks thought an ideal state should be, and what they believed to be the duties of a good citizen.

The Greek philosopher Aristotle wrote a book in which these ideals were set forth.[1] He believed that the end for which the state existed was that all its citizens could lead what he called a "good life," and by that he meant the life which best gives opportunities for man to develop his highest instincts, and which makes it possible for every citizen to develop his own gifts, whatever they may be, in the highest and truest way. To realize such a life, there must be law and order in a state, and Aristotle considered that the first thing necessary to ensure this was that the state must not be too large. He believed that the greatness of a state was not determined by the size of its territory or the number of its population, but that though a certain size and certain numbers helped to make a state dignified and noble, unless these were combined with good law and order, the state was not great. States, he said, were like animals and plants or things made by human art which, if they are too large, lose their true nature and are spoiled for use. But how is one to know when the limit in size and population has been reached? Is there any test by which it can be discovered whether a state has grown or is in danger of growing too large?

Aristotle answered this question by saying that the state must be large enough to include opportunities for all the variety and richness of what he called the "good life," but not so large that the citizens could not see it or think of it in their

[1] *The Politics* of Aristotle.

minds as one whole of which they knew all the parts. He also thought it necessary that the character of all citizens should be well known, an impossibility in too large a community, but how else, he asked, could men elect their magistrates wisely?

The duty of the state was, then, to ensure the possibility of a "good life" to all its citizens. So what was the Greek ideal of citizenship? First of all, every citizen was expected to take a direct and personal share in all the affairs of the state. To the Greek there was no separation between private and public life, all things concerning the state were his affairs, and it was expected that everyone should have an opinion of his own, that he should think clearly on all matters of common interest and not allow himself to be swayed by his feelings without honestly thinking the matter out; and to a Greek, thinking meant straight thinking, the power to know right from wrong, to judge justly without prejudices or passion, to separate the important from the unimportant, and to follow undismayed wherever the truth might lead.

This belief in the duty of the citizen to be personally active in the affairs of the state tended to keep the state small, for if every citizen was to attend the meetings of the Assembly, the latter must be of such a size that everyone could be heard if he desired to speak, and it was necessary that a very short journey should bring the country-dweller into the city to attend to the state business, for frequent journeys and long absences from his farm or his flocks would be impossible for the countryman.

Further, the Greek believed that wealth was allowed to a man only as a trust. Certain privileges and rights came to him because of its possession, but they were privileges and rights that required of their owner distinct duties. The more a man had, the more the state required of him; he had to give his time to the making of laws; his wealth built ships, bore the expense of public festivals, adorned the city with beautiful buildings, and it was spent not on himself alone, but shared with his fellow citizens, and given to that which was their common interest. This resulted in a passionate devotion of every Greek to his city, for every individual had a definite share in some way or other in the making of it, and by the sacrifice of his life in times of danger, he proved again and again that he was in very truth ready to die for it.

The ideal city demanded very high standards of her citizens, and no Greek state attained these perfectly. But in their search for what they conceived to be the highest perfection, the Greeks found out truths both concerning government and the real meaning of citizenship that have remained one of the priceless possessions of mankind.

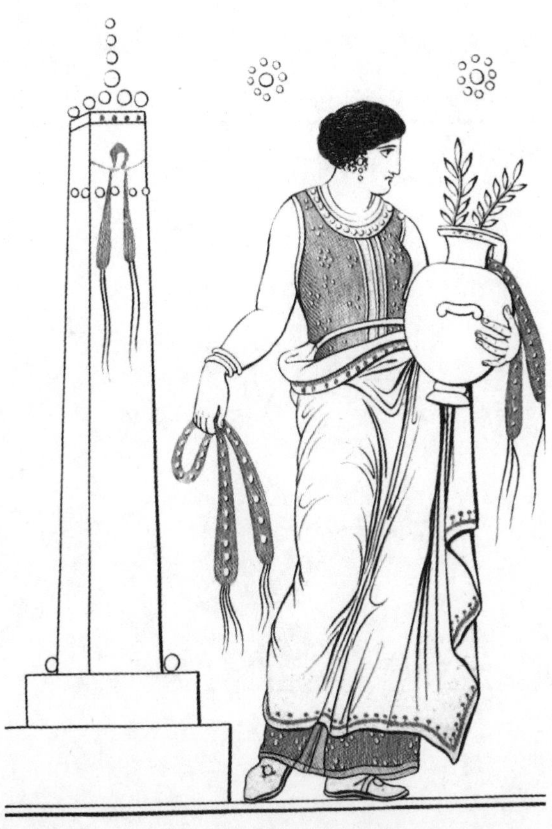

CHAPTER 8

SPARTA[1]

OF ALL THE CITY-STATES in Greece, two stand out from the others as having played the leading part in Greek history. These two are Athens, which most nearly approached the ideal city-state, and Sparta, the foremost military state in Greece.

Sparta was the chief city in the peninsula in the south of Greece called the Peloponnesus, or the Land of Pelops, one of the ancient mythical heroes of that land. During the period of the Greek migrations, the Peloponnesus was probably the last district to be settled, and the tribes which came down into it were called the Dorians. They invaded Laconia, of which the chief city was Sparta, and settled it and the surrounding country. Only the citizens of the city itself were called Spartans; those who owed allegiance to the city but who lived in the country outside were known as Lacedaemonians.

Unlike most other Greek cities, which were well fortified and defended by a citadel built on high ground, Sparta, "low-lying among the caverned hills," had grown out of a group of villages and had no walls. But if she had no outward signs of security from her foes, she had the mightiest warriors in Greece ready to defend her to the utmost. Lycurgus, the wise man of Sparta, was once consulted as to whether it would not be a wise thing to build a wall around the city, and he answered those who came to him with the words: "The city is well fortified which hath a wall of men instead of brick."

[1] Except where noted otherwise, all the quotations in this chapter are from Plutarch: *Life of Lycurgus*.

The Spartans were always afraid of attack from their slaves. These had been the former inhabitants of the land and had been conquered and made slaves by the Spartans. These slaves were called Helots; they were severely and often cruelly treated by their masters, and were always ready to revolt when opportunity came. This was one of the reasons that made the Spartans spend more time than other Greeks in military training. This common danger also had the result of drawing all Spartans very closely together, and of making all other interests subordinate to the supreme duty of protecting the state.

I. The Government of Sparta: Laws of Lycurgus

THE SPARTANS ALWAYS held Lycurgus to have been their great lawgiver, though they never agreed as to when he lived. It is probable that the laws were not made by one single lawgiver, but that many wise men, whose names were unknown to later generations, had helped to create the laws over a long period of time. As Lycurgus was the wise man whose name was known to the Spartans, they came to look back to him as their only lawgiver, because it was by the government he was supposed to have established, and the laws he made, that Sparta became so great a state. He was the brother of a king of Sparta who died leaving a child as his heir. Everyone thought that Lycurgus would take the opportunity to seize the throne and make himself king, but he declared that he would only rule until his nephew should be old enough to become king. Some people, however, would not believe this, and plots were made against his life. This decided Lycurgus to leave Sparta for a time and to visit some other countries with the intention of learning things from them that might be of use to his own land. He went first to Crete, where,

> having considered their several forms of government, and got an acquaintance with the principal men amongst them, some of their laws he very much approved of and resolved to make use of them in his own country. From Crete he sailed to Asia, with design, as is said, to examine the difference betwixt the manners and rules of life of the Cretans who were very sober and temperate, and those of the Ionians, a people of sumptuous and delicate habits, and so to form a judgment. Lycurgus was much missed at Sparta, and often sent for, "for kings indeed we have," the people said, "who wear the masks and assume the titles of royalty, but as for the qualities of their minds, they have nothing by which they are to be distinguished from their subjects."

Lycurgus only, they said, knew both how to rule and how to make the people obey him.

So Lycurgus returned, but on his way he went to Delphi to consult Apollo, and the Oracle called him "beloved of God," and said to him:

> Lo, thou art come, O Lycurgus, to this rich shrine of my temple, Beloved thou by Zeus and by all who possess the abodes of Olympus. Whether to call thee a god, I doubt, in my voices prophetic, God or a man, but rather a god I think, O Lycurgus.[2]

The Oracle then went on to say "that his prayers were heard, that his laws should be the best, and the commonwealth which observed them the most famous in the world."

On his return to Sparta, the first thing Lycurgus did was to reform the government. This was now to consist of three

[2] Herodotus, I.

parts: the Kings, the Senate or Council, and the Assembly. Sparta had always had two kings at a time, who succeeded each other from father to son. It was they who had the right of commanding the army in war, they were always accompanied by a bodyguard of specially picked men, at the public sacrifices and games they had special seats of honor, and at all banquets and feasts double portions of everything were served to them. When it was necessary for the state to consult the Oracle, it was one of the kings who decided on the messenger to be sent.

The Senate or Council consisted of the two kings who were members by right of their birth, and of twenty-eight other men who were elected as Senators for life. Every candidate had to be sixty years old, for Lycurgus believed that until a man had reached that age, he was not wise enough nor fit enough to be

> entrusted with the supreme authority over the lives and highest interests of all his countrymen. The manner of their election was as follows: the people being called together, some selected persons were locked up in a room near the place of election, so contrived that they could neither see nor be seen, but could only hear the noise of the assembly without; for they decided this, as most other affairs of moment, by the shouts of the people. This done, the competitors were not brought in and presented all together, but one after another by lot, and passed in order through the assembly without speaking a word. Those who were locked up had writing tables with them, in which they recorded and marked each shout by its loudness, without knowing in favor of which candidate each of them was made, but merely that they came first, second, third, and so forth. He who was found to have the most and loudest acclamations was declared senator duly elected. Upon this he had a

> garland set upon his head, and went in procession to all the temples to give thanks to the gods.

The duties of the Senate were to prepare all the laws and matters of public interest which were to be brought before the general Assembly; it acted as a court of justice for criminal cases, and its deliberations carried great weight.

Every Spartan citizen over thirty years of age was a member of the Assembly. It was the duty of the Spartans in the Assembly to give or withhold approval of all the matters brought before them by the Senate. It was they who elected the Senators and all other magistrates, and they declared war and made peace. In spite of this Assembly of citizens, the government of Sparta was really in the hands of the Senate, for the members of the Assembly might not discuss the laws submitted for their approval, but only ratify or reject them. At no time were the ordinary citizens given much opportunity to speak at length in public. The Spartans did not like long speeches, and Lycurgus believed that no one should be allowed to talk much unless he could say a great deal that was useful and to the point in a few words. This way of talking became so characteristic of the men of Laconia that it was called by their name, and even today speech that is short and sharp and to the point is called *laconic*.

Many stories are told of this Spartan manner of speech. King Leonidas said once to a man who was speaking about some important matter, but at the wrong time and place, "Much to the purpose, Sir, elsewhere"; and one who kept pressing for an answer to the question "Who is the best man in Lacedaemon?" received as his answer: "He, Sir, that is least like you."

Long after the death of Lycurgus, another special body of men was elected to help in the government. These men were called *ephors*, and there were five of them. It was their business to watch the conduct of the kings, to see that the laws were all carried out and that order and discipline were maintained in the state. Probably no other Greek state would have submitted to such oversight, but the Spartans were well disciplined and did not look upon such an office as one that interfered in any way with their personal freedom. Plato, writing long after of their authority, said that it was "exceedingly like that of a tyrant."

II. Customs in Sparta

HAVING ESTABLISHED the government, Lycurgus next set himself to introduce what he considered good customs amongst the Spartans. The first thing he did was to redistribute the land amongst the citizens. He found that some were very rich and others poor, and he determined that they should all live together sharing in everything alike. So he divided the land into lots and distributed it equally amongst all the citizens. After this had been done, and the time of harvest had come, Lycurgus, "seeing all the stacks standing equal and alike, smiled and said to those about him, 'methinks all Laconia looks like one family estate just divided among a number of brothers.'"

During his travels in other parts of the world, Lycurgus had had opportunities to compare rich states with poor ones, and he had concluded that the richest were not always the best governed, and that wealth did not always bring happiness. He was determined that the Spartans should become good soldiers and that they should be great in war, for he believed that simple habits and simplicity of living were more easily acquired by a nation of warriors than by one devoted only to peace. To this end he wanted to have neither rich nor poor in Sparta, but that all should be alike. Lycurgus, however, was wise enough to know that some people would always manage to make more money or to save more than others, so instead of dividing up all the money in the state equally between everyone, he

> commanded that all gold and silver coin should be called in, and that only a sort of money made of iron should be current, a great weight and quantity of which was but very little worth; so that to lay up twenty or thirty pounds there was required a pretty large closet, and, to remove it, nothing less than a yoke of oxen.

Not only did this prevent any one man from becoming too rich, it lessened the crime of theft in Sparta, for no one would want to steal what was of no value.

This lack of money also resulted in doing away with luxuries; for

> there was no more means of purchasing foreign goods; merchants sent no shiploads into Laconian ports; no gold or silversmith, engraver or jeweler set foot in a country which had no money, so that luxury wasted to nothing and died away of itself.

Everything needed in their houses had to be made by the Spartans themselves, with only the simplest tools, and the houses were roughly built. The law required that the

> ceilings of their houses should only be wrought by the axe, and their gates and doors smoothed only by the saw, and as no man would furnish such plain and common rooms with silver-footed couches and purple coverlets and gold and silver plate,

all Spartans eventually grew accustomed to the plainest and simplest surroundings.

> It is reported that one of their kings was so little used to the sight of any other kind of work, that being entertained at Corinth in a stately room, he was much surprised to see the timber and ceiling so finely carved and paneled, and asked his host whether the trees grew so in his country.

The last law made by Lycurgus to ensure simplicity of living was that all Spartan men and youths should eat at common dining tables, and they were only allowed to eat such food as was permitted by the law. Each table seated about fifteen men, who shared in providing the food; each of them was "bound to bring in monthly a bushel of meal, eight gallons of wine, five pounds of cheese, two and a half pounds of figs, and some very small sum of money to buy flesh and fish with." All the food was prepared in a very simple manner, but "their most famous dish was the black broth, which was so much valued that the elderly man fed only upon that, leaving what flesh there was to the younger." Other Greeks, however, thought this black broth very disagreeable.

It was the custom that at any one table, only those should sit who were friendly to each other. When a newcomer wanted to join a certain table, all those already seated at it voted as to whether they would have him or not. An urn was passed round the table and everyone present dropped into it a small ball of bread. Those who voted for the newcomer dropped their balls without altering their shape, those who voted against him flattened the ball with their fingers before placing it in the urn. One flat ball was enough to exclude a man from the table.

When dinner was over, "every man went to his home without lights, for the use of them was on all occasions forbidden, to the end that they might accustom themselves to march boldly in the dark."

III. Spartan Education

Lycurgus was determined that every Spartan should be so trained that he might become a good soldier, and some of his most important laws concerned the education of children. As soon as a child was born, he was carried to

> the elders of the tribe to which he belonged; it was their business to carefully view the infant, and if they found it stout and well-made, they gave order for its rearing, but if they found it puny and ill-shaped, they ordered it to be taken to a cavern on Mount Taygetus, where it was left to perish, for they thought it neither for the good of the child itself nor for the public interest that it should be brought up if it did not, from the very outset, appear made to be healthy and vigorous.

There was a belief in Sparta that wine was more strengthening than water for a bath, and so the first bath a baby had was always in wine.

There was much care and art, too, used by the nurses; the children grew up free and unconstrained in limb and form, and not dainty and fanciful about their food; not afraid in the dark, or of being left alone; without any peevishness or ill-humor. Upon this account, Spartan nurses were often hired by people of other countries.

At the age of seven, Spartan boys left their homes and their mothers, and the state took charge of the rest of their education.

> As soon as they were seven years old they were to be enrolled in certain companies and classes, where they all lived under the same order and discipline, doing their exercises and taking their play together. Of

> these, he who showed the most conduct and courage was made captain; they had their eyes always upon him, obeyed his orders, and underwent patiently whatsoever punishment he inflicted; so that the whole course of their education was one continued exercise of a ready and perfect obedience. Reading and writing they gave them, just enough to serve their turn; their chief care was to make them good subjects, and to teach them to endure pain and conquer in battle.

As they grew older, Spartan boys were taught to undergo all kinds of hardships. They wore very little clothing, even in the cold of winter, and one coat had to serve them for a year.

> After they were twelve years old they lodged together in little bands upon beds made of the rushes which grew by the banks of the river Eurotas, which they were to break off with their hands without a knife. The old men had an eye upon them at this time, coming often to the grounds to hear and see them contend either in wit or strength with one another, and this seriously and with much concern; so that there scarcely was any time or place without someone present to put them in mind of their duty, and punish them if they had neglected it.
>
> Besides all this, there was always one of the best and most honest men in the city appointed to undertake the charge and governance of the Spartan boys; he again arranged them into their several bands, and set over each of them the most temperate and boldest for the captain, called an *iren,* who was usually twenty years old. This young man, therefore, was their captain when they fought, and their master at home, using them for the offices of his house; sending the

> oldest of them to fetch wood, and the weaker and less able to gather salads and herbs, and these they must either go without or steal; which they did by creeping into the gardens, or conveying themselves cunningly and closely into the eating-houses; if they were taken in the act, they were whipped without mercy for thieving so ill and awkwardly. They stole, too, all other meat they could lay their hands on, looking out and watching all opportunities, when people were asleep or more careless than usual.

If the boys were caught, they were not only punished with whipping, but hunger too, for they were then reduced to their ordinary allowance, which was purposely kept very small in order to force them to use cunning and skill if they wanted to add to it. "So seriously did the Lacedaemonian children go about their stealing, that a youth, having stolen a young fox and hidden it under his coat, suffered it so to tear him with its teeth and claws, that he died rather than let it be seen."

As they grew up the Spartan youths were severely disciplined in every way. Every year the older boys were whipped in public before the altar of Artemis in order to teach them to endure pain without crying out, and it is said that some boys died under this whipping rather than utter a complaint.

> The iren used to stay a little with them after supper, at which time he would bid one of them sing a song; to another he'd put a question which required an advised and deliberate answer; for example, who was the best man in the city? What did he think of such an action of such a man? They accustomed them thus early to pass a right judgment upon persons and things, and to inform themselves of the abilities or

> defects of their countrymen. Besides this, they were to give a good reason for what they said, and in as few words as might be; he that failed of this, or answered not to the purpose, had his thumb bit by his master. Sometimes the iren did this in the presence of the old men and magistrates, that they might see whether he punished justly or not; and when he did amiss, they would not reprove him before the boys, but, when they were gone, he was called to account and underwent correction if he had run far into either of the extremes of indulgence or severity.
>
> Furthermore, in his desire to firmly implant in their youthful souls a root of modesty Lycurgus imposed upon these bigger boys a special rule. In the very streets they were to keep their two hands within the folds of the cloak; they were to walk in silence and without turning their heads to gaze, now here, now there, but rather keep their eyes fixed upon the ground before them. And you might sooner expect a stone image to find a voice than one of those Spartan youths; to divert the eyes of some bronze statue was less difficult.[3]

Not very much time was spent by the boys in learning to read and write; most of their education was given to their gymnastic training, to running, jumping, boxing, and wrestling, and to every kind of exercise that would fit them to be brave and hardy soldiers. They learned some music, chiefly singing, but they only sang such songs as would put life and spirit into them, and their battle songs were sung with great enthusiasm.

During a war, the Spartan young men were treated a little less severely than when in training at home. They were

[3] Xenophon: *Constitution of the Lacedaemonians.*

allowed to curl and adorn their hair, to have costly arms and fine clothes, and their officers were not so strict with them. They marched out to battle to the sound of music. "It was at once a magnificent and terrible sight to see them march on to the tune of their flutes, without any disorder in their ranks, any discomposure in their minds, or change in their countenance, calmly and cheerfully moving with the music to the deadly fight."

Spartan soldier

Spartan discipline did not end when the boys and youths had become men.

> No one was allowed to live after his own fancy; but the city was a sort of camp, in which every man had his share of provisions and business set out, and looked upon himself not so much born to serve his own ends as the interest of his country.

The girls were educated at home, but, like the boys, they were given gymnastic training, and they learned to run and wrestle, to throw the quoit and dart, and to be as strong and brave as their brothers. As the Spartan boys were trained to become good soldiers, ready to die for Sparta, so were the girls trained to become good wives and mothers of Spartan men, and, if they could not themselves die for their country, to be willing to sacrifice those whom they loved best. Every Spartan when he went to war carried a shield that was so heavy that if he fled from the enemy, he would have to throw it away, so it was considered a great disgrace to return home without one's shield; if he died in battle the Spartan was carried home upon it. The Spartan mothers knew this, and when they said farewell to their sons who were setting out to war, they bade them return home with their shields or upon them.

The Spartans held their women in great honor; they listened to their counsel and often acted upon it. A lady of another city once said to a Spartan, "You are the only women in the world who can rule men." "With good reason," was the answer, "for we are the only women who bring forth men."

Having established all these laws and customs, Lycurgus forbade the Spartans to travel, for he was afraid that contact with foreign people would teach them bad habits and make them discontented with their simple way of living. "He was as careful to save his city from the infection of foreign bad habits, as men usually are to prevent the introduction of a pestilence."

At last the time came when Lycurgus felt that his laws and customs were firmly established, and that they were all familiar to the people, but he was afraid that after his death they might be changed. So he thought of a plan whereby he might make them last forever. He called a special Assembly of the people together and told them that everything was well established, but that there was still one matter on which he would like to consult the Oracle. Before he departed on this journey, he made the two kings, the Senate, and the whole Assembly take a solemn oath that they would observe his laws without the least alteration until his return. "This done, he set out for Delphi, and, having first offered a sacrifice to Apollo, he asked the god whether his laws were good and sufficient for the happiness and virtue of his people." The Oracle answered that the laws were excellent, and that the state which kept them should be greatly renowned. Lycurgus sent this oracle in writing to Sparta, and then having once more offered a solemn sacrifice, he took leave of his friends, and in order not to release the Spartans from the oath they had taken, he put an end to his own life, thus binding them to keep his laws forever. Nor was Lycurgus deceived in his hopes, for Sparta continued to be one of the greatest of the Greek states, so Plutarch tells us, as long as she kept the laws of Lycurgus.

CHAPTER 9

THE GROWTH OF ATHENS

I. Earliest Athens

ATHENS WAS THE MOST beautiful city in Greece. It grew up at the foot of the high rock known as the Acropolis, which in the earliest times was the citadel that defended the city. The Acropolis had very strong walls, and the main entrance was guarded by nine gates, which must have made it almost impossible for an enemy to take, and there was a well within the fortress, so that there was always water for those who defended it. But history has told us almost nothing about the mighty lords who built this fortress or about the life of the people over whom they ruled.

But if history is silent, legend has much to say. The earliest rulers of Athens were kings, and of these one of the first was Cecrops. All kinds of stories gathered round his name, and it was believed that he was not altogether human, but a being who had grown out of the earth and was half-man and half-serpent. It was when he was king that the contest took place as to whether Athena, the gray-eyed Goddess of Wisdom, or Poseidon, Lord of the Sea, should be the special guardian of the city. The victory was awarded to Athena, who, taking her spear, thrust it into the ground, whereupon an olive tree marvelously appeared. Poseidon gave the horse as his gift to Athens, and legend adds that, striking the rock with his trident, he brought forth clear salt water, which he also gave to the Athenians. For all time the olive was associated not only with Athena, but with

Attica and Athens, her city, and to the Athenian, the sea became almost like a second home.

The ancient kings claimed descent from the gods. They were not only the lawgivers, but they acted as judges, as chief priests, and in time of war as generals. All who were oppressed had the right to appeal to the judgment seat of the king, and his decisions were final. Though the king was the supreme ruler, there were assemblies of the chief men, always called the *elders*, and of the people, who met whenever the king called them together. These gatherings are important, not because of any real power they possessed in early times, for they only met to hear what the king intended to do, and never to discuss, but because it was from these assemblies that the power of the people to govern themselves developed.

The greatest of the early kings was Theseus, he who slew the Minotaur and freed Athens from paying tribute to Minos the Sea-King of Crete. His greatest claim to be held in the remembrance of his countrymen was that it was believed to have been Theseus who united all Attica under the leadership of Athens. Before this time all the towns and villages in Attica had been independent, but he "gathered together all the inhabitants of Attica into one town, and made them people of one city ... and gave the name of Athens to the whole state."[1] Legend tells of him that he was good and merciful to all who were in need, and a protector of all who were oppressed, but he offended the gods in some way, and died in exile far from Athens. Long centuries after, Cimon, an Athenian general, took possession of the island in which it was said that Theseus had been buried. Cimon

> had a great ambition to find out the place where Theseus was buried and by chance spied an eagle

[1] Plutarch: *Life of Theseus.*

on a rising ground, when on a sudden it came into his mind, as it were by some divine inspiration, to dig there, and search for the bones of Theseus. There were found in that place a coffin of a man of more than ordinary size, and a brazen spearhead, and a sword lying by it, all of which he took aboard his galley and brought with him to Athens. Upon which the Athenians, greatly delighted, went out to meet and receive the relics with splendid processions and with sacrifices, as if it were Theseus himself returning alive to the city. His tomb became a sanctuary and refuge for slaves, and of all those of mean condition that fly from the persecution of men in power, in memory that Theseus while he lived was an assister and protector of the distressed, and never refused the petitions of the afflicted that fled to him.[2]

II. The Rule of the Few: the Oligarchy

It is not known with any certainty how long the rule of the kings lasted in Athens, but they seem to have slowly lost their power, and at last other magistrates were appointed to help them rule. The earliest kings had been hereditary rulers; when they became less powerful, though they were no longer the sole rulers of Athens, these hereditary kings still kept their office for life. Later they ruled for life but were elected; the next change made was to elect a new king every ten years, and at last the greatest change of all took place when the old office of king was done away with, and the power that had once been in the hands of one man was entrusted to three: the Archon, a Greek title meaning *ruler*, who was the chief representative of the state and who gave his name to the year, the King-Archon,

[2] Plutarch: *Life of Theseus.*

who was the chief priest and who had authority over all the sacrifices offered by the state, and the Polemarch, or War-Archon, who was the chief general. Six other archons were also elected whose duty it was to assist the others and to see that the laws of the state were obeyed.

Not everyone could be an Archon; only men from noble families could be elected, and so the power passed into the hands of a few men. The rule of a few is called an *oligarchy*, and it was the second step the Athenians took on their way to being a self-governing community.

At first this rule was good, for by experience the nobles learned a great deal about the art of governing; they realized that order was better than disorder in a state, and they set high standards of devotion to public duty. But the nobles all belonged to one class of people, they were the best educated and the more wealthy, and instead of using their advantages of position and education and wealth as a trust for the good of the whole state (the ideal developed in later years by the Athenians), they grew to consider these things their own exclusive property, and they became very narrow and intolerant. They considered themselves in every way superior to the common people, and began to make laws which benefited themselves alone, ignoring the rights of others, especially those of the poor.

Now the nobles had acquired their power because of their opposition to the rule of one man, but when the authority had been placed in their hands, they proved themselves equally unable to be just towards all, and their rule became as intolerant as that of the kings. Then it was that their authority was questioned in its turn, and the people began to ask each other questions. What is the difference, they asked, between rich and poor, between the noble and the plain man, between the freeman and the slave? Who, they asked, are citizens, and what does it mean to be a citizen? The more the people questioned, the greater grew the oppression and injustice of the nobles, and conditions in Athens grew very bad. Many things helped to create this spirit of discontent: there had been wars, the harvests had been bad and famine had resulted, and there were very harsh laws which allowed debtors who could not pay their debts to sell themselves as slaves. Quarrels arose, and more and more the people questioned the justice of all this. They said:

> But ye who have store of land, who are sated
> and overflow,
> Restrain your swelling soul, and still it and keep
> it low;
> Let the heart that is great within you be trained
> a lowlier way;
> Ye shall not have all at your will, we will not
> forever obey.[3]

III. Solon, the Wise Man of Athens, and the Rule of the Many[4]

IT WAS AT THIS TIME of confusion and distress that Solon, one of the Seven Wise Men of Greece, appeared. By birth he was a noble, but he was a poor man, and in the early part of his life he had been a merchant. There came a time later when the merchant was not looked upon as the equal of the noble, for Plutarch, in writing the life of Solon about seven hundred years after his death, makes an apology for his having been engaged in trade.

> In his time, as Hesiod says, "Work was a shame to none," nor was any distinction made with respect to trade, but merchandise was a noble calling, which

[3] Poem of Solon, from *Aristotle on the Athenian Constitution*, translated by F. G. Kenyon (By permission of Messrs. G. Bell and Sons).

[4] Except where otherwise noted, the quotations in this section are from Plutarch: *Life of Solon.*

> brought home the good things which the barbarous nations enjoyed, was the occasion of friendship with their kings, and a great source of experience.

Solon enjoyed the experience of traveling and seeing new things, a delight that remained with him even to the days of his old age, for when he was old he would say that he

> Each day grew older, and learned something new.

Just before this time Athens had been at war with Megara, a neighboring state, over the possession of Salamis, which had formerly belonged to Athens, an island so near the Athenian harbor that it was absolutely necessary that it should belong to Athens. But the war had been long and unsuccessful, and no victory had been gained by either side. The Athenians were so "tired with this tedious and difficult war that they made a law that it should be death for any man, by writing or speaking, to assert that the city ought to endeavor to recover the island." Solon felt this to be a great disgrace, and knowing that thousands of Athenians would follow if only one man were brave enough to lead, he composed some fiery verses which he recited in the marketplace.

> I come as a herald, self-sent, from Salamis,
> beautiful island,
> And the message I bring to your ears, I have turned
> it into a song.
> Country and name would I change, rather than all
> men should say,
> Pointing in scorn, "There goes one of the cowardly,
> lazy Athenians,
> Who let Salamis slip through their fingers, when it
> was theirs for a blow!"

On then to Salamis, brothers! Let us fight for the
beautiful island,
Flinging afar from us, ever, the weight of
unbearable shame.[5]

Only parts of these verses have come down to us, but they so inspired the Athenians that it was determined to make one more effort to regain Salamis, and this time they were successful. Salamis was recovered, but conditions in Athens remained as unhappy as before. Solon was now held in such high honor that we are told, "the wisest of the Athenians pressed him to succor the commonwealth." He consented, and was elected archon in 594 B.C.

The first thing Solon did was to relieve the debtors. He did this by canceling all debts and by setting free all who were slaves for debt, and by forbidding by law any Athenian to pledge himself, his wife, or his children as a security for debt. This brought such relief to the state that the act was celebrated by a festival called the "Casting off of Burdens."

Solon wanted to bring order into the distracted city he loved, for he held that order was one of the greatest blessings a state could have; so he set to work to reform the government of the state, to reduce the power of the nobles, and to give justice to the people. "First, he repealed all Draco's laws," (Draco had been an earlier lawgiver in Athens) "because they were too severe, and the punishments too great; for death was appointed for almost all offenses, so that in after times it was said that Draco's laws were written not with ink, but blood."

Solon reformed the government of the state in such a way that even the poorest citizens had political rights. They could not all be archons, but Athens, like Sparta and other

[5] Poem of Solon, translated by Leslie White Hopkinson.

Greek states, had her general Assembly of the people, and they could all vote at this, and they could all take part in electing the magistrates. While recognizing the rights of the poorer citizens, Solon believed in preserving a certain part of the power of the nobles, and he arranged the taxation and public service to the state in such a way that the greater the wealth of a man and the higher his position, the more the state demanded of him, both in service and money. Solon himself said of these laws:

> I gave to the mass of the people such rank as befitted their need,
> I took not away their honor, and I granted nought to their greed;
> While those who were rich in power, who in wealth were glorious and great,
> I bethought me that naught should befall them unworthy their splendor and state;
> So I stood with my shield outstretched, and both were safe in its sight,
> And I would not that either should triumph, when the triumph was not with the right.[6]

Solon did not please everyone with his laws, and when

> some came to him every day, to commend or dispraise them, and to advise, if possible, to leave out or put in something, and desired him to explain, and tell the meaning of such and such a passage, he, knowing that it was useless and not to do it would get him ill will, it being so hard a thing, as he himself says, in great affairs to satisfy all sides, bought a

[6] Poem of Solon, from *Aristotle on the Athenian Constitution*, translated by F. G. Kenyon (By permission of Messrs. G. Bell and Sons).

> trading vessel and, having obtained leave for ten years' absence, departed, hoping that by that time his laws would have become familiar.

He stayed away the ten years and then returned to Athens. He took no further part in public affairs, but was reverenced by all and honored until his death.

During his travels, Plutarch tells us that Solon visited Croesus, the rich king of Lydia. This visit could never have taken place, for Solon died in Athens just as Croesus came to the throne. As a matter of fact, Plutarch knew that quite well, but he says that he must tell so famous a story, even if it were not true, because it was so characteristic of Solon and so worthy of his wisdom and greatness of mind, and that it would be foolish to omit it because it did not agree with certain dates about which in any case everybody differed!

> They say that Solon, coming to Croesus at his request, was in the same condition as an inland man when first he goes to see the sea; for as he fancies every river he meets with to be the ocean, so Solon, as he passed through the court and saw a great many nobles richly dressed, and proudly attended with a multitude of guards and footboys, thought everyone had been the king, till he was brought to Croesus, who was decked with every possible rarity and curiosity, in ornaments of jewels, purple and gold, that could make a grand and gorgeous spectacle of him. Now when Solon came before him and seemed not at all surprised, Croesus commanded them to open all his treasure-houses and carry Solon to see his sumptuous furniture and luxuries, though he did not wish it; and when he returned from viewing all, Croesus asked him if ever he had known a happier man than he. And when Solon answered that

> he had known one Tellus, a fellow citizen of his own, and told him that this Tellus had been an honest man, had had good children, a competent estate, and died bravely in battle for his country, Croesus took him for an ill-bred fellow and a fool. He asked him, however, again, if besides Tellus, he knew any other man more happy. And Solon replied, yes, two men who were loving brothers and extremely dutiful sons to their mother, and when the oxen delayed her, harnessed themselves to the wagon and drew her to Hera's temple, her neighbors all calling her happy, and she herself rejoicing; then, after sacrificing and feasting, they went to rest, and never rose again, but died in the midst of their honor a painless and tranquil death. "What," said Croesus angrily, "and dost thou not reckon us amongst the happy men at all?" Solon, unwilling either to flatter or exasperate him more, replied, "The gods, O King, have given the Greeks all other gifts in moderate degree, and so our wisdom, too, is a cheerful and homely, not a noble and kingly wisdom, and him only to whom the divinity has continued happiness unto the end, we call happy."

This story is not only characteristic of Solon, but of the Greek spirit. That spirit did not like the extreme of extravagance and luxury and display, and it believed that there was glory that money could not buy. The Greek who had been rewarded by a wreath of olive leaves had achieved the greatest success known in Greece. This was once told to a noble who had come with the Persian king to invade Greece, and when he heard it, he exclaimed to the king, "What kind of men are these against whom thou hast brought us to fight, who make their contest not for money but for honor!" That was the spirit of Greece.

IV. The Tyrants

ATHENS DID NOT ATTAIN her political freedom without a struggle. She passed from the rule of one man, the king, to the rule of the few, the oligarchy, and then through the legislation of Solon to the rule of the many, the people. But during this period of change, attempts were made from time to time by powerful leaders to get the rule entirely into their own hands. These leaders who wanted to seize the power and rule alone were called by the Greeks *tyrants*. There was always the danger that such a ruler, with no authority in the state to control him, would become harsh and oppressive, but this was not always the case. Though the rule of one man alone is never the best kind of rule, some of the Greek tyrants made a real contribution to the states they governed. They were generally well-educated men, who encouraged art and literature; they were always ambitious men, and they often dreamed of extending their power beyond the limits of their own state, and though it was a purely personal and selfish ambition, the efforts at realizing it brought the Greeks into contact with things which had hitherto lain beyond their horizon, for in the Age of the Tyrants, no Greek had yet dreamed dreams or seen visions of empire.

A man was not always successful in his efforts to become a tyrant. About forty years before Solon was made archon, Cylon, a rich Athenian of good family and popular as a winner at Olympia, tried to seize the power. He consulted the Oracle, which told him to make the attempt at the time of the great festival of Zeus. He took this, as all Greeks would, as meaning the Olympic Games, so he waited until the time came for them, and then he and his friends attacked the Acropolis and actually took possession of the citadel. But it seemed that the Oracle, giving one of those answers of which the meaning was uncertain, had referred to the festival held in honor of Zeus near Athens and not to that at Olympia, and

Cylon's attempt was unsuccessful. Some of the conspirators fled, and others took refuge in the Temple of Athena. Here they were safe, for no one would dare touch anyone who had placed himself under the protection of the goddess in her sanctuary. But there was no food or drink in the temple, and as nobody brought them any, some of them died of hunger, and Cylon was forced to escape secretly. Then the archon told the remainder that if they would surrender, their lives should be spared. They consented, but, not quite trusting the archon, they fastened a long rope to the statue of Athena and held it as they descended the hill, so that they might still be secure under the protection of the goddess. Halfway down the hill, however, the rope broke, and the archon, declaring that this showed that Athena had withdrawn her protection, had the men put to death. This was looked upon as a great crime by the Athenians, for they considered it not only treachery, but also sacrilege, and it made the archon many enemies. These declared that as a punishment for this act, a curse would rest on him and on all his descendants. His family was descended from Alcmaeon, and so the curse was spoken of as the curse on the Alcmaeonids, and the enemies of this family always attributed to it any calamities that happened to the city.

The most famous tyrant in Athens was Peisistratus. While Solon was away on his travels, quarrels broke out again, and when he returned, though he took no active part in affairs, he tried by privately talking with the leaders of the various factions to restore peace, but he was unsuccessful. "Now Peisistratus was extremely smooth and engaging in his language, a great friend to the poor, and moderate in his resentments, so that he was trusted more than the other leaders."[7] In this way he became very popular, and he deceived people into thinking that he was only desirous of serving the

[7] Plutarch: *Life of Solon.*

state, when in reality he was doing all in his power to further his own ambition and to become sole ruler of Athens. In order to gain supporters, he appeared one day in the marketplace in his chariot, which was sprinkled with blood, and he himself appeared to be wounded. On being asked what was the matter, he said his enemies had inflicted these injuries upon him. One of his friends then declared that the Athenians should not permit such a thing to happen, and advised that a bodyguard of fifty men should accompany him to protect him from any further assault. This was done, whereupon with their help, Peisistratus took possession of the Acropolis. But his power was not great enough to hold it, and he and his followers were driven out of Athens.

Peisistratus soon returned, however, having thought of a curious plot by which he might deceive the Athenians into believing it to be the will of the gods that he should rule. During a festival, accompanied by a large number of youths, he entered Athens in his chariot, and at his side stood a tall and beautiful woman, dressed as Athena herself and carrying a shield and spear. The people shouted that the goddess herself had come from Olympus to show her favor to Peisistratus, and he was received as tyrant. But again he was driven out by his enemies. He stayed away ten years, and then once more he collected an army and advanced on Athens. Once more he was successful and entered the city. This time no one opposed him; he became sole ruler and remained so until his death some ten years later.

Peisistratus showed himself to be a wise ruler; he improved the city and brought water into it by an aqueduct, and he built new roads. Along these roads, especially in places near springs and fountains, were placed small statues of Hermes, and on the pedestals under some of them verses were engraved, perhaps similar to the following lines, to cheer the traveler on his way:

I, Hermes, by the gray seashore
Set where the three roads meet,
Outside the wind-swept garden,
Give rest to weary feet;
The waters of my fountain
Are clear and cool and sweet.[8]

It was Peisistratus who made the law that men wounded in battle and the families of those who were killed should be cared for by the state. He built a new temple to Athena and made her festival more splendid, and he had the ancient poems of Homer collected and written down, so that they might be more carefully preserved. But good ruler as he was, he was still a tyrant, and during his rule the people were deprived of their right to govern themselves; but so long as he lived, no one opposed him.

After Peisistratus' death, his sons Hippias and Hipparchus succeeded him, but they forgot that, after all, they could only remain tyrants if the people permitted it, and they grew insolent, harsh, and overbearing. Two young Athenians formed a plot to assassinate these oppressors at the next festival. The day came, and Hipparchus was slain, though Hippias escaped. The conspirators were instantly seized and put to death, and Hippias continued to rule alone. He became more and more cruel, and the Athenians were bowed down under his oppression. At last the Spartans came to their help. They came, because for some time whenever they sent to Delphi to ask any advice of the Oracle, the answer always came, "First set Athens free." With this help, Hippias was driven out and sent into exile.

Athens was free. The rule of the tyrants was over, and Athens was once more able to rule herself, to become that state

---

[8] Written by Anyte, a poetess, probably in the 4th century B.C., translated by Sir Rennell Rodd in *Love, Worship and Death.*

of which, when it was asked, "What shepherd rules and lords it o'er their people?" the answer could be given, "Of no man are they called the slaves or subjects."[9]

Athena mourning

[9] Aeschylus: *The Persians.*

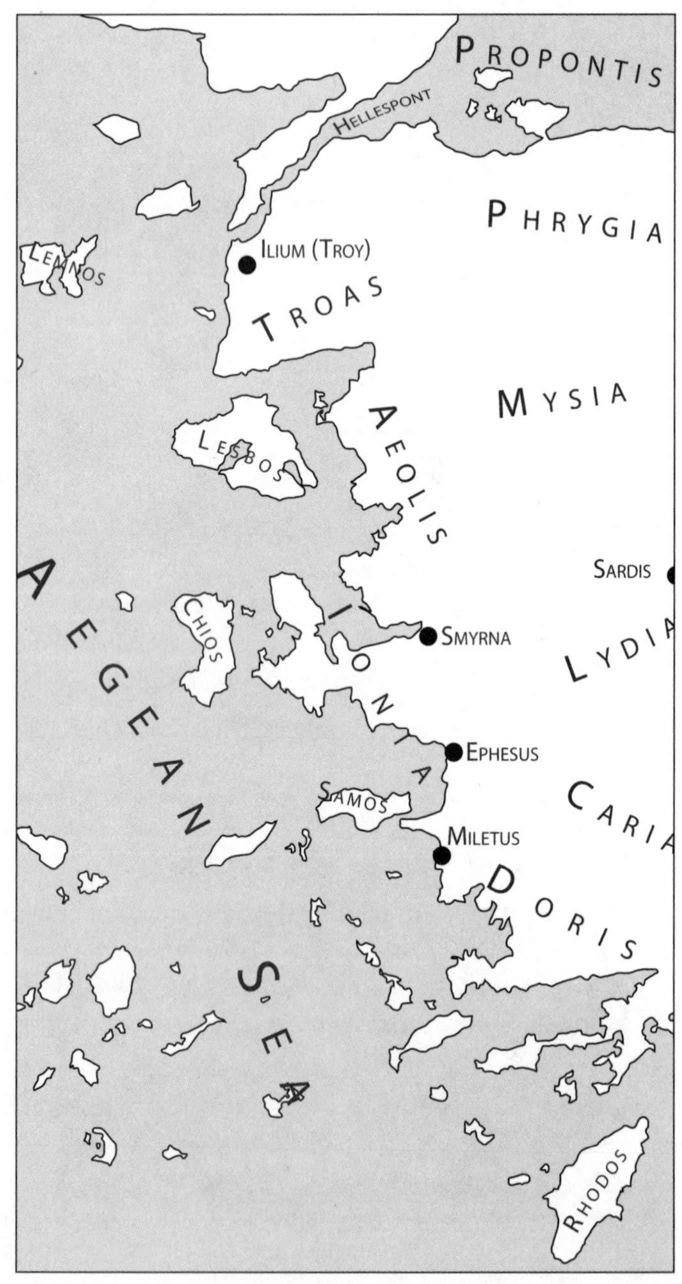

Greek colonies in Asia Minor

CHAPTER 10

Greek Colonies

I. The Founding of a Colony

The Greeks were a sea-faring people, and they were an adventurous people. Their own land was small, but the islands of the Aegean formed steppingstones, as it were, to the coast of Asia Minor, and the Aegean world was very familiar to the Greek sailor. Greek galleys were found in most ports, and the Greek trader became a formidable rival of the Phoenician.

As they sailed from island to island and on to the mainland, the Greeks came to realize that some of these places would make suitable homes, and by degrees they began to colonize them; that is to say, parties of settlers went from their mother-cities to found new homes overseas. Pioneers (adventurous explorers) had always gone out first and brought back reports of the new land. A suitable site required a good water supply, and fertile land where corn could be grown and the vine and the olive cultivated. The settlers needed timber from which they could build their ships, and of course a good harbor was necessary. They also hoped to find friendly natives who would help them in their farmwork and who would in no way oppose them or interfere with their plans. The natives must have looked with eyes of wonder upon the newly arrived Greeks. Most of them had never seen men of this kind before. The only foreign traders they knew were the Phoenicians, and they came only to trade, to exploit the people, and to exhaust the resources of the place in order to gain gold. They knew only these "greedy merchant men with countless gauds in black ships."[1] But these newcomers were different. A Greek poet has described this Greek adventure over the sea, and the wonder of those who received the strangers:

> A flash of the foam, a flash of the foam,
> A wave on the oarblade welling,
> And out they passed to the heart of the blue:
> A chariot shell that the wild waves drew.
> Is it for passion of gold they come,
> Or pride to make great their dwelling?[2]

All kinds of considerations took the Greeks over the sea to found new homes for themselves: some of them were discontented with their government and wanted to go where they could establish a new one; owing to the increasing population their home-cities became overcrowded, which created difficulties in the supply of food, and many thought a new land would give them greater and better opportunities; others found that the trade of the colonies was a source of wealth; and others went just for the love of adventure. Whenever a body of men decided to sail away and found a colony, they first consulted the Oracle at Delphi as to whether they would be successful, and whether Apollo approved of the place they had chosen and would bless their enterprise. They then chose a leader, whose name was always held in honor and handed down as the founder of the colony. On leaving the mother-city, the colonists went in procession to the Town Hall, and there they received fire from the sacred hearth, which they took with them, and from which they kindled the fire on their own sacred hearth in their new home.

---

[1] *Odyssey*, XV.

[2] Euripides: *Iphigenia in Tauris*, translated by Gilbert Murray.

These colonies were quite independent of the mother-city as far as government was concerned, but the colonists looked back to the home from which their race had sprung with great affection; wherever they went they were still Greeks—they spoke the Greek language and they worshipped the Greek gods.

Colonies were founded not only in the islands of the Aegean, but along the coasts of the Black Sea, which the Greeks called the Euxine. These latter colonies, of which Byzantium (the ancient name for Constantinople, now Istanbul) was the greatest, became very important to the Greeks, for they supplied them with grain which grew abundantly on the northern shores, and with iron from the Hittite land in the Southeast.

The greatest of all the colonies in the East were the Ionian colonies, those in the eastern part of the Aegean and on the coast of Asia Minor. The Greeks who colonized them were descended from the Ionian tribes who had settled in Greece, and so this whole region became known as Ionia. Herodotus tells us that the "Ionians had the fortune to build their cities in the most favorable position for climate and seasons of any men whom we know." Miletus was the greatest of the Ionian cities, and it developed a very rich civilization some time before the great days of Athens.

Great thinkers came out of Ionia. Thales, one of the Seven Wise Men of Greece, the philosopher, and man of science, studied the heavens and he foretold an eclipse of the sun in a certain year, which came to pass. The Babylonians before him had made similar studies, but he carried on their work and made greater advances. He questioned in his mind what his discoveries might mean, and for the first time in the world he declared that the movements of the sun and moon and stars were determined by laws, and that the eclipse of the sun was due to certain movements of the heavenly bodies, and had nothing to do with the anger of the Sun-God. This was the first step in the freeing of men's minds from superstition, and though man had a long way to go and many things to learn before he could take the second step, it was Thales of Miletus and other Ionian philosophers in the sixth century B.C. who first set men to thinking about the real meaning of the things they saw about them in the world of nature. What we today call *science* was born in Ionia more than two thousand years ago. Many wise sayings of Thales have been preserved. It was he who said, "Time is the wisest of all things, for it finds out everything."[3]

Another wise man of science who lived in Miletus was Anaximander. He was one of the earliest map-makers, and he and Hecataeus, who wrote a geography as a "text to Anaximander's map," were amongst the first thinkers who developed the science of geography.

The Ionian colonies could claim poets as well as men of science. Chios is said to have been the birthplace of Homer, and Lesbos, one of the largest of the island colonies, was famous as the home of Sappho, not only the first woman whose poetry has come down to us, but one of the great poetesses of the world. Unfortunately we have only a few fragments of her poems.

THE GIFTS OF EVENING

Thou, Hesper, bringest homeward all
　　That radiant dawn sped far and wide,
The sheep to fold, the goat to stall,
　　The children to their mother's side.[4]

The face of Greece was turned towards the East, but adventurous spirits have always turned towards the unknown West; the Phoenicians had already explored Western regions and the Greeks soon followed. The Elysian Fields lay to the west, and what might man not discover if he sailed in that direction? The Greeks did not find the Elysian Fields, but they

[3] Diogenes Laertius.

[4] Poem of Sappho, translated by Sir Rennell Rood in *Love, Worship and Death.*

did what proved to be of the most momentous importance in the history of the civilization of the world: they founded colonies in the south of Italy, and these became so flourishing that the whole region was known as Magna Graecia. These Greeks brought their writing, their art, and their poetry and planted them securely in the land that was one day to be ruled by a city, which was then only a little settlement at the foot of seven hills. Rome became mightier than Greece in the art of governing a great empire, and the day was to come when she would rule Greece herself, but in the development of her civilization, Rome acknowledged the Greeks as her teachers.

Other Greek colonies were founded at Syracuse in Sicily, and along the north coast of the Mediterranean to what is now Marseilles, and in the South a few were established along the shores of Africa to Naucratis in Egypt. The colonies in the south of Spain and along the north coast of Africa from the Pillars of Hercules to Carthage were in the hands of the Phoenicians, but by the end of the sixth century B.C., the prevailing civilization in the Mediterranean was Greek.

II. Ionia and Lydia

The Ionian colonies occupied the coastland of Asia Minor, but the mainland behind them was the kingdom of Lydia. For a long time the Ionians lived in peace, developing their science, thinking out their ideas, and growing in power. But at the beginning of the sixth century B.C., a new race of kings came to the Lydian throne. They were vigorous and ambitious, and did not approve of the important coast towns with good harbors being in the hands of Greeks. So they attacked them, beginning with Miletus which was besieged. The siege lasted eleven years, but the city did not surrender. At last the Lydians realized that Miletus was being saved by her harbor, and though it could get no food or supplies of any kind by land, everything needed was brought to the city by water. So the king of Lydia gave up the idea of conquering Miletus, and he made a treaty of peace with her.

It was probably not only the impossibility of conquering a seaport that made the king of Lydia give up the siege of Miletus, but the knowledge that a war cloud had arisen in the East which was steadily drawing nearer his land. This was the army of the Medes, a nation which had already helped to destroy Assyria, and whose army was now coming towards Lydia. Several battles took place with no very decisive result, but at length the two armies met in a battle

> in which it happened, when the fight had begun, that suddenly the day became night. And this change of the day, Thales the Milesian had foretold to the Ionians. The Lydians, however, and the Medes, when they saw that it had become night instead of day, ceased from their fighting and were much more eager both of them that peace should be made between them.[5]

So peace was made, and soon after the king of Lydia died, and Croesus succeeded him.

Now the Ionian cities, when they saw their independence threatened, ought to have combined together and made a joint stand against their enemies, but each separate city so prized its independence and so feared anything that might even seem to lessen it, that they stood alone, and when Croesus, being at peace with the Medes, determined to get possession of these Ionian cities, he was able to attack them one by one and overpower them. He allowed them to keep their own independent government, but he required them to pay him a regular yearly tribute. This was the first time in Greek history

[5] Herodotus, I.

Amphitheater at Miletus

that Greeks had paid a tribute to anybody; before the reign of Croesus, all Greeks everywhere had been free. Croesus left a certain amount of independence to the Ionian cities, because of his admiration for the Greeks and their civilization. He sent rich and splendid gifts to Apollo, and in return was made a citizen of Delphi, and at the Pythian Games his envoys were given special seats of honor.

By this time Cyrus, the Mede, had become king of Persia, and Croesus watched his increasing power with great anxiety. He saw that war was bound to come, so he sent a message to the Oracle at Delphi asking if he should march against the Persians. What Herodotus called a "deceitful" answer came back, that if he crossed the river Halys, a great empire would be destroyed. Thinking, of course, that this meant the destruction of the Persian empire, Croesus crossed the river and met Cyrus in battle. Now the Lydians were famous for their horses, and horsemen were an important part of their army. Cyrus knew this, so he thought of a plan whereby he might defeat them. He ordered all the camels, which were in the rear of his army carrying the provisions and baggage, to be unloaded and the camels brought to the front, and there well-armed men were mounted on them. He did this because the horse has a fear of the camel and cannot endure either to see his form or to smell his scent; and so soon as the horses smelled the camels and saw them, they galloped away to the rear, and the hopes of Croesus were at once brought to nought."[6]

The Lydians were defeated and withdrew into Sardis, the capital. But after a short siege, Cyrus took the city, and Croesus lost his kingdom. He did not want to fall into the hands of the Persians, so he had a great pyre erected, and after pouring out a libation to the gods, he mounted it and bade his slaves set it on fire that he might perish in the flames, rather than fall alive into the hands of his conqueror. But suddenly clouds arose in the sky and rain fell, extinguishing the flames. It was thought that this must be the doing of Apollo, to whom Croesus had always shown much honor; and hearing of it, Cyrus commanded that Croesus should be taken down from the pyre and brought into his presence. "Croesus," he asked him, "what man was it who persuaded thee to march upon my land and so to become an enemy to me instead of a friend?" And Croesus answered,

> O King, that I did this was to your gain and my loss, and the fault lies with the god of the Hellenes who led me to march against you with my army. For no one is so senseless as to choose of his own will war rather than peace, since in peace the sons bury their fathers, but in war the fathers bury their sons. It was the will, I suppose, of the gods that these things should come to pass thus.[7]

Lydia was now added to the Persian Empire and only the Ionian cities were still independent. But even in the face

---

[6] Herodotus, I.

[7] Herodotus, I.

of the great danger from Persia, they did not unite, and one by one Cyrus conquered them until Ionia had been reduced to subjection, and when the cities on the mainland had been conquered, then the Ionians in the islands, being struck with fear by these things, gave themselves to Cyrus, who, moving through the upper parts of Asia, subdued every nation, passing over none.[8]

And thus it came about that the Greeks who lived in Asia lost their independence and became subject to the Great King of Persia.

Tomb of Cyrus the Great at his capital Pasargades

[8] Herodotus, I.

CHAPTER 11

The Beginning of the Persian Wars[1]

I. Darius and the Ionian Revolt

The rule of the Lydian kings over the Ionian cities in Asia Minor had not been a hard one, but that of the Persians was different, for they established tyrants in all the Greek cities, and required the assistance of their soldiers and sailors in their wars, things which were very bitter to the freedom-loving Greeks.

When Darius had become king, he determined, like the Great Kings before him, to add yet more lands to his empire, and so made ready an army which was to invade Scythia, the region north of the Black Sea. As the Persians themselves were not naturally sailors, the Greeks in the Ionian cities were forced to send a large number of ships to the help of this expedition.

Darius and his army set out, and, arriving at the River Ister (now known as the Danube), were joined by the Ionian ships. Here Darius commanded that a bridge of boats should be built, and then taking a cord in which he tied sixty knots, he called the Ionian leaders together and said to them:

> Men of Ionia, do ye now keep this rope and do as I shall say: so soon as ye shall have seen me go forward against the Scythians, from that time begin, and untie a knot on each day; and if within this time I am not here,

[1] Chapter VIII is taken chiefly from the *History* of Herodotus.

> and ye find that the days marked by the knots have passed by, then sail away to your own lands. Till then, guard the floating bridge, showing all diligence to keep it safe and to guard it. And thus acting, ye will do for me a very acceptable service.

Having said this, Darius hastened forward on his march.

Scythia was a land totally unknown to the Persians, and strange tales were told in later years of the adventures of the king and his army. The Scythians were a nomad people, and they believed themselves to be invincible. When they heard that Darius was in their land with the intention of conquering it, they "planned not to fight a pitched battle openly, but to retire before the Persians and to drive away their cattle from before them, choking up with earth the wells and the springs of water by which they passed and destroying the grass from off the ground." For some time Darius pursued this mysterious people, but he could never come up with them.

> Now as this went on for a long time and did not cease, Darius sent a horseman to the king of the Scythians and said as follows: "Thou most wondrous man, why dost thou fly forever, when thou mightest do of these two things one?—if thou thinkest thyself able to make opposition to my power, stand thou still and cease from wandering abroad, and fight; but if thou dost acknowledge thyself too weak, cease then in that case also from thy course, and come to speech with thy master, bringing to him gifts of earth and of water." To this the king of the Scythians made reply: "My case, O Persian, stands thus: never yet did I fly because I was afraid, either before this time from any other man, or now from thee; nor have I done anything different now from that which I was wont to do also in time of peace;

> and as to the cause why I do not fight with thee at once, this also I will declare unto thee. We have neither cities nor land sown with crops, about which we should fear lest they be captured or laid waste, and so join battle more speedily with you; but know this, that we have sepulchers in which our fathers are buried; therefore come now, find out these and attempt to destroy them, and ye shall know then whether we shall fight with you for the sepulchers or whether we shall not fight. Before that, however, we shall not join battle with thee. About fighting let so much as has been said suffice; but as to masters, I acknowledge none over me but Zeus my ancestor and Hestia the queen of the Scythians. To thee then in place of gifts of earth and water I shall send such things as it is fitting that thou shouldst receive; and in return for thy saying that thou art my master, for that I say, woe betide thee."

The king of Scythia sent gifts to Darius as he had promised, strange and mysterious gifts. He sent him a bird, a mouse, a frog, and five arrows. At first the Persian could not imagine what these gifts might mean, but one of his wise men interpreted them as meaning: "Unless ye become birds and fly up to the heaven, or become mice and sink down under the earth, or become frogs and leap into the lakes, ye shall not return back home, but shall be smitten by these arrows."

The Scythians continued to lead the Persians from place to place in this strange campaign, until at last they brought them back again to the Ister (the Danube) where the Ionians were guarding the bridge of boats. The Scythians arrived first, and they tried to persuade the Ionians to break up the bridge, so that Darius would find no means of escape and would then fall into their hands. Some of the Greeks were in favor of doing this, but the Tyrant of Miletus, who wanted to keep on good terms

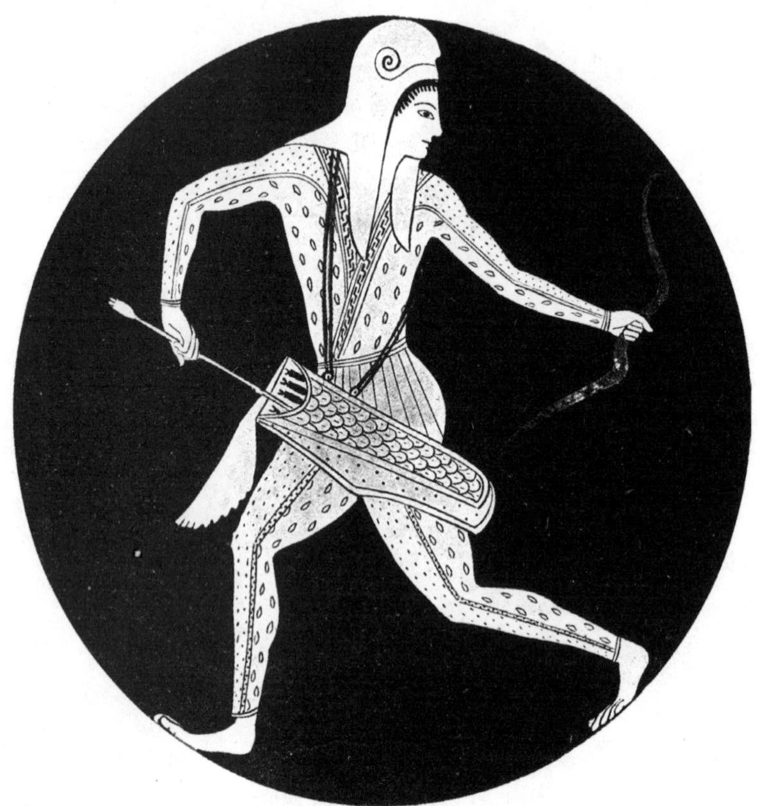

Scythian archer

with Darius, advised against such treachery, and his word prevailed. In order to get the Scythians away, they pretended, by moving a few of the boats, that they were going to destroy the bridge, but when Darius came, after a moment's fear that he had been deserted, he found the bridge still there, and he crossed safely and returned to his own land.

When Darius learned that it was owing to the advice of the Tyrant of Miletus that the bridge had been saved, he sent for him and praised him highly for what he had done, telling him he knew him to be a man of understanding and well disposed towards him, and that in consequence he wished him to go with him to Susa, to eat at his table, and to be his counselor. Darius did this because in reality he distrusted him and preferred that he should be near him in Susa, where his movements could be watched.

Meanwhile, a kinsman of this Tyrant had been left in his place at Miletus, and when a rebellion broke out in Naxos, he undertook to put it down, hoping that this would bring him favor from the king. Unfortunately for him, he was unsuccessful, and as he very much feared the wrath of the king, he decided that as he could not put down the rebellion, he would himself join it.

The Greeks in Miletus were more than willing to revolt from the Persian yoke, and they were joined by other Ionian cities. But they did not feel strong enough to stand alone against Persia, so they sent ambassadors to Greece asking for help from their kinsmen there. Sparta was asked first. The ambassador appealed to the king and told him that the Ionians felt it was a disgrace not only to themselves but also to the Spartans, who were looked upon as the leaders of all men of Greek birth, that they should be slaves instead of freemen. "Now therefore," he said, "I entreat you by the gods of Hellas to rescue from slavery the Ionians who are your own kinsmen." He then went on to describe the Persians whom he might conquer, the wealth of their land, and all the benefits that would come to him if he would help the Ionians to become free. The king told him he would think it over and give him an answer on a day following. When the day came, the king asked the ambassador from Miletus how many days' journey it was from the sea of the Ionians to the residence of the king. Now it must be remembered that no part of Greece was far from the coast, and that no Greek, not even a Spartan who was a soldier rather than a sailor, was happy if he felt out of reach of the sea. So the feelings of the Spartan king can be understood when he was told that to reach the city of the king of Persia was a journey of three months from the sea. His mind was quickly made up. "Guest-friend from Miletus," he said, "get thee away from Sparta before the sun has set; for thou speakest a word which sounds not well in the ears of the Lacedaemonians, desiring to take them a journey of three months away from the sea."

The ambassador then went to Athens, where he was more successful. The Athenians sent twenty ships to help the Ionians, and the Eretrians, out of gratitude for help once received from Miletus when they were in need, added five. With this assistance, the Greeks marched to Sardis and seized it. But a house accidentally caught fire, and the fire began to spread over the whole town. This gave the Persians time to rally from the surprise of the attack, and they drove out the Greeks, who scattered in dismay. Some were overtaken and slain, and the rest retreated to their ships.

Darius was in Susa at this time, and the news of the burning of Sardis was taken to him there. He did not take much account of the Ionians who had taken part,

> because he knew that they at all events would not escape unpunished for their revolt, but he enquired who the Athenians were; and when he had been informed, he asked for his bow, and having received it and placed an arrow upon the string, he discharged it upwards towards heaven, and as he shot into the air he said: "Zeus, that it may be granted me to take vengeance upon the Athenians!" Having so said, he charged one of his attendants, that when dinner was set before the king he should say always three times: "Master, remember the Athenians."

Darius remembered the Athenians, but he had first to punish the Ionian cities for their share in the revolt. One by one he attacked them, and they fell before him, until at last only Miletus was left. Her only hope of safety lay in her sea-defences, and all the ships the Ionians could collect were gathered at Lade, an island just outside the harbor of Miletus. Now the Ionians had copied many of the customs of their Lydian neighbors, and they were more luxurious and led softer lives than their kinsmen on the mainland. Efforts were made by one of the Greek leaders to make the Ionians drill and exercise themselves every day, that they might all be in good condition when the day of battle should come. For a time they submitted, but they were lazy and unaccustomed to such toil, and the hard work and exercise so exhausted them that they declared they would prefer slavery to such hard work as was being forced upon them. So they refused to drill anymore, and "they pitched their tents in the island like an army, and kept in the shade, and would not go on board their ships or practice any exercises."

There could only be one result to this. The Persians gave battle, and the Ionians were defeated, some of them even disgracing themselves by sailing away without fighting at all. The men of Chios refused to play the coward and fought to the end, but there were too few of them to turn the tide of battle, and the Persians overcame them completely. Miletus was taken by storm, the city was destroyed by fire, the men were all put to death, and the women and children were sent as slaves to Susa.

The news of the fall of Miletus was a terrible blow to the Greek world. Up to that time she had been the greatest of the Greek cities. She was rich, not only in material wealth, but in all that concerned the intellectual life, and now she had fallen! It was, above all, a blow to the Athenians, for Athens and Miletus were closely bound by ties of kinship, and when an Athenian dramatist

> composed a drama called the "Capture of Miletus," and put it on the stage, the body of spectators fell to

> weeping, and the Athenians moreover fined the poet heavily on the grounds that he had reminded them of their own calamities; and they ordered also that no one in the future should represent this drama.

Thus it came about that again the Ionians became the subjects of the Persian king. They had been punished to the utmost for daring to revolt from his power, and there was no fear that they would do it again. Darius was now free to remember the Athenians.

II. Marathon

In 492 B.C. Darius sent Mardonius, a general who was high in his favor, across the Hellespont with orders to march through Thrace and Macedonia and, having firmly secured their allegiance, to march on to Greece, where Athens and Eretria were to be severely punished for their share in the burning of Sardis. Darius had several reasons for this expedition: the punishment of Athens and Eretria was the one about which most was said, but as it never entered his mind that he could be defeated, Darius probably intended so to destroy the cities on the mainland that the Greeks in Ionia would see that it would be useless to rely on the help of their kinsmen should they ever think of another revolt, and so to punish the European Greeks that they would never dare to interfere again in the affairs of the Persian Empire. But underneath all these reasons were dreams of conquest. The Great King had visions of subduing the whole of Greece and of extending his empire into Europe.

Preparations were made and Mardonius set out. A fleet was to sail close to the coast and keep in constant touch with the army. All went well until Mount Athos was reached and here a great storm arose.

> The north wind handled them very roughly, casting away very many of their ships. It is said that the number of ships destroyed was three hundred, and more than twenty thousand men; for as this sea which is about Athos is very full of sea monsters, some were seized by these and so perished, while others were dashed against the rocks; and some of them did not know how to swim and perished for that cause, others again by reason of cold.

The army fared little better, for it was attacked by some Thracian tribesmen, and though Mardonius forced them to submit to him, he suffered so much loss in the fighting, that as his fleet also had been almost entirely destroyed, he was obliged to depart back to Asia having gained no honor in this undertaking.

Two years went by, and then another expedition was planned. Before it started, Darius sent messengers to Athens and Sparta and other Greek states demanding of them earth and water, the symbols of submission to the Great King. Some states agreed to the demand, either because they were struck dumb with terror at the mere thought that the Great King might invade their land, or because they thought that he was certain to conquer and that by submitting at once they would secure themselves and their land from destruction. Athens and Sparta, however, refused uncompromisingly. The messengers were thrown by the Athenians into a pit, and by the Spartans into a well, and told that if they wanted earth and water they could get them for themselves.

On hearing what had happened to his messengers, Darius gave orders to the generals to set out at once for Greece, and to punish every state which had refused submission by enslaving all the inhabitants and bringing them bound to Susa. In particular, Athens and Eretria, for their other misdeeds, were to receive the severest treatment. So the expedition started.

Archers of Darius

Remembering the disaster at Mount Athos, the fleet sailed this time across the Aegean, touching at Naxos, the first of the Ionian cities that had revolted, and which now received its punishment by being burned and its people enslaved. Then the Persians went on to Delos, where they offered sacrifices to Apollo, and from there they sailed to Eretria, which they immediately attacked. The city held out for six days, and then traitors within the walls opened the gates to the Persians who entered and took the city. They burned it to the ground and carried off all the inhabitants into slavery. And so Eretria was punished for her share in daring to burn a city of the Great King.

News of these movements of the Persians had, of course, reached Athens, but up to this time the Athenians had not considered them as having any dangerous consequences to themselves. But Eretria was not very far from Athens, and when the news of the utter destruction of this city arrived, the Athenians realized the full extent of their peril. Now Hippias, the exiled Tyrant, had taken refuge with the Persians, but he had never given up hope of one day returning to Athens. He was at this very time plotting with friends in the city, and the Persians, knowing this, hoped for their aid in taking Athens. So the Athenians were threatened with dangers both from within and without.

It is easy to imagine the dismay of the Athenians when they heard that Eretria had been destroyed, and that the Persians, the conquerors of the world, were even then on their way to Athens. How could they hope, with their small army, to stand against the great empire? Help must be had, and that quickly. To whom should they turn, if not to Sparta, the foremost military state in Greece, and which, should Athens fall, would be the next state attacked? Self-defence, if no other reason, would surely bring them with speed to Athens. So the Athenians sent Pheidippides, a swift runner, with a message imploring help. The distance from Athens to Sparta is a hundred and fifty miles, and the

Greek soldier of Marathon

hours must have seemed very long to the Athenians as they waited for his return with the answer. But so swiftly did he run that he was back before they had dared expect him. How had he done it? For two days and nights he had raced "over the hills, under the dales, down pits, and up peaks," and in less than forty-eight hours he had reached Sparta. He rushed into the midst of their Assembly with but scant ceremony and passionately entreated them to come to the help of Athens.

But to this cry for help the Spartans gave but a cool answer. They would come, certainly, but must wait five days until the moon was full when it was their custom to sacrifice to Apollo, and to break this custom would be to slight the god. When the full moon had come, then they would send help to the Athenians. Pheidippides only waited long enough to receive the answer, and then with despair in his heart, he started back to Athens. Over the hills and the plains, through woods and across streams he raced, appealing in his heart to the gods to whom Athens had ever shown honor, yet who seemed to have deserted her in her utmost need. Was there no help? Suddenly he stopped; whom did he see sitting in a cleft of a rock? It was Pan, the Goat-God.

"Stop, Pheidippides," he cried, and stop Pheidippides did. Graciously and kindly did the god then speak to him, asking him why it was that Athens alone in Greece had built him no temple, yet he had always been and would forever be her friend. And now in her peril, he would come to her aid. He bade Pheidippides go home and tell Athens to take heart, for Pan was on her side.

If Pheidippides had run swiftly before, now he ran as if wings had been given to him. He hardly touched the earth but seemed to race through the air, and burst upon the waiting Athenians, who had not dared expect him so soon, with the news that Sparta indeed had failed them, but that Pan, mighty to save, would fight for them!

But now grave news was brought: the Persians were landing in Attica. It was September of the year 490 B.C., and the hot summer days had not yet passed away. The Athenians could not wait for the Spartans, they must go out alone and meet the foe. They marched twenty-four miles in the heat over a rough and rugged road, until they reached the plain of Marathon. There they found the Persians.

Now the Persians had probably never intended to fight at Marathon. They hoped that the friends of Hippias in Athens would in the end betray the city to them, and their plan in landing where they did was to bring the Athenian army away from the city, and if possible to keep it away, until they should have received the expected signal from the traitors. The plain of Marathon is surrounded by hills except where it slopes down to the sea. The Athenians occupied the stronger and higher positions, the Persians were encamped near the sea, and their ships were anchored close to the coast. For several days the armies watched each other and waited. The Athenians counted the days until the moon should be full, when there was hope that the Spartans might come; the Persians knew that every added day gave the conspirators more time to do their treacherous work in the city. And so both sides waited.

Suddenly help came to the Athenians from an unexpected quarter, help which cheered and inspirited them. Through a cloud of dust on one of the roads leading down into the plain, they saw the gleam of spears and helmets. It could not be the Spartans, for they would not come from that direction. As the men drew nearer, they were found to be an army from Plataea, a little city in Boeotia, to which Athens had sent succor when some years before Thebes had threatened her independence. Now, though not thought of by the Athenians as an ally, because she was small and not powerful, she had remembered those who had befriended her in the hour of need, and had come down with all her fighting men to help Athens in her peril.

Miltiades was the Athenian general at Marathon. He knew why the Persians were waiting, and when messengers brought him word that they were embarking some of their men, knowing that this meant their intention to sail around to Athens, because the conspirators in the city were ready to act, he gave the signal to attack. There were probably two Persians to every Greek, so the Greek army had been arranged in the best way to face these odds. The center line was thin, but the wings were very strong. On the first onslaught from the Persians, this center gave way, but the wings immediately wheeled around and attacked the Persians with such force that these gave way before them and fled down to the shore. The Greeks pursued, and there was terrific fighting and slaughter. Seven of the Persian ships were destroyed by fire, but the others escaped. The Persians fled to these remaining ships, leaving over six thousand dead on the plain and quantities of rich plunder. They set sail for Athens, and knowing that the Athenian army was still on the plain of Marathon, they hoped to find the city undefended and that the traitors would open the gates to them. But the Athenians who had won at Marathon were not going to let their city fall into the hands of the enemy, so when they saw the Persian ships setting sail, wearied as they were with the strain of battle, they marched over the twenty-four miles of rough road to the defence of their beloved city, leaving only a small force behind to guard the bodies of the slain and to prevent thieves from carrying off the plunder.

On his return from Sparta, Pheidippides had been asked what reward should be given him for the race he had run. All he asked was to be allowed to fight for Athens, and when the Persians had been driven away, then to wed the maid he loved and to dwell in his own home. It was given him as he asked. He fought in the fight at Marathon, but when the victory had been gained, one more race was asked of him. Over the rough road he ran to Athens to shout in the ears of the waiting Athenians: "Athens is saved!" But his heart could not contain such great joy, and having delivered his message, he died.

The Athenian army reached Athens before the enemy, and when in the moonlight the Persian ships sailed into the bay near Athens, there, ready to meet them, were the same men who had defeated them at Marathon earlier in the day. The Persians were not willing to meet them again so soon; they realized that they had indeed suffered grievous defeat, and commands were given for the broken army and crippled fleet to set sail for Asia.

The Spartans came as they had promised, but too late to take any part in the battle.

> There came to Athens two thousand of them after the full moon, making great haste to be in time, so that they arrived in Athens on the third day after leaving Sparta; and though they had come too late for the battle, they desired to behold the Medes; and accordingly they went on to Marathon and looked at the bodies of the

> slain; and afterwards they departed home, commending the Athenians and the work which they had done.

But no part of the honor of Marathon belonged to Sparta.

The Athenians lost about two hundred men in the battle. They were buried where they had fallen, a great mound was erected over their graves, and their names were inscribed on tall pillars nearby. Much rich plunder was left by the Persians on the plain, some of which was offered to Apollo as a thank-offering for the victory. The Athenians built a beautiful little temple, known as the Treasury of the Athenians, at Delphi, and Pan was not forgotten. A grotto on the side of the Acropolis was dedicated to him, where sacrifices were offered in memory of his help and encouragement when both had been sorely needed.

The Greeks who had fought at Marathon had many tales to tell of the battle, and many a wondrous deed was said to have been performed. It was thought that the gods themselves and the ancient heroes of Athens had taken part. Pan, they said, had struck such fear into the hearts of the Persians that they had fled in disorder and terror, a terror ever after known as a *panic*. Some even said that Theseus and other heroes had been seen, and for a long time the spirits of those who had been slain were thought to haunt the battlefield.

The battle of Marathon was one of the great events in history. For the first time the East and the West had met in conflict, and the West had prevailed. The Athenians were the "first of all the Hellenes who endured to face the Median garments and the men who wore them, whereas up to this time the very name of the Medes was to the Hellenes a terror to hear." Never before had a little state faced the world empire of the Persians and conquered. The Greek soldiers had shown themselves capable of facing the Persians, long looked upon as the conquerors of the world, and of prevailing against them. The civilization of the East had met with a check on the very threshold of Europe, and Athens had saved Greece. But the Great Kings of Persia were not accustomed to defeat; would they accept this, and was Greece and, through Greece, Europe, safe, or would the Persians come again?

CHAPTER 12

THE GREAT PERSIAN INVASION UNDER XERXES[1]

I. The Preparations

a. The Persians

THE PERSIANS CAME AGAIN. When the report came to Darius of the battle which was fought at Marathon, the king, who even before this had been greatly exasperated with the Athenians on account of the attack made upon Sardis, then far more than before displayed indignation, and was still more determined to make a campaign against Hellas. He at once sent messengers to the various cities of the empire and ordered that they should ready their forces. Each city or community was called upon to send more men than at the former time, and to also send ships of war, horses, provisions, and transport vessels. When these commands had been carried all around, all Asia was moved for three years, for all the best men were being enlisted for the expedition against Hellas, and were making preparations. But before the expedition was ready, a rebellion broke out in Egypt, and soon after Darius died, and "thus he did not succeed in taking vengeance upon the Athenians."

Darius was succeeded by his son Xerxes. The first thing he did was to crush Egypt, and then he turned his attention to Greece. Mardonius, the general who had been forced to retire

[1] Except where otherwise noted, Chapter IX is taken or adapted from the *History* of Herodotus.

from Thrace after the wreck of the fleet off Mount Athos, was anxious to persuade the king to undertake another invasion. He probably wanted to retrieve the reputation he had lost on the former occasion, and hoped that if Greece became a Persian province, he would be made governor. "Master," he would say to the king, "it is not fitting that the Athenians, after having done to the Persians very great evil, should not pay the penalty for that which they have done." He would add that Greece was "a very fair land and bore all kinds of trees that are cultivated for fruit and that the king alone of all mortals was worthy to possess it."

Xerxes did not need much persuasion. He came of a race of kings whose word was the law of the Medes and Persians that changeth not, and his wrath was great against the states that had not only refused to submit to the Persian king, but had actually defeated his army in battle. He would wreak his vengeance upon them for what they had done, and he declared that he would march an army through Europe against Greece, in order, as he said, "that I may take vengeance on the Athenians for all the things which they have done both to the Persians and to my father. I will not cease until I have conquered Athens and burned it with fire."

Our knowledge of the preparations made for this invasion by Xerxes comes from Herodotus. He may have exaggerated some things in his account, but his history was written for the Greeks of his own time, and he wanted to make clear to them how great was the difference between the East and the West; how much better their freedom and independence were than the slavery endured by states which were ruled by the Great King. For these states had no voice in the affairs of the empire; if the king went to war, they had to follow him and lay down their lives for causes in which they had no concern, and which generally only ministered to the greed and avarice of their rulers.

Having decided on the invasion of Greece, Xerxes sent heralds throughout the empire proclaiming the war and bidding all fighting men make ready and join the king at Sardis. There the troops were mustered, and in the spring of 480 B.C., ten years after the battle of Marathon, Xerxes and his army were ready to set out. They were to march to the Hellespont, and then, by way of Thrace and Macedonia, descend into Greece. The fleet was to join the army at the Hellespont and, by sailing close to the shore, keep in constant touch with the army on land.

At last all was ready and the day came for the army to leave Sardis. First the baggage-bearers led the way together with their horses, and after these, half the infantry of all the nations who followed the Great King. Then a space was left, after which came the king himself. Before him went first a thousand horsemen, chosen from amongst the noblest Persians, and then a thousand spearmen; these were followed by ten sacred horses with rich trappings, and behind the horses came the sacred chariot of the great Persian god, drawn by eight horses, with the reins held by a charioteer on foot, for no human creature might mount upon the seat of that chariot. Then followed Xerxes himself, attended by spearmen chosen from the best and most noble of all the Persians. They were in turn followed by a body of men known as the Immortals, of which there were always ten thousand. They bore this name, because if any one of them made the number incomplete, either by death or illness, another man filled his place, and there were never either more or fewer than ten thousand. These were the very flower of the Persian army; nine thousand of them carried spears ending with silver pomegranates, and the spears of the thousand who guarded the front and rear were ornamented with pomegranates of gold.

Now of all the nations, the Persians showed the greatest splendor of ornament and were themselves the best men, and they were conspicuous for the great quantity of gold they used. The Medes and Persians wore tunics and trousers, for which the Greeks always felt the greatest contempt because they were worn by the Barbarian and not the Greek, and soft felt caps on their heads. They carried wicker shields and had short spears and daggers and bows and arrows. Besides these a host of nations followed the Great King: there were Assyrians, famous throughout all ancient history as a great fighting race, with bronze helmets, linen breastplates, and wooden clubs studded with iron; there were Bactrians with bows of reed and short spears; Scythians with their pointed sheepskin caps, and their battle axes; there were Caspians dressed in skins and wielding short swords; there were men of strange and savage appearance, some wearing dyed garments, with high boots, others dressed in skins, and all bearing bows and arrows, daggers and short spears. Arabians came too, with their loose robes caught up ready for action and long bows in their hands; and dark Ethiopians, fearful to look upon in their garments made of the skins of the leopard and the lion; these fought with long bows with sharp pointed arrows, and with spears and clubs, and when they went into battle, each man painted half his body white and half of it red. And other Ethiopians there were, who wore upon their heads horses' scalps with the ears and manes still attached. Many more nations and tribes were represented in this mighty army. Some carried small shields, small spears, and daggers, others wore bronze helmets to which the ears and horns of an ox were attached.

All these and many more made up the army of the Great King; they came from North, South, East, and West, and from the islands of the sea, and they marched in magnificent array from Sardis to the shores of the Hellespont, where the fleet was to meet them. When Xerxes reached the strait, he had a throne of white marble built for him, and there he took his seat and gazed upon his army and his ships. Now Xerxes

Soldiers of Xerxes' army, according to Herodotus

had given orders that a bridge should be built across the Hellespont over which his army should pass into Europe. But when the strait had been bridged over, a great storm arose which destroyed the bridge. When Xerxes heard of it, he was exceedingly enraged and bade his soldiers scourge the Hellespont with three hundred strokes of the lash, and he let down into the sea a pair of fetters. While this was being done, the sea was thus addressed:

> Thou bitter water, thy master lays on thee this penalty, because thou didst wrong him, though never having suffered any wrong from him; and Xerxes the King will pass over thee, whether thou be willing or no.

The sea was punished in this way, and command was given to cut off the heads of those who had had charge of building the bridge. Not with impunity was the Great King disobeyed. A new bridge was then built, stronger and more secure than the first, and over this the army passed in safety.

In order that no accidents might happen, honor was paid to the gods, incense and fragrant perfumes were burned upon the bridge, and the road was strewn with branches of myrtle. The crossing was to take place early in the morning, and all were ready before the dawn broke. As the sun was rising, Xerxes poured a libation from a golden cup into the sea, and prayed to the Sun that no accident might befall him until he had conquered Europe, even to its furthest limits. Having prayed, he cast the cup into the Hellespont and with it a golden mixing bowl and a Persian sword, as gifts to the powers of the sea. When Xerxes had done this, the great army passed over the bridge in brilliant array. It took seven days and seven nights without any pause for the whole army to pass over, and it is said that at the end, a man who dwelled on that coast and who had watched the crossing, exclaimed:

> "Why, O Zeus, in the likeness of a Persian man and taking for thyself the name of Xerxes instead of Zeus, hast thou brought all the nations of men to subdue Hellas? Was it not possible for thee to do it without the help of these?"

When the whole army had crossed over safely, Xerxes inspected it. He drove through all the ranks in his chariot, and scribes who accompanied him wrote down for him the names of all the nations who were represented. When he had done this, the ships were drawn down into the sea, and Xerxes, changing from his chariot to a ship of Sidon, sat down under a golden canopy and sailed along by the prows of the ships and inspected his fleet. The ships then set sail, and were to go along the coast to Therma, where the land army was to meet them again.

Xerxes and the army then proceeded on their march through Thrace and Macedonia. Messengers had been sent on ahead some time before to make arrangements for provisioning this great host. All the towns through which the Persians passed were compelled to provide food and drink for the men and the animals with them. It was a tremendous undertaking, and scarcity and want were left behind as the invaders passed on. The inhabitants had to provide great quantities of wheat and barley, they were made to give up the best of the fatted cattle, their birds, and fowls, and to provide everything in the way of gold and silver needed for the service of the table. All this was a great hardship to the people of the land, and in one place they went in a body to their temple and entreated the gods that for the future they would keep them from such evil. Nevertheless they offered up a thanksgiving to the gods for all the mercies they had shown to them in the past, and especially for having granted that Xerxes, while in their city had only thought good to take food once in each day, for it would have been altogether impossible for them to have provided him with breakfast in the same manner as dinner.

The fleet sailed safely to Therma and was joined there by the army as had been arranged. So far all had gone well for the Persians. They had succeeded in a great achievement, for apparently without any serious mishaps, this tremendous army had been transported from Sardis right around the Aegean, and had been fed and cared for on the way. The difficulties must have been very great, and only splendid organization could have done it successfully. But it had been done, and now Xerxes, in order to wreak his vengeance on one Greek city, stood with his army composed of the fighting men of forty-six nations on the very threshold of Greece. From Therma he could look across to the mountains of Thessaly, he could see snow-topped Olympus, the home of the gods who watched over the fortunes of the freedom-loving Greeks. The Athenians had withstood the Persians at Marathon, but now the whole of the Eastern world was marching against them. Could they withstand that mighty host, or would they be forced to submit?

b. The Greeks

Ten years had passed between the battle of Marathon and the arrival of Xerxes on the borders of Greece. In the years preceding 490 B.C., the Persian power had been a terror to the Greek. Not content with subduing Asia even to the dim borders of India, the Great Kings had pushed their way to the Aegean and had even conquered the Greeks who dwelled along its eastern coasts. Then, like an ominous war-cloud, this mighty power had crossed the sea to Greece itself. But there the unexpected had happened. At Marathon the Persians had sustained at the hands of a small state, until then comparatively unknown, the first great defeat they had ever met with. The Plataeans had helped, it is true, but their numbers had been small and it was the Athenians who had really defeated the Persians. Since then the Athenians had enjoyed a great reputation for their military power. Myths and legends had woven themselves around the name of Marathon with the result that the power of the Athenians was reputed greater than perhaps it actually was, and that of Persia was certainly depreciated. If she had been as formidable as had always been supposed, how could the Athenians have defeated her almost unaided? So for a number of years the Greeks had felt less terror at the name of Persia, and they had been enjoying a certain feeling of security, little realizing how false it was.

But suddenly they were shaken out of their calm. Rumors of the Persian preparations for an invasion of Greece reached them, rumors which were doubtless exaggerated, but which nevertheless had much truth in them. It is amazing how in spite of slow and difficult communication, news was swiftly carried in those days from place to place. So the Greeks were fairly well informed as to what the Persians were doing. At this crisis the Athenians took the lead, and

> if anyone should say that the Athenians proved to be the saviors of Hellas, he would not fail to hit the truth; these were they who, preferring that Hellas should continue to exist in freedom, roused up all of Hellas. Nor did fearful oracles, which came from Delphi and cast them into dread, induce them to leave Hellas.

The first thing the Greeks did was to hold a conference at Corinth, which was attended by envoys from all the leading states except Argos and Thebes, which stood aloof. At this conference the Greeks made three important decisions. They resolved that they would reconcile all their own differences and bring to an end the wars they had with one another; as

Hellenes they would unite against the common foe. Then they determined to send spies to Asia, who should bring back accurate reports of the preparations and power of Xerxes. And lastly, they would send messengers to the colonies in Sicily, Corcyra, and Crete asking for assistance.

Three spies set out, but they were captured in Sardis and condemned to death. When Xerxes, however, heard what had happened, he sent for the spies, who were brought into his presence. To their surprise, instead of being led out to immediate execution, Xerxes commanded that they should be led around and shown the whole army, both foot and horse, and when they had seen everything, they were to be set free to return home. He did this because he said that

> if the spies had been put to death, the Hellenes would not have been informed of his power, how far beyond any description it was; while on the other hand by putting to death three men, they would not very greatly damage the enemy; but when these returned back to Hellas, he thought it likely that the Hellenes, hearing of his power, would deliver up their freedom to him themselves, before the expedition took place, and thus there would be no need for them to have the labor of marching an army against them.

Little did Xerxes know the kind of freedom-loving people with whom he had to deal. So the spies looked at everything and then returned to Greece.

Meanwhile, the messengers to the colonies returned. The answers to the appeal for support were very disappointing. Neither Sicily, Corcyra, nor Crete would help. They either refused outright or made uncertain answers. They seem to have thought more of their own preservation than of the safety of Greece as a whole; they thought the Persian would probably win, and they preferred either to be on the winning side, or to be in such a position that they could make good terms with the Persian, did he conquer.

The Greeks now made ready to go out with their armies to meet the Persian foe. The chief command was given to Sparta, the greatest military state in Greece, and they marched to the Vale of Tempe in the north of Thessaly, where they hoped to meet Xerxes and prevent him from coming into Greece. When they got there, however, they found that it would not be possible to hold the pass against the enemy, for it was so situated that the Persians could attack them by sea as well as by land, and there was another path over the mountains by which the Persians could attack them in the rear. So the Greeks withdrew to Corinth in order to deliberate further where they would meet the enemy. This retreat from Thessaly took place while Xerxes and his army were crossing the Hellespont, and it had important consequences for the Persians, for the Thessalians, hitherto never very loyal to Greece, seeing the other Greeks leave their land, "took the side of the Medes with a good will and no longer half-heartedly, so that in the course of events they proved very serviceable to the king."

The Greeks now decided on making a stand much further south at Thermopylae. This was a narrow pass and easier to defend, so they resolved

> to guard it and not permit the Barbarian to go by into Hellas, and they resolved that the fleet should sail to Artemisium, for these points are near to one another, so that each division of their forces could have information of what was happening to the other.

At Thermopylae the Greeks awaited the Persians.

II. Thermopylae

It was midsummer in the year 480 B.C. when the Persian host left Therma and marched down through Thessaly to the Pass of Thermopylae. The Persians encamped before the Pass and a scout was sent forward to bring back information as to what the Greeks were doing. Only a small force of Greeks was defending the Pass, the main part of the Greek army was kept back further to the south to defend the isthmus. A small body of about three hundred Spartans had been sent under King Leonidas to defend the Pass of Thermopylae, and, if possible, to prevent the Persians from advancing further into Greece. These three hundred men were the picked bodyguard of the king, a force in which only fathers of sons might serve, so that their families might not die out of Sparta.

The Persian scout went cautiously forward and, to his great surprise, saw some of the Spartans practicing athletic exercises and others combing their long hair. He could not see the rest, as an ancient wall built across the Pass hid them from sight. He returned to Xerxes and reported on what he had seen. The king sent for a Greek who was in his camp and asked him what this behavior of the Spartans might mean. He told him that they were following an ancient Spartan custom, for "whenever they are about to put their lives in peril, they then attend to the arrangement of their hair." The Spartans knew against what odds they had to fight, but their duty had placed them where they were, and no Spartan ever retreated or turned his back upon his foe.

The Great King intended to attack at the same moment, both by land and by sea. The fleets were at Artemisium, and there were four times as many Persian ships as Greek. A hot and sultry summer's day had passed, and the signaled attack was expected in the morning. But at early dawn the sea began to be violently agitated and a strong East wind arose; thunder rumbled in the distance, and soon a terrible storm broke. The Greek ships were in safety, but a large number of Persian ships were wrecked, and great treasure was lost. For three days the storm continued, and for three days Xerxes had to wait before he could attack the Pass. When on the fourth day the storm died down, the sea fight began. Three times over, the Greeks attacked the Persian ships, and each time they prevailed against them. After the third fight, news was brought to Themistocles, the Athenian admiral, that two hundred Persian ships, sailing to the Greek rear, had been lost in the storm, so that there was nothing more to fear from an attack in that direction. The Greeks succeeded in throwing the Persian ships into confusion and so crippled the fleet that they finally won the battle. It was then that Xerxes gave the order to his army to attack the Pass.

For the whole of a hot summer's day, the Persians attacked. First the Medes tried to force the Pass, but it was narrow, and as they met the Spartan spears, down they went, man after man. Hour after hour this continued, but every attack was repulsed, and hardly a Spartan fell. Then the Medes withdrew and the Immortals took their place. They were fresh and greatly superior to the Spartans in numbers, but neither could they prevail against them. At times the Spartans would make a pretence of turning to fight, but when the Barbarians followed after them with shouting and clashing of arms, they then turned and faced the Barbarians and slew large numbers of them. The Spartans lost a few men, but at the end of the day the Persians drew back, exhausted and defeated, and the Spartans still held the Pass.

The next day, the same thing happened. So great was the slaughter of the Persians on this day that three times Xerxes leaped up from the seat from which he was watching the fight, in deadly fear for his army. But by the end of the day, the Pass had not been taken, and again the Persians withdrew, exhausted and driven back, leaving large numbers of their companions lying dead before the Pass.

Xerxes was in great straits as to what he should do next, when he was told that a man desired audience of him. He was a Greek who lived in that region, and he offered, if the Persian would reward him with enough gold, to lead his army by a path (known to him, but of which the Spartans were ignorant) over the mountain to a spot from which the Pass might be attacked in the rear. It was a long and difficult path, but the traitor knew it well and would guide them surely. The reward was promised, and about the time when the lamps were lit in the camp, the Immortals with their commander set out under the guidance of the traitor. All through the long black night they climbed by a steep and rocky path, and when dawn appeared they had reached the summit of the mountain. In this region a thousand men of Phocis were stationed to protect their own country and the path which led down to the valley below. They could not see the Persians as they climbed, for the sides of the mountain were covered with oak trees, but in the great silence which falls upon nature just before the dawn, suddenly these men heard an unexpected sound. It was the Persians stepping on the dried oak leaves which lay thickly on the ground beneath their feet. The Greeks started up, and when the Persians, coming suddenly upon them, discharged their arrows at them, they retreated to a higher position close at hand, where they waited for the expected attack. To the Greeks' surprise, however, the enemy turned away and left them. On went the traitor, followed by the Persians, until they were on the road in the rear of Leonidas.

While it was yet night, scouts came down from the mountains where they had been keeping watch and told Leonidas that the Pass was turned, and that the enemy was approaching it from the rear. Leonidas knew what that meant—

the end had come—but he commanded Spartans, and he knew that while one remained alive, the Pass would not be taken.

At sunrise, according to the arrangement made with the traitor, Xerxes attacked. The Spartans, knowing that they were going forth to death, now advanced further out into the broader space in front of the Pass, where there was more room. And then followed a fight which will never be forgotten. The Barbarians made attack after attack, and the Spartans slew them and drove them back every time. Many were driven into the sea and perished, and many more were trodden down and trampled to death; there was no reckoning of the number that perished. Two brothers of Xerxes fell fighting, and then Leonidas fell. The Spartans fought for the body of their king; most of their spears were by this time broken, so they fought and slew the Persians with their swords. Four times the Persians had almost taken the body of the king, and four times they were driven back by the Spartan, when word came that the Immortals were attacking the Pass in the rear. Then the remaining Spartans placed themselves with the body of Leonidas behind the wall, and there they made their last defence. On this spot, those who still had daggers defended themselves, and those who had no weapons remaining fought with their hands and teeth until, overwhelmed by the Barbarians who were now assailing them both in the front and in the rear, they were surrounded and cut down, until not a Spartan was left alive.

And so the Persians took the Pass, and the road to Athens lay clear before them.

The Spartans were buried where they fell, and a pillar was erected to the memory of those who had died so great a death in defending the Pass. On it was inscribed the simple words:

> Stranger, bear word to the Spartans that we lie here obedient to their charge.

III. Themistocles

Themistocles

THE PERSIANS had taken the Pass of Thermopylae; Thebes, the chief city in Boeotia, was anxious to be on the winning side and was a *medizing* state; there was nothing to save Athens from the conquering Persian army.

But in this dark hour, a statesman arose in Athens who was to restore her confidence and make her place secure among the free nations of the world. This man was Themistocles, already known to the Athenians as the admiral who had defeated the Persians at Artemesium. He came of a humble family, but the laws made by Solon and later lawgivers made it possible for him, in spite of his birth, to rise to the highest position in the state.

> From his youth Themistocles had been of a vehement and impetuous nature, a quick intelligence, and a strong and aspiring bent for action and great affairs. The holidays and intervals in his studies he did not spend in play or idleness, as other children, but would be always inventing or arranging some oration or speech to himself, so that his master would often say to him, "You, my boy, will be nothing small, but great one way or other, for good or else for bad." He received reluctantly and carelessly instructions

> given him to improve his manners and behavior, or to teach him any pleasing or graceful accomplishment, but whatever was said to improve him in sagacity or in management of affairs, he would give attention to beyond one of his years. And when in company he was obliged to defend himself because he could not play on any stringed instrument, he would retort that though he could not do that, were a small and obscure city put into his hands, he would make it great and glorious. It is said that Themistocles was so transported with the thoughts of glory, and so inflamed with the passion for great actions, that though he was still young when the battle of Marathon was fought, upon the skillful conduct of the general Miltiades being everywhere talked about, he was observed to be thoughtful, reserved, and alone by himself; he passed the nights without sleep, and avoided all his usual places of recreation, and to those who wondered at the change, and inquired the reason of it, he gave the answer that "the trophy of Miltiades would not let him sleep."[2]

This Themistocles was the man who was now to help Athens, and he possessed the very qualities she most needed in the serious position in which she found herself.

> For Themistocles was a man whose natural force was unmistakable; this was the quality for which he was distinguished above all other men; from his own native acuteness, and without any study either before or at the time, he was the ablest judge of the course to be pursued in a sudden emergency, and could best divine what was likely to happen in the remotest future.

---

[2] Plutarch: *Life of Themistocles.*

> Whatever he had in hand he had the power of explaining to others, and even where he had no experience he was quite competent to form a sufficient judgment; no one could foresee with equal clearness the good or evil intent which was hidden in the future.

This foresight was shown in the belief held by Themistocles, who, "when others were of opinion that the battle of Marathon would be an end to the war, thought it was but the beginning of far greater conflicts,"[3] and because of this belief he did his best to encourage the Athenians to be ready for whatever might happen.

Themistocles believed that the chief thing necessary for Athens was a fleet, and he persuaded the Athenians, though with great difficulty for they could not at first see the necessity, to build ships. There was not very much money in Athens just then, and without money, ships could not be built. But at this critical time, an unexpectedly large sum of money was paid into the public treasury; this was the revenue from the silver mines at Laurium in the south of Attica, which the Athenians were intending to divide amongst themselves. "Then Themistocles persuaded them to give up this plan of division and to make for themselves with this money two hundred ships." This they did, and they also improved the harbor of Athens, and

> henceforward, little by little, turning and drawing the city down towards the sea in the belief that with their ships they might be able to repel the Persians and command Greece, Themistocles, so Plato tells us, turned the Athenians from steady soldiers into mariners and seamen, and gave occasion for the reproach against him that he took away from them

[3] Thucydides, I.

> the spear and the shield and bound them to the bench and the oar.[4]

Themistocles did not accomplish this without opposition. He had a rival in Athens, Aristeides, a man who had grown up with him and played with him as a boy, but who had always taken the opposite side in whatever they were doing. Unlike Themistocles, Aristeides belonged to a noble family, and whenever Themistocles took the side of the people, Aristeides favored the nobles. Even as boys they

> were at variance with each other, and they soon made proof of their natural inclinations; the one being ready, adventurous, and subtle, engaging readily and eagerly in everything; the other of a staid and settled temper, intent on the exercise of justice, not admitting any degree of falsity or trickery, no not so much as at his play.[5]

Of all his virtues, it was the *justice* of Aristeides which most appealed to the people; it never failed under any circumstances, and so they gave him the surname of the *Just*.

Now Aristeides believed that the building of a navy for Athens was too great a change from the former policy of the city. The Athenians had won the battle of Marathon and had thereby secured their reputation as soldiers, and he thought it very ill-advised and dangerous to depart from the old traditions and to put all their strength into warships. Themistocles thought otherwise, and the two leaders came into violent conflict with each other.

There was at Athens a custom known as *Ostracism*. This was a law which once a year allowed the Athenians to banish

[4] Plutarch: *Life of Themistocles.*

[5] Plutarch: *Life of Aristeides.*

for ten years any citizen who had, as they thought, assumed too much power or had become too popular. They were always afraid that such power might lead to a return of tyranny, and in their passionate desire to prevent that, they were often led to banish those who deserved a better reward for their services. In times of national danger, those who had been ostracized were sometimes recalled before their term of exile was over; otherwise they were not allowed to return until ten years had passed. The sentence of ostracism could not be passed unless at least six thousand votes were cast. Each vote was written on a piece of broken pottery, called an *ostrakon,* and then placed in an urn set up in a special place for the purpose. The conflict between Themistocles and Aristeides grew so great that the Athenians decided that one or the other of them must give way and leave Athens, and they decided to hold an ostracism. This resulted in the banishment of Aristeides, and Themistocles was left to carry out his aims for Athens without opposition. It is said that during the voting,

> an illiterate fellow, meeting Aristeides and not recognizing him, gave him his sherd and begged him to write Aristeides upon it; and Aristeides, surprised, asked the man if Aristeides had ever done him any injury. "None at all," said he, "neither know I the man: but I am tired of hearing him everywhere called the Just." Aristeides, hearing this, is said to have made no reply, but returned the sherd with his own name inscribed.[6]

Aristeides was a noble and a conservative, and opposed to the changes which Themistocles felt to be so necessary if Athens was to keep her freedom. But Aristeides was a man

[6] Plutarch: *Life of Aristeides.*

whose honor has never been called in question, who gave of his best to his country without ever asking for reward, and who, when he was later recalled to power and his great rival was falling into disgrace, never, as far as is known, by word or deed, treated Themistocles in any way that was mean-spirited or ungenerous.

Thanks to Themistocles, the Athenians now had a navy and a good harbor, but that would not protect them from the army of Xerxes, which was advancing through Boeotia towards Attica. In their alarm, the Athenians sent messengers to Delphi to ask the advice of the Oracle, but the answer they received filled them with despair. They were told to leave their home, for all was doomed to destruction; that fire and the War-God were about to bring ruin upon them; that there was no hope for them, but that they would steep their souls in sorrow. The Athenians could not believe that such a fate awaited them, and they sent again to the Oracle, entreating Apollo to look upon them with favor. At last they received the following answer, with which they returned to Athens:

> Pallas cannot prevail to soften Zeus the Olympian,
> Though she assail him with words and ply him with
> counsels of wisdom,
> Yet will I give thee afresh an answer firm
> and unchanging:
> Conquered must lie the land where stands the
> fortress Cecropian,
> Conquered the peaceful mead of sacred Cithaeron;
> but thenceforth
> Zeus, wide-gazing, permits to keep in honor of Pallas
> Walls of wood unshaken to shelter thee and
> thy children.
> Wait not for horse nor for foot that come to ruin
> thy country,

Out of the mainland afar; but rather yield to
the foeman,
Turning thy back in flight, for yet shalt thou meet
him in battle.
O divine Salamis! how many children of women
Shalt thou slay at the sowing of corn or the ripening
of harvest![7]

With this answer the Athenians returned home, and there great discussion arose as to the meaning of the Oracle. Some interpreted it as meaning that they should build a fence of wood around the city, others that the "walls of wood" could only mean ships, and that they should leave everything and commit themselves to their fleet. Then there were some who thought that the last lines foretold a terrible defeat for Athens; but Themistocles rose up in the Assembly and declared that had the god meant that, he would have said, "Salamis the cruel or the merciless," but since he had said, "Salamis the divine," the slaughter must refer to the enemy and not to the Athenians. Themistocles was also on the side of those who held that the wooden walls were the ships, and he persuaded the Athenians to remove to a place of safety out of Attica their wives and children, and as much of their property as they could. This they did, and then, leaving only a few men to guard the Acropolis, the fighting men betook themselves to their ships and anchored near the island of Salamis.

All this was done none too soon, for

> the Barbarians had now arrived in Attica and all the land was being laid waste with fire. They reached Athens, and took the lower city, and then finding that there were still a few of the Athenians left in the

[7] From the translation in *Greek History for Young Readers* by Alice Zimmern.

> temple, they took their post upon the rising ground opposite the Acropolis and besieged them. The Athenians continued to defend themselves although they had come to the extremity of distress, so for a long time Xerxes was not able to capture them. But at length, finding a place where no one was keeping guard, because no one would have supposed that any man could ascend that way, the Persians forced their way up to the Acropolis, and after entering the gates they slew all the defenders, plundered the temple, and set fire to the whole of the Acropolis.

And so Athens fell into the hands of the Barbarians.

IV. Salamis to the End

Athens was burned, her walls had been destroyed, but the Athenian men had not yet been defeated; they were with the fleet at Salamis, and ready to fight to the death for the freedom of their state. They were joined there by ships from the other Greek states, but when the news of the burning of Athens reached the Greek commanders, those who came from the Peloponnesus, especially the Spartans, were unwilling to remain at Salamis any longer, but wanted to sail to their homes and, should the enemy pursue them, make their last stand there. Themistocles opposed this policy with all his might, and a hot discussion followed. The Corinthian admiral taunted Themistocles with wishing to stay and fight at Salamis, because he had now no native land, to which Themistocles replied that where there were Athenian ships and Athenian men, there was Athens, and that moreover it was a larger land than Corinth, seeing that the Athenians had sent two hundred ships, more than the ships of all the other Greeks put together. In spite of his passionate appeal, the commanders of the other Greek ships decided to set sail and leave the Athenians to fight the Barbarians alone.

In these desperate straits, Themistocles thought of a stratagem by which he might force a battle, before his allies had time to desert him. He sent a secret messenger, whom he could trust, in a boat to the encampment of the Barbarians and charged him to give this message to Xerxes:

> The commander of the Athenians sent me privately, without the knowledge of the other Hellenes (for, as it chances, he is disposed to the cause of the King, and desires rather that your side should gain the victory than that of the Hellenes), to inform you that the Hellenes are planning to take flight, having been struck with dismay; and now it is possible for you to win a great victory, if you do not permit them to flee away: for they are not of one mind with one another and they will not stand against you in fight, but ye shall see them fighting a battle by sea with one another, those who are disposed to your side against those who are not.

Xerxes received this message with joy and immediately acted upon it; he began to surround the Greeks so that not one might escape. While this was being done, Aristeides, the banished rival of Themistocles, whose sentence had been lifted in this hour of peril when Athens needed all her sons, suddenly returned from Aegina to the Athenian fleet with the news that it was impossible for any of the Greeks to sail away because they were even then surrounded by the enemy. Aristeides gave this news first to Themistocles, saying to him that if at other times they had been rivals, there was only one kind of rivalry in which they could now engage, a rivalry as to which should do more service to his country. The news he brought was true, and the Greeks could not now escape a battle.

The sea-fight began as the day dawned. Xerxes had erected a great throne for himself, from which he could watch the events of the day; "and full in view of all the host the throne stood on a high knoll hard beside the sea."

Xerxes

Aeschylus, a great Athenian poet, who was himself present at the battle, wrote a play called the *Persians,* in which a messenger takes the news of Salamis to the mother of Xerxes, waiting at Susa for the return of her son. Never before had he been defeated, but now she must listen to a tale of woe:

'Twas this began all our disaster, Queen:
A demon or fell fiend rose—who knows whence?—
For from the Athenian host a Hellene came,

And to thy son, to Xerxes, told this tale,
That when the mirk of black night should be come,
The Greeks would not abide, but, leaping straight
Upon the galley thwarts, this way and that
In stealthy flight would seek to save their lives.
Soon as he heard, discerning neither guile
In that Greek, nor the jealousy of heaven,
This word to all his captains he proclaims,
That when the sun should cease to scorch the earth,
And gloom should fill the hallowed space of sky,
In three lines should they range their throng of ships
To guard each pass, each seaward surging strait:
And others should enring all Aias' Isle:
Since, if the Greeks should yet escape fell doom,
And find their ships some privy path of flight,
Doomed to the headsman all these captains were.
Thus spake he, in spirit overconfident,
Knowing not what the gods would bring to pass.
With hearts obedient, in no disarray,
Then supped our crews, and every mariner
To the well-rounded rowlock lashed his oar.
But when the splendor faded of the sun,
And night came on, each master of the oar
A-shipboard went, and every man-at-arms.
Then rank to rank of long ships passed the word:
And, as was each appointed, so they sailed.
So all night long the captains of the ships
Kept all the sea-host sailing to and fro.
And night passed by, yet did the Hellene host
Essay in no wise any secret flight.
But when the day by white steeds chariot-borne,
Radiant to see, flooded all earth with light,
First from the Hellenes did a clamorous shout
Ring for a triumphant chant; and wild and high

Pealed from the island rock the answering cheer
Of Echo. Thrilled through all our folks dismay
Of baffled expectation; for the Greeks
Not as for flight that holy paean sang,
But straining battleward with heroic hearts.
The trumpet's blare set all their lines aflame.
Straightway with chiming dip of dashing oars
They smote the loud brine to the timing cry,
And suddenly flashed they all full into view.
Foremost their right wing seemly-ordered led
In fair array; next, all their armament
Battleward swept on. Therewithal was heard
A great shout—"On, ye sons of Hellas, on!
Win for the home-land freedom!—freedom win
For sons, wives, temples of ancestral gods,
And old sires' graves! this day are all at stake!"
Yea, and from us low thunder of Persian cheers
Answered—no time it was for dallying!
Then straightway galley dashed her beak of bronze
On galley. 'Twas a Hellene ship began
The onset, and shore all the figurehead
From a Phoenician: captain charged on captain.
At first the Persian navy's torrent-flood
Withstood them; but when our vast fleet was cramped
In strait-space—friend could lend no aid to friend—
Then ours by fangs of allies' beaks of bronze
Were struck, and shattered all their oar-array;
While with shrewd strategy the Hellene ships
Swept round, and rammed us, and upturned were hulls
Of ships;—no more could one discern the sea,
Clogged all with wrecks and limbs of slaughtered men:
The shores, the rock-reefs, were with corpses strewn.
Then rowed each bark in fleeing disarray,
Yea, every keel of our barbarian host,

> They with oar-fragments and with shards of wrecks
> Smote, hacked, as men smite tunnies or a draught
> Of fishes; and a moaning, all confused
> With shrieking, hovered wide o'er that sea-brine
> Till night's dark presence blotted out the horror.
> That swarm of woes, yea, though for ten days' space
> I should rehearse could I not tell in full.
> Yet know this well, that never in one day
> Died such a host, such tale untold, of men.[8]

Xerxes, the Great King, was defeated, and his one desire now was to return home to Asia. He left his general, Mardonius, in Thessaly with a picked body of men, who should carry on the war in the spring, but he himself, with what was left of his army, marched back through Macedonia and Thrace to the Hellespont, and so back to his own land. It was a very different march from the triumphant one he had made earlier in the year. The inhabitants of the lands through which they had passed had no fear of a defeated king, and it was difficult to obtain provisions. The Persians seized what crops there were,

> and if they found no crops, then they took the grass which was growing up from the earth, and stripped off the bark from the trees and plucked down the leaves, and devoured them. Then plague seized upon the army and some of them who were sick the king left behind.

In such manner did Xerxes return home.

In the meanwhile, Mardonius and his army spent the winter in Thessaly. When the spring came (this was the spring of 479 B.C.), he sent a messenger to the Athenians who spoke these words to them:

---

[8] Aeschylus: *The Persians*, translated by A. S. Way.

> Athenians, there has come a message from the King which speaks in this manner: I remit to you all the offences which were committed against me, and this I say: I will give you back your own land and any other in addition, and you shall remain independent; and I will rebuild all your temples, provided you will make a treaty with me.

The Spartans heard that this message had come, and they sent messengers to Athens imploring the Athenians to make no terms with the Barbarian, for they feared that if Athens became subject to Persia, there would be no safety left for them. They offered to send supplies to Athens to make up for the loss of their harvest, destroyed by the Persians, to support the families of those Athenians who had been slain, to do almost anything, in fact, if only the Athenians would stand firm.

The Spartans need not have feared. The freedom-loving Athenians were not likely to submit to a barbarian foe. They sent back to the Persian this answer:

> So long as the sun goes on the same course by which he goes now, we will never make an agreement with Xerxes, but trusting to the gods and heroes as allies, we will go forth to defend ourselves against him.

To the Spartans they said:

> It was natural, no doubt, that you should be afraid lest we should make a treaty with the Barbarian; but it was an unworthy fear for men who knew so well the spirit of the Athenians, namely that there is neither so great a quantity of gold anywhere upon the earth, nor any land so beautiful, that we should be willing to accept it and enslave Hellas by taking the side of

> the Medes. Be assured of this, that so long as one of the Athenians remains alive, we will never make an agreement with Xerxes. We are grateful for your thought toward us, but we shall continue to endure as we may, and not be a trouble in any way to you. But send out an army as speedily as you may, for the Barbarian will be here invading our land at no far distant time. Therefore, before he arrives here in Attica, come to our rescue quickly in Boeotia.

Thus the Athenians made answer, and upon that the envoys went away back to Sparta.

When the messengers returned to Mardonius with the answer from Athens, the Persian general marched out of Thessaly down through Boeotia into Attica, and for the second time the Barbarian burned Athens. Xerxes had left but little to burn; Mardonius left nothing. He then marched back into Boeotia and set up his camp in the region between Thebes and Plataea. Here he waited for the Greeks. There was some delay before they came, for the Spartans made various excuses for not setting out, but at length under their king, Pausanias, they marched out and joined the Athenians. And then at Plataea was fought the last great battle in this great war. All day long it raged, and at first it seemed as if the Persians were gaining, but while the outcome of the battle was still in doubt, Mardonius was killed, and with him fled all the hopes of the Persians. They took to flight, but were pursued and overtaken by the Greeks, and very few were left alive. The Greeks then entered the camp of the Persians, and they gazed in astonishment at the riches they found there. There were "tents furnished with gold and silver, and beds overlaid with gold and silver, and mixing bowls of gold, and cups and other drinking vessels." One-tenth of this rich plunder was sent to Delphi and the rest divided amongst those who had fought the battle. A bronze statue of Zeus was sent as an offering to Olympia, and one of Poseidon was sent to the isthmus. It was further resolved that the land belonging to Plataea should be held sacred forever, and that never again should fighting take place on it.

After the Persians had taken the Pass of Thermopylae, the body of Leonidas had been taken and cruelly used in revenge for his having dared to withstand the Great King, and to slaughter so many of his Persian soldiers. It was suggested to Pausanias that he should take vengeance for this barbarous act by mutilating the body of Mardonius, who had fallen in the battle.

> Stranger [he answered], thou holdest me as nought by advising me to do such a thing. These things it is more fitting for Barbarians to do than for Hellenes, and even with them we find fault for doing so. I do not desire in any such manner as this to please those who like such things. As for Leonidas, he has been greatly avenged already by the unnumbered lives which have been taken of these men. As for thee, come not again to me with such a proposal, nor give me such advice; and be thankful, moreover, that thou hast no punishment for it now.

In the Persian camp, the Greeks found the tent of Xerxes himself, which he had left for Mardonius, not wishing to be cumbered with too much baggage in his flight from Greece. When Pausanias saw it, he,

> seeing the furniture of Mardonius furnished with gold and silver and hangings of different colors, ordered the bakers and the cooks to prepare a meal as they were used to doing for Mardonius. Then when they did this as they had been commanded, it

> is said that Pausanias, seeing the couches of gold and of silver with luxurious coverings, the tables of gold and silver, and the magnificent apparatus of the feast, was astonished at the good things set before him, and for sport he ordered his own servants to prepare a Laconian meal; and as, when the banquet was served, the difference between the two was great, Pausanias laughed and sent for the commanders of the Hellenes; and when these had come together, Pausanias said, pointing to the preparation of the two meals, "Hellenes, for this reason I assembled you together, because I desired to show you the senselessness of this leader of the Medes, who, having such fare as this, came to us who have such sorry fare as ye see here, in order to take it away from us." Thus it is said that Pausanias spoke to the commanders of the Hellenes.

After the battle of Salamis, the Persian ships had withdrawn to Samos, and those of the Greeks to Delos, where they had spent the winter. In the spring, when the armies were marching out to meet at Plataea, the fleets moved slowly towards the Ionian coast, and on the same day as the battle of Plataea, so Herodotus tells us, they met in a fierce sea-fight, in which the Persians were completely routed. Thus on the same day, by land and sea, the Barbarian was defeated and Greece was free. She had proved that right was greater than might, and that in the cause of freedom, the weaker might stand against the stronger and prevail.

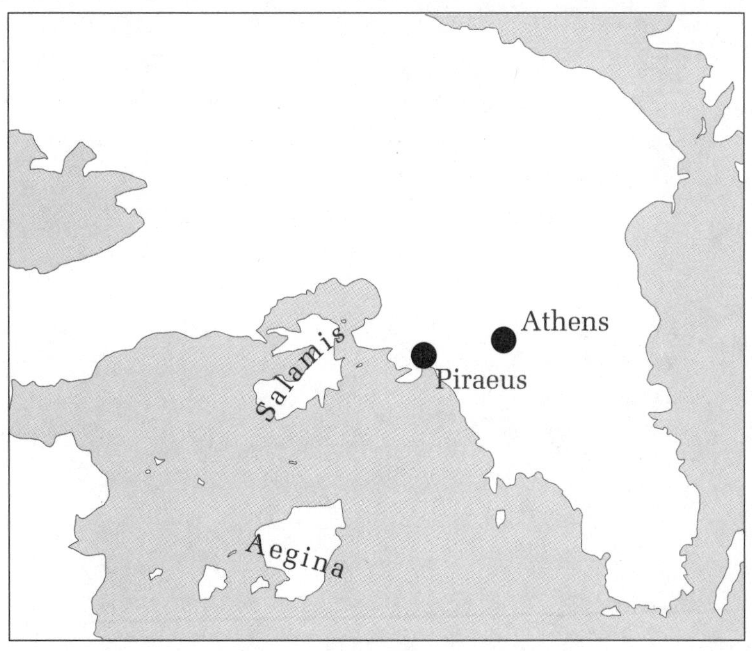

Salamis

CHAPTER 13

The Athenian Empire

I. The Fortification of Athens

The Persians had been defeated, and Greece was free. The Athenians had suffered more than any other state, for they had been forced to leave their city to be occupied by the enemy, and twice it had been burned to the ground. Now, however, they were free to return. The city was utterly destroyed, but a great hope for the future filled their hearts when they found that the sacred olive tree on the Acropolis, which had been burned by the Persians, was not dead after all, but had sent up fresh green shoots. Athena had not deserted them.

Themistocles was now the acknowledged leader of Athens, and the hero of all Greece.

> At the next Olympic Games, when Themistocles entered the course, the spectators took no further heed of those who were contesting for the prizes, but spent the whole day in looking at him, showing him to the strangers, admiring him, and applauding him by clapping their hands, and other expressions of joy, so that he himself, much gratified, confessed to his friends that he then reaped the fruit of all his labors for the Greeks.[1]

He was by nature a great lover of honors and glory, and he liked to appear superior to other people. After the battle of Salamis,

[1] Plutarch: *Life of Themistocles.*

when numbers of the Persian dead were washed ashore, "he perceived bracelets and necklaces of gold about them, yet passed on, only showing them to a friend that followed him, saying, 'Take you these things, for you are not Themistocles.'"[2]

It was Themistocles who had given Athens her navy by means of which she had defeated the Barbarian, and he now realized that if she was to keep her independence, the city must be well fortified. The Athenians were more than willing to follow his advice, and everyone in the city, men, women, and even children, worked hard to rebuild the walls. Now the Spartans were becoming more and more jealous of the increasing power of the Athenians, and when they heard of the new walls that were rising all around Athens, they sent envoys there to tell the Athenians that they believed any such fortification of their city unnecessary. They thought it wiser that there should be no strongly walled city in Attica, for should an enemy ever capture it, the citadel could be used as a base from which the enemy would go out and conquer other places. If war should come again, and the Athenians should feel insecure in their city, Sparta would gladly welcome them in the Peloponnesus. Themistocles suggested that he should go to Sparta and talk everything over with the Spartan leaders, and he set out accordingly. He left instructions that during his absence the work on the walls should go on with all possible speed and that messengers were to be sent to tell him when the work was finished. But the Spartans were not satisfied with the excuses and explanations given them by Themistocles, so he suggested that they should send messengers to Athens to find out the truth for themselves. They had hardly started when the Athenian messengers arrived with the news that the walls were built. Themistocles then told the whole truth to the Spartans, telling them that Athens was in every way the equal

[2] Plutarch: *Life of Themistocles.*

of Sparta and would take no orders from her as to what she should or should not do in her own land. The Spartans were angry, but they did not show it at that time, and Themistocles returned home to Athens.

Themistocles next set to work to fortify the harbor of the Peiraeus. Athens is a few miles inland from the sea, and the Peiraeus is her harbor. It is a peninsula with a deep bay on one side, in which ships can lie safely at anchor. A strong wall was built all round this peninsula, and the narrow entrance to the harbor was made secure by chains which could easily be drawn across in such a way as to prevent, whenever necessary, the entrance of any ships. The city and the harbor were then connected by long walls, which practically formed a fortified road down to the sea. This gave Athens all the advantages of a seaport, and an enemy would find it as difficult to take Athens as it had been to take Miletus.

The Persians had been defeated in Greece, but the Ionian Greeks in Asia Minor were still subject to the Great King. Now that the war was over, these Greeks appealed to the states on

Fortifications of Athens and the port of Peiraeus

the mainland to help them. Athens took a special interest in these Ionian colonies as they had been settled by men of close kinship to the Athenians. So the

> Hellenes deliberated about removing the inhabitants of Ionia, and considered where they ought to settle them in those parts of Hellas of which they had command, leaving Ionia to the Barbarians; for it was evident to them that it was impossible on the one hand for them to be always stationed as guards to protect the Ionians, and, on the other hand, if they were not stationed to protect them, they had no hope that the Ionians would escape from the Persians. Therefore, it seemed good to those of the Peloponnesians who were in authority that they should remove the inhabitants of the trading ports which belonged to those peoples of Hellas who had taken the side of the Medes, and give that land to the Ionians to dwell in; but the Athenians did not think it good that the inhabitants of Ionia should be removed at all, nor that the Peloponnesians should consult about Athenian colonies; and as these vehemently resisted the proposal, the Peloponnesians gave way.[3]

The Spartans not only gave way, but when an Athenian fleet set sail for the Hellespont, the Spartans sent twenty ships with Pausanias, the general who had commanded at Plataea, to join the expedition. The combined fleets took Sestos and then in the following year Byzantium. Pausanias was left in command at Byzantium, and soon after, a strange change was observed in him. His manner became overbearing and proud, and he gave up his Spartan habits of simple living, and

[3] Herodotus, IX.

adopted Persian ways, even dressing as a Persian. All this was so suspicious that he was recalled to Sparta, but as nothing was proved against him, he returned to Byzantium. Here he entered into correspondence with Xerxes and offered, in return for gold and the Great King's daughter as his bride, to betray Greece to the Persians. Though this was not known in Sparta until later, his conduct became sufficiently suspicious for the Spartans to recall him a second time, but at first they could find no definite proofs of his treachery. At last one of his slaves gave evidence against him. For some time Pausanias had been sending messengers to Asia Minor, and this particular slave had noticed that none of these messengers ever returned. When in time it became his turn to be sent, instead of bearing the message to the East, he took it to one of the ephors, who opened it and found in it proofs of treachery and betrayal of Greece to the Barbarian, with instructions to kill the slave who brought the message. The news that his messenger had been intercepted reached Pausanias, who immediately fled from his house and took refuge in a chamber adjoining the shrine in one of the temples. Here he was secure, but the ephors, in order to prevent his escape, gave orders that the doorway should be blocked up, and, imprisoned in the little chamber, Pausanias slowly starved to death. He was only taken out when he was just at the point of death, in order that the body of a traitor might not profane the temple.

While these things had been taking place in Sparta, Themistocles had been at the head of affairs in Athens. He had many enemies amongst the Athenians, and they accused him of many wrong acts. These were never definitely proved against him, and the records of the end of his career are so scanty that it is difficult to know how much truth there was in the accusations, but there were undoubtedly a number of suspicious facts of which his enemies made use. Amongst other things he was accused of taking bribes. He denied it, yet when he left

Athens, he possessed a strangely large fortune, the sources of which were never explained. Themistocles had a very biting tongue, and when his enemies attacked him, he would remind them, much oftener than was necessary, of the great services he had performed for Greece and for Athens in particular, and this arrogant boasting made him hated by many people who might otherwise have been his friends. A last serious accusation brought against him was that he was in communication with the Persians and was about to play the traitor. There was no proof of this, but Themistocles believed in the policy of making peace with the Persians. There was no fear that they would again attack the Greeks, and Themistocles saw that wealth and prosperity would most surely come to Athens through her trade, and so he advocated peaceful relations with the great empire of the East, in order that Athenian merchants might go safely in and out of her trading ports, and so add to the wealth and importance of Athens. But this was a very unpopular policy to hold in Athens, and feeling grew more and more bitter against Themistocles, until at last he was ostracized.

He left Athens and wandered from place to place. No city would give him a welcome, partly because he was feared, and partly because Athens was now a powerful state and no one wanted to offend her by giving shelter to one of her exiles. Sometimes Themistocles was forced to flee for his life, and once the only way in which he could safely be sent out of a city was to hide him in a litter which was placed in a closed carriage in the manner in which ladies usually traveled, and so "he was carried on his journey and those who met or spoke with the driver upon the road were told that he was conveying a young Greek woman out of Ionia to a nobleman at court."[4]

After this and similar adventures, homeless, a wanderer from city to city, Themistocles, the man who had saved Greece,

[4] Plutarch: *Life of Themistocles.*

who had laid the foundations of the greatness of Athens, who had been the bitterest and most relentless enemy of the Persians, came to Susa, and prostrating himself before Artaxerxes, who had succeeded Xerxes as king, he said to him:

> "O King, I am Themistocles the Athenian, driven into banishment by the Greeks. The evils that I have done to the Persians are numerous, but I come with a mind suited to my present calamities; prepared alike for favors or for anger. If you save me, you will save your suppliant; if otherwise, you will destroy an enemy of the Greeks."[5]

The king rejoiced greatly over the arrival of Themistocles, and he "was so well pleased, that in the night, in the middle of his sleep, he cried out for joy three times, 'I have Themistocles the Athenian.'"[6] The courtiers around the king were less pleased, and they spoke of Themistocles as "a subtle Greek serpent."

At the end of a year, Themistocles was able to speak the Persian language quite easily, and he became very intimate with the king, who honored him above all strangers who came to the court.

There are no records to tell us of all the many things that must have passed through the heart and mind of Themistocles, exiled from Greece and living with the Persians, but tradition has handed down to us the hope that at the end, his ancient love and loyalty to Athens triumphed, for it is said that the Great King summoned him to help the Persians in an expedition against Greece, but that Themistocles, rather than sink to such a depth of shame, drank poison, and so put an end to his own life. It was a tragic end to a great man, who had done great deeds for his country. But his character was not

[5] Plutarch: *Life of Themistocles.*

[6] Plutarch: *Life of Themistocles.*

strong enough to stand the strain of the continued accusations, insults, and injustices of his enemies, and in the hour of testing, he failed and turned his back upon his country. Though almost certainly innocent of the worst of that of which he was accused while still in Athens, his later actions place him, if not with those who became actual traitors to their country, at least with those whose loyalty and honor have been indelibly stained.

This flaw in the character of Themistocles was one that was very common in Greece. The Greeks were not a grateful people. They, and the Athenians in particular, were always afraid that too much power in the hands of one man would lead them back to a tyranny, and so they frequently failed to recognize or reward in a way that was fitting or lasting those who had done great deeds for them. The Greek patriot loved his state passionately, yet it was a love that not uncommonly turned to hate, if it was met by ingratitude, and the saddest pages in Greek history are those on which are recorded the names of Greek traitors.

Athens could never have become the great state she did, but for the work of Themistocles, and in spite of all that he did in the closing years of his life, one would like to believe that the story preserved by Plutarch is true. He tells us that long years after the death of Themistocles, there was a tomb near the haven of Peiraeus, where the sea is always calm, which was reputed to be that of the great Athenian statesman, and that it was said of it:

> Thy tomb is fairly placed upon the strand,
> Where merchants still shall greet it with the land;
> Still in and out 'twill see them come and go,
> And watch the galleys as they race below.[7]

Was it, perhaps, possible that the Athenians of a later generation, recognizing what Themistocles had done for

[7] Plutarch: *Life of Themistocles.*

Athens, forgave him and brought his body home to rest near the great harbor which he himself had made?

II. The Confederacy of Delos

THE RECALL OF PAUSANIAS from Byzantium left the Spartans in Asia Minor with no commander. Sparta had never been very much in earnest about freeing the Ionians, and the Ionians, very naturally, felt more confidence in a sea-power than in one whose strength lay chiefly in her army, and so they turned to Athens for leadership.

Themistocles was in exile, and his old rival Aristeides was now the most powerful leader in Athens. He believed that it was the duty of the Athenians to do all in their power to free their kinsmen in the Ionian cities from the Persian rule, and to this end, he and the Ionian leaders formed a league, known as the Confederacy or League of Delos. It took its name from the island of Delos, where the meetings were held, and where the treasury of the League was kept. Delos was chosen because it could easily be reached by all the members of the League, and also because it was a place specially honored by Apollo, for legend said he had been born there, and before Delphi had become so important, his chief sanctuary had been in his island birthplace.

The object of the League was the freeing of all Hellenes in Asia Minor and the islands of the Aegean from the Persians, and, having secured their liberty, to help them maintain their independence. For this purpose money and ships were needed. "By the good will of the allies, the Athenians obtained the leadership. They immediately fixed which of the cities should supply money and which of them ships for the war against the Barbarians,"[8] and as they were

[8] Thucydides, I.

> desirous to be rated city by city in their due proportion, they gave Aristeides command to survey the countries and to assess everyone according to their ability and what they were worth; and he laid the tax not only without corruption and injustice, but to the satisfaction and convenience of all. Aristeides, moreover, made all the people of Greece swear to keep the league, and himself took the oath in the name of the Athenians, flinging wedges of red-hot iron into the sea, after curses against such as should break their vow.[9]

The contributions were collected every spring by ten specially appointed men, called Hellenic Stewards, who brought the money to Delos, where it was placed in the treasury of the League. The League began its work at once, and one by one the Greek cities in Asia Minor and the islands in the Aegean were set free, until at length not one was left under the rule of Persia. As each city became independent, it joined the League, which grew in strength and importance as its numbers increased. Athens was its acknowledged leader; not only did she determine the amount each member should contribute, but the Hellenic Stewards were all Athenians, and affairs of the League were governed by Athenian law. Slowly the relationship of Athens to the other members of the League changed. At first the states had regarded themselves as allies of each other and of Athens, but as the power of Athens grew, she began to look upon these Greek states less as allies than as subjects who were bound to follow her lead and do her bidding. At length this relationship was so well recognized that in some states Athens exacted this oath of allegiance from those who enjoyed her protection as members of the Delian League:

---

[9] Plutarch: *Life of Aristeides.*

> I will not revolt from the people of the Athenians in any way or shape, in word or deed, or be an accomplice in revolt. If anyone revolts I will inform the Athenians. I will pay the Athenians the tribute, and I will be a faithful and true ally to the utmost of my power. I will help and assist the Athenian people if anyone injures them; and I will obey their commands.[10]

In name, Athens together with all the island states in the Aegean and the Ionian cities in Asia Minor were allies and independent. Their envoys still met at Delos, supposedly to take counsel with each other, but in fact they were subject to Athens and obeyed her commands. The League had been formed in 477 B.C., and for twenty-three years Delos was its headquarters. Then it was suggested that the treasury should be moved to Athens, and that the meetings should in future be held there. No longer was Athens merely the leading state amongst her allies. The removal of the treasury from Delos to Athens made her in name as well as in fact not simply the leading state of a Confederation, but the Athenian Empire.

III. The Athenian Empire Under Pericles

ATHENS WAS NOW an empire and was recognized as such. The island states in the Aegean as well as the Ionian cities on the mainland of Asia Minor were bound to her by ties of allegiance. The heart of the empire was Athens, and settlers from many different places were welcomed there, if they brought with them something that contributed to the welfare of the city: the sculptor, the worker in gold, silver, or other metals, the potter, the dyer, the leather-worker, and the merchant who brought costly wares from distant lands—all these and many more were welcomed.

---

[10] From W. Warde Fowler: *The City-State of the Greeks and Romans.*

Pericles

Themistocles had been exiled, Aristeides was dead, and a statesman named Pericles now took the leading part in Athenian affairs. His boyhood had been spent during some of the most thrilling years of Athenian history. As a child he had become a hero-worshipper of the men who had fought at Marathon; he must have been amongst the older children who were forced to flee from Athens on the approach of Xerxes. And though not old enough to fight, he was old enough to understand how much hung upon the outcome of the battle of Salamis, and he probably spent that great day in sound, if not also in sight, of the conflict between the two hostile fleets. Pericles' father was the commander of the fleet which in the following year defeated the Persian on the same day on which was fought the battle of Plataea, and one can imagine the youth, returning to his beloved Athens, glorying in the deeds of his father and his countrymen, and resolving to take his part in making Athens a great and glorious city.

Pericles belonged to a noble family, and he had been educated by some of the great philosophers of his day. Like Thales of Miletus, these men believed that nature was governed by laws that had nothing to do with the goodwill or anger of the gods, and one of them, though still believing in the existence of many gods, held the belief that the world had been created by one Mind alone, and he taught Pericles to share this belief. This helped to free the mind of Pericles from superstition, and on several occasions he tried to free others from the fears which superstition brings. He was once on board his ship when an eclipse of the sun took place. The darkness filled everyone with terror, and it was looked upon as a sign of the wrath of the gods.

> Pericles, therefore, perceiving the steersman seized with fear and at a loss what to do, took his cloak and held it up before the man's face, and, screening him with it so that he could not see, asked him whether he imagined there was great hurt, or the sign of any great hurt in this, and he answering no, "What," said Pericles, "does that differ from this, only that which has caused that darkness there, is something greater than a cloak."[11]

Although by birth belonging to the nobles, Pericles took the side of the people in Athens, partly, at first, because he did not want to do anything that might make it even seem that he was aiming at the sole power of a tyrant. He soon became the acknowledged leader, and he then

> entered on quite a new course and management of his time. For he was never seen to walk in any street but that which led to the marketplace and the council hall, and he avoided invitations of friends to supper, and all friendly visiting and intercourse whatever. He also presented himself at intervals only, not coming

[11] Plutarch: *Life of Pericles.*

> at all times into the Assembly, but reserving himself for great occasions.[12]

In many ways Pericles showed himself superior to the men around him, and because of this superiority and for his great power in public affairs, he was given the surname of the Olympian. Like Zeus, he was said to speak with

> thundering and lightning, and to wield a dreadful thunderbolt in his tongue. Pericles, however, was very careful what and how he was to speak, insomuch that whenever he was to speak in the Assembly, he prayed the gods that no one word might unawares slip from him unsuitable to the matter and the occasion.[13]

Under the leadership of Pericles, Athens rose to be a great state. The Age of Pericles was a short one, lasting only for about fifty years in the last part of the fifth century B.C., but it was a period which was great not only in material prosperity, but also in every form of intellectual and artistic beauty. The work of Pericles

> which gave most pleasure and ornament to the city of Athens, and the greatest admiration and even astonishment to all strangers, and that which is now Greece's only evidence that the power she boasted of and her ancient wealth are no romance or idle story, was his construction of the public and sacred buildings.[14]

The story of these buildings will be told in its own place; for more than two thousand years they have testified to the greatness of the people who built them.

---

[12] Plutarch: *Life of Pericles.*

[13] Plutarch: *Life of Pericles.*

[14] Plutarch: *Life of Pericles.*

By the laws Pericles made, it became possible for every free-born Athenian citizen, no matter how poor he was, to take an active part in the government of the state, thus completing the work of the earlier lawgivers and making Athens a democracy, a state ruled by the many.

It was the custom in Athens that the bodies of Athenians who had been slain in battle should be brought home and buried in special tombs which were situated in a very beautiful spot outside the walls. Only after the battle of Marathon were the dead, in recognition of their great valor against the Barbarian, buried on the field. All others were brought home and given a public funeral. There was always buried with them an empty coffin, as a symbol of all those whose bodies were missing and could not be recovered after the battle. It was believed that this wish to do honor to the dead and to give them fitting burial would ensure their happiness in the life after death, which every Greek believed to be imperiled if there was lack of proper burial. At the close of the funeral ceremonies, some great orator was always asked to deliver a suitable oration. On one such occasion, Pericles was the orator, and in the great Funeral Speech he made, he set forth to the Athenians what he considered Athens stood for in the world. There are no better words in which to describe the greatness of Athens at this time and the ideals at which she aimed, so listen to the words of Pericles, describing the city he loved:

> Our form of government does not enter into rivalry with the institutions of others. We do not copy our neighbors, but are an example to them. It is true that we are called a democracy, for the administration is in the hands of the many and not of the few. But while the law secures equal justice to all alike in their private disputes, the claim of excellence is also recognized; and when a citizen is in any way distinguished, he

is preferred to the public service, not as a matter of privilege, but as the reward of merit. Neither is poverty a bar, but a man may benefit his country whatever the obscurity of his condition. ... A spirit of reverence pervades our public acts; we are prevented from doing wrong by respect for authority and for the laws, having an especial regard to those which are ordained for the protection of the injured as well as to those unwritten laws which bring upon the transgressor of them the reprobation of the general sentiment.

And we have not forgotten to provide for our weary spirits many relaxations from toil; we have regular games and sacrifices throughout the year; at home the style of our life is refined; and the delight which we daily feel in all these things helps to banish melancholy. Because of the greatness of our city, the fruits of the whole earth flow in upon us; so that we may enjoy the goods of other countries as freely as of our own. ... We are lovers of the beautiful, yet simple in our tastes, and we cultivate the mind without loss of manliness. Wealth we employ, not for talk and ostentation, but when there is a real use for it. To avow poverty with us is no disgrace; the true disgrace is in doing nothing to avoid it. An Athenian citizen does not neglect the state because he takes care of his own household; and even those of us who are engaged in business have a very fair idea of politics. We alone regard a man who takes no interest in public affairs, not as a harmless, but as a useless character; and if few of us are originators, we are all sound judges of a policy. ... In doing good, again, we are unlike others; we make our friends by conferring, not by receiving, favors. ... To sum up, I say that Athens is the school of Hellas ... for in the hour of trial, Athens alone among her contemporaries is superior to the report of her. … We have compelled every land and every sea to open a path for our valor, and have everywhere planted eternal memorials of our friendship and of our enmity. Such is the city for whose sake these men nobly fought and died; they could not bear the thought that she might be taken from them; and every one of us who survives should gladly toil on her behalf. … Day by day fix your eyes on the greatness of Athens, until you become filled with the love of her; and when you are impressed by the spectacle of her glory, reflect that this empire has been acquired by men who knew their duty and had the courage to do it. …

And now, when you have duly lamented, everyone his own dead, you may depart.[15]

[15] Thucydides, II.

CHAPTER 14

Life in Ancient Athens in the Time of Pericles

I. A Walk in Ancient Athens

Almost in the center of Attica lies a plain surrounded in the distance by hills: towards the east, Mount Hymettus, the home of goats, purple with thyme and filled with the murmur of bees; and to the north, Mount Pentelicus, famous for its shining white marble, that gleamed a rosy-red when the sun went down. Rising straight out of the plain is a great oval-shaped rock, the famous Acropolis of Athens, once its citadel and fortress, but transformed by Pericles into a great shrine for Athena. From this rock the land sloped gently to the sea. The plain was watered by the Cephisus, the only stream in Attica which did not run dry in the summer, and along its banks were olive groves, adding their touch of dark gray-green to the landscape. In the center of this plain, at the foot of the Acropolis, was Athens.

Roads from all directions led to Athens, but the Greeks, unlike the Romans, were not great road-makers, and except for those used for processions on festivals, such as the Sacred Way that led to Eleusis, the roads in Attica were not in good repair, and foot-passengers, when they went on a journey, generally preferred the shorter paths over the hills.

In the early morning, the roads outside the city were thronged with people coming in from the country on various kinds of business. Chief of these were the farmers, bringing their fruit and vegetables and other produce to sell in the market, but merchants from distant lands were also to be seen bringing their wares along the road from the Piraeus. The city was entered by gates in the great wall which had been built by Themistocles after the Persian Wars, and from the gates, the streets all led to the marketplace, or *Agora,* as it was called by the Greeks. The streets were narrow, crooked, and dark, and were not paved, and the houses on each side presented a very dull appearance, for the windows rarely faced the street. The streets were dirty, too, for all kinds of refuse were thrown into them. This absence of light and air did not make for health, and so very often pictures of Apollo, the Bringer of Health, were painted on the walls. The Athenians spent their wealth on their great public buildings, and there was very little to distinguish one private house from another. Demosthenes, writing at a later time, said of the Athenians of the Age of Pericles:

> The public buildings they constructed for us; the number and beauty of the temples, and of the offerings they contained, are such that their successors can never surpass them; but in private life they practiced so great a moderation, that even if any of you knew which was the house of Aristeides or Miltiades or any of the famous men of old, you would find it no more pretentious than those of its neighbors.

The water in Athens came from wells and springs and fountains, many of which were at the street corners, and it was the task of the slave maidens to draw the water from the fountain and carry it home in vessels which they carried on their heads.

It is evident that Athens was a city very different from a well-equipped modern city, and that it lacked a great deal of what we would consider necessary. But the Athenian of the fifth century B.C. had extraordinarily little use for *things,* and he laid no stress on comfort. He was content to have houses without drains, beds without sheets or springs, and rooms as cold or as hot as the open air. He could tell the time without a clock, cross the sea without a compass, fasten his clothes (or rather his two pieces of cloth) with two pins instead of rows of buttons, and wear sandals without stockings, or even go barefoot. He warmed himself over a pot of ashes, judged lawsuits in the open air on a cold winter's morning, studied poetry without books, learned geography without maps, and politics without a newspaper. The Athenians were civilized without being comfortable.[1] Of course, much of this simple life was possible because of the climate, and modern standards of cleanliness need in no way conflict with a simple life; nevertheless it is the glory of the Athenians that they not only believed but practiced the belief that the things of the mind and spirit are greater than those of the body.

The daily life of Athens centered in the Agora. If the streets approaching it were mean and dirty, the Agora itself, the center of public life, was wide and spacious and surrounded by dignified and beautiful buildings. In shape it was a great open square, two sides of which were taken up with public buildings and temples. On the remaining sides were the *stoas,* or porches. These consisted of a roof supported by a row of columns in front and a wall at the back. Each stoa was a covered walk, protected from the glare of the sun, the biting of the cold wind, and from the rain; whatever the weather might be, the Athenian could always find a pleasant sheltered place where he could walk and talk with his friends. One of these porches was known as the King's Porch. It was used as one of the law-courts, and on the wall at the back were inscribed the laws of Solon, and it was here that every archon had to take his

[1] A. E. Zimmern: *The Greek Commonwealth.*

The restored Stoa of Attalos in Athens, exterior and interior

oath of office. The most frequented of the stoas was the Painted Porch, so called because its wall was decorated with frescoes, one of which was a great painting of the battle of Marathon.

The center of the Agora was a great open space, part of it free for the public to walk in, and part of it full of booths and stalls where was sold everything needed by the Athenians.

There were three classes of people in Athens: the citizens, who were all free-born Athenians, the foreign residents who were called metics, and the slaves. In outward appearance there was often very little difference between them, but only the citizens might vote, and they alone had any privileges. The metics were generally well-to-do—they were merchants and bankers and helped very largely to create the wealth which made Athens great.

The morning life of Athens centered in the Agora, but when the afternoon came, this was gradually deserted, and the Athenians who had gathered there earlier in the day went along the roads that led out of the city to the different *gymnasia*. These were originally places devoted to the games practiced by all Athenians, but they gradually became used more as parks where the young men played games and the older men watched and talked. The Academy was the greatest of the gymnasia, and philosophers used to frequent it, and with their pupils discuss all the many things in which the keen and adventurous minds of the Athenians were interested. Plato, one of the greatest of the philosophers, was a well-known figure at the Academy.

Rising above the city, watching over it and guarding it, was the Acropolis, crowned by temples and statues. A great statue of Athena looked down upon the city at her feet, at the busy Agora and the public buildings in which the government of the state was carried on, at the narrow streets lined with the houses of the citizens, and beyond the walls at the pleasant roads leading, on one side, out to the gymnasia and the country beyond, and, on the other, down to the harbor, busy with the trade of Athens, and where the galleys went in and out on their voyages all over the Mediterranean world.

II. Athenian Dress

A VISITOR TO THE Agora in the morning would have found Athenians of all kinds going about their daily business and he would have had opportunity to see how they dressed. The morning crowd in the Agora consisted almost entirely of men; to see Athenian women, a stranger would have to be invited to their houses, a rare privilege but seldom accorded, or to have visited Athens during a festival, when women were allowed to take part in the great processions which went up to the shrine of Athena on the Acropolis. But men of all classes could be seen every day in the Agora: the workingman going to his work, the countryman selling the produce of his farm, slaves doing the daily marketing for the household, and men of leisure walking about and talking to their friends.

The chief garment worn by all these men was the *chiton,* or tunic. It was made by taking an oblong piece of cloth, cutting it the required length, and then folding it around the body so that it hung from the neck to the knees. It was fastened at the neck with a pin, sometimes beautifully wrought in gold, in such a way that arm-holes were made and one side was always left open. A girdle kept the folds of the chiton in place, and it was generally tight enough to disguise the fact that one side was open. A man's chiton seldom came below his knees, but the wearer could always regulate the length; workmen and all those engaged in active occupations were generally *well-girded,* that is, they pulled up the chiton so that it was short, with part of it hanging over the girdle. Older men usually allowed the chiton to hang to its full length.

In the house, the chiton was the only garment required, and workmen and all young men engaged in active pursuits seldom wore anything else outdoors, but out of the house, the older men generally added a mantle known as the *himation*. This was another oblong piece of cloth, but larger than that used for the chiton, which was thrown over the left shoulder, brought around under the right arm to the front of the body, and then thrown again over the left shoulder. The himation was not, as a rule, pinned and so it had to be very carefully adjusted in order that its folds might hang well. It was a very difficult thing to put on a himation gracefully, and it was often the work of a special slave to arrange it before his master went outdoors. The folds had to hang well, and it had to be of the right length, for if it was too short, the Athenian thought the wearer looked like a rustic come to the city for the first time, and to wear it too long was a sign of ostentation and needless display.

The only other garment sometimes worn by the young men was the *chlamys*, a short cloak. It was circular, gathered around the neck and fastened by a pin or clasp, and hung over the back and left shoulder reaching to the waist. The chlamys was generally of a bright color; the chiton and himation were more often white, though sometimes colors were used, but beautifully designed borders were frequently embroidered in colors on both the chiton and himation—an Athenian crowd presented a bright and gay scene.

Athenian men seldom wore anything on their heads, unless they were traveling, when they wore a close-fitting cap, either with or without a brim, but they generally wore sandals on their feet, though this was not considered absolutely necessary.

The dress of the Athenian women consisted, like that of the men, of a chiton and himation, but the woman's chiton was longer; it reached to her feet and was fuller, and it often had short sleeves. No Athenian woman could ever appear outdoors without her himation, and this was often so arranged that it was drawn over her head, forming a hood. This was generally the only form of head covering worn by Athenian women, though if they went out in the sun they sometimes took parasols.

Athenian women probably used more colors in their dress than the men; a particularly beautiful saffron-yellow was a favorite color, especially for their bridal dresses, and on such occasions their dress was enriched by gold ornaments, necklaces, bracelets, and rings. Ornaments of various kinds were freely used by the Athenian women in their dress, but the Greeks disliked anything that had no purpose but show, and their jewels were so arranged as to enrich their appearance without taking away from its simple dignity and beauty.

Greek dress:
(left) himation over chiton
(right) short chiton
(bottom) clamys with petasos
(broad-brimmed hat)

III. The Athenian House

"I DO NOT SPEND my days indoors," said an Athenian once, "my wife is quite capable of managing our domestic affairs without my aid."[2] This probably expressed the feeling of most Athenian men, for they gave very little time to their houses. These were the places where the women of the family spent nearly all their hours, but where the men did little more than sleep and have their meals. In the summertime an Athenian house was probably a pleasant place, though we should have found it lacking in nearly everything that we consider necessary, but in the winter it would have been uncomfortably chilly and draughty.

It has already been noticed that an Athenian house usually presented a blank wall to the street, for it was built around a court onto which all the rooms opened. The houses were generally of one story only, though a few occasionally had more, and the rooms drew all their light and air from the court. Socrates once said that a perfect house should be one that was cool in summer and warm in winter, and of such a convenient size that the owner could keep all his possessions in it with ease and security.

The front door was always kept carefully shut and bolted, but a knocker, often in the form of a ring in a lion's mouth, announced the visitor, who was admitted by the porter, a slave who sat in a small room just inside the door. The door opened into a courtyard, which in a good-sized house would be fairly large, but badly paved. This was the men's court. A row of columns all around the sides supported a roof which made a kind of verandah, from which small rooms opened. These rooms do not seem to have had any light or air except that which entered from the court, and they must have been dark

[2] Xenophon: *The Economist.*

and uncomfortable. They were used only by the grown sons of the family and by the male slaves.

In the middle of the court stood an altar to Zeus the Protector of the Home, on which fragrant incense always burned, and fresh garlands of flowers and leaves would be placed on it every day.

Leading out of the men's court was the dining hall. There would be no table, for the guest did not go to the table, but a low table was brought to him as he sat or reclined on a beautifully carved couch. The most sacred spot in the house was in this room, the altar of Hestia, on which burned the sacred fire of the family hearth. There might be a row of large vases against one wall, and if one of them bore the inscription, "I am from the Games at Athens," the family would take care to preserve it as one of their greatest treasures, for the words meant that the vase had been a prize won by some member of the family in the Athenian Games.

A door opposite that which led from the men's court into the dining room opened into another court, that of the women. This was similar to the men's court, but more often planted with flowers and shrubs. The women's rooms, nearly as small and dark and uncomfortable as those of the men, opened from the women's court, and the kitchen was probably at the back of it. On one side of this court there was a large chamber, the best furnished in the house, where the master and mistress slept.

All the furniture in these rooms was simple, but of beautiful design. The chief things used were couches, footstools, low chairs, tables, and chests. The latter took the place of closets and cupboards. There were lamps and bronze candelabra, and large numbers of cases used by the Athenians as ordinary water jugs, wine jars, and drinking cups, all of the most graceful shapes and forms, and beautifully painted.

The life of the Athenian house centered in the women's court, though during the daytime, when the men of the house were absent, the women used the men's court almost as much as their own. However, the moment they heard the sound of the knocker on the front door, they fled to their own part of the house, lest they should be caught unawares by a male visitor.

Such was probably the house of a well-to-do Athenian, a very much more comfortable and well-furnished house than that of the Spartan, yet lacking in almost everything that we associate with the idea of comfort. But the Athenian succeeded in being civilized without being comfortable; his well-being was in no way dependent on *things*, and believing that his wealth was something to be used for the good of the whole community, he spent it on the temples and public buildings of the city rather than on his own private dwelling. It may be true that the little use the Athenian made of his own house made him less interested in it than in the other buildings of the city, but whether he carried it to an extreme or not, it was his public-spirited point of view that gave him that greater interest in the public welfare than in his own private affairs.

IV. Athenian Trade

THE EARLIER GREEKS believed that a state should be self-supporting, that the farmers should produce enough food, and the craftsmen everything needed in daily life. But from the time of Solon onwards, this became increasingly difficult in Athens, for owing to the arrival of settlers who came from many different places, attracted by the possibilities of work in the growing state, the population increased, and it became impossible to produce enough food. This had a very important influence on Athens, for instead of being self-sufficient and secure within her own walls, she became dependent for her life on the food supplies, especially the corn, that came to her from Egypt and the Black Sea colonies, and in the time of war it was absolutely necessary that the routes to these places should be kept open. Very strict laws were passed to regulate the corn trade and to make sure that enough would always be brought to Athens. No Athenian merchant might take corn to any other harbor than the Piraeus, and none might leave Egypt or the Black Sea ports unless he had a certain amount of corn on board his ship.

The fact that the Athenian merchant had to go to distant places for corn increased his trade in other articles. He was at home on the sea, and his many-oared ship passed swiftly over the waters of the Aegean, stopping at many places: at the ports of Ionian colonies, where he found his kinsfolk, eager to hear the latest news from the mainland and especially from Athens; and at the ports of the Barbarians, where he rejoiced that he was a Greek and did not dwell amongst these strangers. The Athenian merchant sailed in his own ship and, beyond his final destination, generally had no definite route in mind. He was guided by the favorable winds, or by rumors of suitable trading ports where he would find good opportunities for exchanging his goods. He left Athens with oil, honey from Hymettus, and the far-famed Athenian pottery, the chief exports, and he exchanged these for the corn and fish of the Black Sea ports, the wool of Miletus, the perfumes and spices of Syria, the linen and papyrus and the all-important corn of Egypt, the wine of Chios, the cypress wood of Crete, the dates of Phoenicia, the rugs and cushions of Carthage; while in such ports as Carthage and Miletus he found articles which had reached these places by caravans from still more distant lands. In Carthage he obtained ivory and ebony from Africa, and in Miletus richly woven carpets and rugs from Babylon.

All this trade brought wealth to Athens, and it taught the quick Athenian mind, always alert and interested in any new thing, "new ways of enjoying life."

V. Athenian Pottery

Most of the industries carried on in any large city were to be found in Athens, but the industry for which she was best known throughout the Mediterranean world was that of the potter, and Athenian vases were exported in very large quantities. But these vases were not mere ornaments; each had its own particular use as a household utensil, an offering to a god, or as an offering at a tomb.

Vases for different purposes were made of different shapes; each was beautiful in form, but with its beauty it combined usefulness. The handles on the water jars are placed just where they are most needed, the oil pours out of the narrow neck of the oil jug drop by drop so that the quantity could be easily regulated, and the drinking cup has a slight curve to the rim, so that one can drink out of it quite easily without spilling the liquid.

There are certain well-known forms of these vases: the *amphora* is a large two-handled vase which was used for storing oil and other liquids; the *hydria* has three handles and was used for carrying water; the *krater* is a large vase in which wine and water were mixed; the *lekythos* is a jug with a narrow neck used for pouring out oil slowly in small quantities; and the *kylix* is a wide and shallow drinking cup. A large amphora, often full of oil, was given as a prize for some of the athletic contests at the Panathenaic games held in Athens. Such an amphora can always be recognized, as it bears on one side the figure of Athena with the inscription: "I am from the Games at Athens," and on the other a painting depicting the contest for which the vase was a prize.

The quarter in Athens given up to the potters was known as the Cerameicus, and here there were a number of workshops owned by different vase-makers. At the head of each establishment was the master; but he was a craftsman as well as manager and was able to do everything connected with the industry: he could not only make the vase, but also design and paint it. His workmen, however, did most of the turning, shaping, and polishing of the vases. When the vase had been made, it was given to the artist who painted the design on it, after which it had to be dried, baked, and glazed. The black glaze that was used in Athens was one of the great discoveries of the ancient potters' art. Time never spoiled it, and it seems as fresh today as when it was first put on the vases. In some cases it has peeled off in small flakes, but that only happens when the clay beneath is damp; otherwise it remains unchanged.

The earlier vases were painted in black on the red background of the clay; later, the artist sketched his design on the red clay and gave the vase back to the workman, who painted in the background in black and then returned it to the artist, who retouched his design and in some cases added here and there a touch of color.

Besides the rooms for the workmen and artists, and the court where the ovens were placed, a potter's workshop required storerooms where the finished vases were kept, and a room where the master received his customers and sold his pottery.

The subjects of the paintings on the vases were always carefully chosen and were suited to the use to which the vase was to be put; the large vases had graver and more serious subjects, the kylix had more animated scenes. This cup was used at banquets and on festive occasions, and so the artists painted gay and merry scenes on it, and as they tried to attract buyers by the novelty of their designs, the kylix paintings show a great deal of originality. The subjects were taken from mythology, or showed battle scenes, or subjects connected with daily life. If all our other sources of knowledge of life in Athens were suddenly lost to us, the vases would still be a rich mine of information, as in one way or another they represent all the varied experiences of human life.

In all their art the Greeks were chiefly interested in representing the human form. They themselves did not realize that in doing this they were taking a step onward in man's great adventure of learning how to live, but in all the many ways in which they represented man, they showed him going forth into the outside world of nature, conscious that he had the power to make of it a world in which he felt at home. Part of the greatness of the Greeks came from the fact that they did this unconsciously. The craftsmen and vase-painters themselves were in no way regarded as the equals of the great sculptors. The Athenians regarded them as quite lowly workers, but they were artists nevertheless, proved so by the fact that though there was often copying of a general design, the artist never copied mechanically, but put into his work something that was his own. In all the great quantity of Greek vases in the world today, no two have been found exactly alike, and so the craftsmen, though they were unconscious of how later ages would regard their work, knew the satisfaction that comes from creating beauty in any form, and they said of their work that "there is no sweeter solace in life for human ills than craftsmanship; for the mind, absorbed in its study, sails past all troubles and forgets them."[3]

[3] Amphis: quoted by G. M. A. Richter in *The Craft of Athenian Pottery.*

Greek pottery

CHAPTER 15

A Day With an Athenian

I. The Athenian Gentleman

The day began early in Athens, and as soon as the sun was up everyone was stirring: the workman was off to his work, the schoolboy to school, and every booth and stall in the Agora was laden with articles to attract the buyers who were expected in the market.

Before leaving his house, the Athenian gentleman had his breakfast, a little bread soaked in wine, after which one of his house slaves saw that his himation hung in graceful folds, and then, accompanied by one or more slaves carrying baskets, he set forth for the Agora. Here the morning marketing was done, but unless he was giving a very important banquet in the evening, the gentleman did not himself attend to the household marketing; his slaves did that for him and took the purchases home. Their master, in the meantime, would walk up and down the Agora, or take a turn or two in one of the porches, where he would meet some of his friends, or go to the barber's shop, where he would be sure to hear the latest news of the day: Pericles had proposed to build another temple, and there was much discussion as to whether the state could afford it; the Spartan army was said to be stronger than ever, and Sparta had always been jealous of Athens; was she secretly getting ready for a war, and if so, should not Athens be prepared, or were those right who believed that the greatness of Greece lay in a policy of peace with Sparta? Perhaps the Olympic Games were being held, and the news had just come and spread like wildfire through the city, so that the Athenians had covered themselves with glory, especially in the chariot race, and that the victors were even then on their way home, so all must be in readiness to receive them. Or was it known that a galley had just returned from a trading voyage on the Aegean, and that the sailors were reporting that there was a good deal of discontent in some of the islands, and that threats were being made of withholding some of the tribute money unless the islanders were allowed greater independence? These and many more burning questions of the day were made known and discussed without the use of newspapers.

But the Athenian gentleman did not spend all his morning in talk. If he were wealthy, he would have definite duties required of him by the state: he had to fit out and keep in good order one or more triremes for the navy, and there would be interviews with the captain as to the number of men he required and how much they should be paid; there were estimates for repairs to be gone over, and designs for a new and splendid figurehead on the prow of the ship to be approved. Or perhaps it was his turn to provide for one of the choruses in the coming dramatic festival, and he must see to it that this chorus was well trained and that no expense was spared in making it better than any of the others, so that he might win the prize.

Then there were other duties towards the state that were demanded of every free-born citizen. He must sit on the jury and judge lawsuits whenever he was called upon to do so, and as the Athenians were very fond of such suits, the demand came very often. Aristophanes, a dramatist who wrote a number of plays in which he made fun of a great many of the Athenian characteristics, said of the juryman:

He is a law-court lover, no man like him.
Judging is what he dotes on, and he weeps
Unless he sits on the front bench of all.[1]

In some way or other, every Athenian citizen took part in the actual government of the state, and in the time of Pericles about nine thousand men held, during the year, some kind of state position. These officials were chosen by the people and were seldom re-elected, so that not only was everybody in turn responsible for certain functions, but everyone was capable of intelligently discussing the affairs of the state—and this was done at great length every day whenever Athenian citizens met together.

About once every ten days, the Agora was deserted in the morning, and every free-born Athenian citizen over thirty years of age, both rich and poor, was expected to go to the Pnyx, the meeting place of the Assembly. In times of war, or when some very important question in which everyone was interested had to be settled, no one stayed away, and there would be great hurrying in the early morning in order to get a good seat.

The Pnyx was a great open-air place of assembly, west of the Acropolis and not far from the city wall. In shape it was a sloping semi-circle, part of which was supported by a wall. There were no seats, and the citizens had to make themselves as comfortable as they could on the bare ground. Facing the slope was a rock cut in the form of a platform and mounted by steps on each side. This was called the *bema*, and here the orators stood when they addressed the Assembly. In front of the bema was the altar on which was offered the sacrifice that always opened the Assembly, and behind it on a rock were seats for the state officials who had charge of the meeting.

---

[1] Aristophanes: *The Wasps*, translated by B. B. Rogers. (By permission of Messrs. G. Bell and Sons.)

There were doubtless many days when the business at hand was not very interesting, but there were times when excitement ran high and no one was absent. It is not difficult to imagine the scene. Not far off rose the rock of the Acropolis, symbol of the strength and glory of Athens and of the guardianship of Athena; in the dim distance was the sea, the great bond of union between Athens and the islands of the Aegean and the East, and a symbol of the protecting power of Poseidon; overhead stretched the blue Greek sky; and there below in the Pnyx was the densely packed crowd of Athenians, deliberating on matters on which hung their very life or death. It was there that the decision was made to march to Marathon and to face the unnumbered Persian foe; that Themistocles pleaded passionately for a navy; that the messengers from Delphi brought back the answer about the "wooden walls"; that Aristeides persuaded the Athenians to free the Ionians from their Persian masters and to form the Delian League which led Athens to become an empire; and it was there, too, that Pericles in stately and measured tones urged the Athenians to beautify their city as no other city in the world had ever been beautified before.

These and similar occupations took up the morning of the Athenian gentleman. After a light meal in the middle of the day, he would go to the Academy or one of the other gymnasia, where he would spend the cool of the day in exercising himself, or in watching the youths at their games; in walking in the pleasant groves talking over the events of the day with his friends; or in discussing with some philosopher all kinds of questions concerning new interpretations of old beliefs and new ideas about man, whence he comes and whither he goes. Some of these were questions which were discussed for the first time in the history of the world, and never before and but seldom since has there been such an eager desire to know the truth about all things as there was in this Athens of the fifth century B.C.

But as the evening drew on and it grew dusk, the Athenians left the gymnasia and returned to the city. All day long they had been in company, and in the evening the most was made of every opportunity to meet again, for they held that "to eat your dinner alone was not dining but feeding," so it was very likely that the day would end with a banquet. If that were so, the guests would all have been invited in the morning, either by the host himself when he met them, or by a message carried by a slave. Preparations were usually made for more than the invited number of guests, as it was a common custom for guests to bring some additional friends of their own, and uninvited guests would often come without any special bidding. Since leaving the gymnasia, all the guests would have been at their homes. There they would have bathed and clad themselves in fresh chitons and mantles, and slaves would accompany them to the house of their host.

At a banquet the guests reclined on couches, and the food was brought to them on low tables. The evening meal was the chief meal of the day in Athens. It began with fish or meat and vegetables, and when this course was over, the tables were removed, water was poured over the hands of the guests, and garlands were often passed around. Then came the second course of fruits, confectionery, and various kinds of sweetmeats, after which the tables were again removed and replaced by smaller ones on which stood beautifully shaped drinking cups. The guests were given more garlands and wreaths, and the slaves brought in the large kraters, in which the wine and water were mixed, and the after-dinner entertainment of the evening began.

This entertainment was called the Symposium, and it began with the pouring out of three libations: to the Olympian gods, to the Heroes, and to Zeus. Then the health of the hosts and of his guests was drunk, after which began the entertainment. This consisted of conversation, singing, listening to music, watching dancers, playing games, telling stories, or passing round jests. Just what was done at the Symposium depended on the kind of guests present. "When the company are real gentlemen and men of education," said Plato, "you will see no flute girls, nor dancing girls, nor harp girls; they will have no nonsense or games, but will be content with one another's conversation." More often, however, the guests were less serious. They enjoyed the music of the flute and other instruments, they played games, watched dancing, and they "chatted and talked pleasant nonsense to one another."

When the party came to an end, a libation was offered to Hermes, and the slaves were called, who attended their masters home, lighting their way with torches or lamps. The older men would go sedately home, while the younger would keep up their merriment and go noisily and boisterously through the streets until, having knocked at the doors of their houses, the sleepy porter would wake up and let them in, and silence would at length reign in the streets of the city.

II. The Athenian Lady

WHAT, IN THE MEANTIME, was the Athenian lady doing? She was at home, managing all the household affairs and bringing up the children. She educated her sons until they were seven years old, when they went to school, and her daughters until they were about fifteen, when they were considered old enough to be married.

The Greek writer Xenophon wrote an account of what were considered the duties of an ideal Athenian wife. He imagines the husband of a young bride telling her what he expected of her, and in what way he hoped the household affairs would be managed.

> You will need to stay indoors, despatching to their toils without, such of your domestics whose work lies there. Over those whose appointed tasks are indoors it will be your duty to preside, yours to receive the stuffs brought in, yours to apportion part for daily use, and to make provision for the rest, to guard and garner it so that the outgoings destined for a year may not be expended in a month. It will be your duty when the wools are brought in to see that clothing is made for those who have need. Your duty also to see that the dried corn is made fit and serviceable for food. Then, too, if any of the household fall sick, it will be your care to tend them to the recovery of their health.
>
> But there are other cares and occupations which are yours by right. This, for instance, to take some maiden who knows nothing of carding wool, and to make her skillful in the art, doubling her usefulness; or to receive another quite ignorant of housekeeping or of service, and to render her skillful, loyal, serviceable, till she is worth her weight in gold. But the greatest joy of all will be to prove yourself my better; to make me your faithful follower; knowing no dread lest as the years advance you should decline in honor in your household, but rather trusting that though your hair turn gray, yet in proportion as you come to be a better helpmate to myself and to the children, a better guardian of our home, so will your honor increase throughout the household as mistress, wife, and mother, daily more dearly prized.[2]

Some further good advice was then given, and the husband concluded by recommending exercise as the best means of preserving both health and beauty. He said:

---

[2] Xenophon: *The Economist.*

> I counsel you to oversee the baking woman as she makes the bread, to stand beside the housekeeper as she measures out her stores; to go on tours of inspection to see if all things are in order as they should be. For, as it seems to me, this will be at once walking exercise and supervision. And as an excellent gymnastic, I urge you to knead the dough, and roll the paste; to shake the coverlets and make the beds; and if you train yourself in exercise of this sort you will enjoy your food, grow vigorous in health, and your complexion will in very truth be lovelier.[3]

Added to all these occupations was the education of the children. The Athenian lady had nurses for them, Spartan slave women, if they were to be had, for their discipline was sterner than that of other Greeks, and the Spartan nurses had the reputation of being able to keep their young charges in particularly good order. All kinds of toys were provided for the children: hoops, balls, spinning-tops, go-carts, dolls, and toy animals. The Athenian mother learned to be a good storyteller, for it was in these early days that the children wanted stories told to them, and many a tale would she relate of the gods and heroes of old, of the nymphs and spirits of the forests and mountains, of the sea and of the air. And when night came and the children must go to bed, then she would sing them to sleep with a slumber song:

> Sleep children mine, a light luxurious sleep,
> Brother with brother: sleep, my boys, my life:
> Blest in your slumber, in your waking blest.[4]

---

[3] Xenophon: *The Economist.*

[4] Theocritus: From *Idyll*, XXIV, translated by C. S. Calverley. (By permission of Messrs. G. Bell and Sons.)

Athenian woman

The girls had to be trained to all the duties of an Athenian wife, and there was much to learn in the short years of their girlhood. It was a domestic training that they were given; of other things they learned as much or as little as their mother knew herself and was able to teach them, probably not more than a little reading and writing. A girl was not encouraged to take up any kind of intellectual pursuits, and during her life before her marriage she was generally "most carefully trained to see and hear as little as possible, and to ask the fewest questions."[5]

But it was not all work for the maiden, and many a time did she sit in the swing in the courtyard and idle away a warm afternoon gently swinging to and fro, and many a merry game of ball did she have with her companions. It was she who made the fresh garlands and wreaths for the altars or the house, and who, when the moon was full, laid offerings on the tomb of her grandparents, and, most glorious of all her girlhood privileges,

[5] Xenophon: *The Economist.*

it was she who helped to weave the robe taken to the temple of Athena at the time of the great Panathenaic festival and who bore baskets of offerings to the goddess in the great procession.

When the Athenian maiden married, all this life came to an end, and she took upon her young shoulders the training of her own household, even as she had seen her mother do. Her marriage had usually been arranged for her, and she often knew but little of her future husband. Before the marriage day, she offered all her girlhood treasures to Artemis, the goddess who had watched over her childhood.

> Her tambourines and pretty ball, and the net that confined her hair, and her dolls and dolls' dresses, Timareta dedicates before her marriage to Artemis, a maiden to a maiden as is fit; do thou, daughter of Leto, laying thine hand over the girl Timareta, preserve her purely in her purity.[6]

When these symbols of her youth had passed from her keeping into that of the goddess, the maiden was dressed in beautiful raiment, crowned with a wreath and covered with the bridal veil for the marriage ceremony. This took place in the evening on a day when the moon was full, and when she was ready, the bride was led by her attendant maidens to the court where the bridegroom and her parents and the invited guests awaited her. The marriage took place in the court, a sacrifice was offered and a libation poured out to the gods, and then the marriage feast followed, at which cakes of sesame were always eaten. This was the only occasion on which women were allowed to be present at a feast, but through it all the bride remained closely veiled. When the feast was over, the bridal chariot was driven up to the door,

[6] Author unknown: From *Select Epigrams from the Greek Anthology*, translated by J. W. Mackail.

and the bride took her seat in it beside her husband, her mother walked behind it bearing the marriage torch with which the fire on the hearth of her new home would be lighted, the guests surrounded it and with flute-playing and singing, escorted the bride to her new home.

If the bridegroom lived in a distant place, the bridal procession broke up at the gates of the city, but if he lived in Athens, he and his bride were escorted to the door of his house, where they were met by his mother, and then, to the music of a marriage song, the bride was led into her new home.

Did the Athenian lady have no amusements or recreations? Did she leave all that was gay behind her when she became a wife? The Athenian lady seldom left the house, and never unless attended by a female slave. She had practically no society but that of her slaves. The peasant women in the fields and the few women who sold in the market had the society of their friends, but such companionship was denied to the well-born lady. She saw no men, except those of her own family. If her husband dined at home alone, she shared his meal, but if he had guests she was unseen. From time to time she took part in the great religious festivals and processions, and occasionally she was permitted to be present in the theater when a tragedy was performed, but she was never permitted to see a comedy, for the wit and humor were often coarse and considered unfitting for her ears.

In many ways it was a strange life that the Athenian lady lived, one that seems as if it were in contradiction to all that the Athenians held of the highest importance, for the

> Athenian lady lived in the house among a people that lived out of doors. Among a people who gave great importance to physical training, she was advised to take her exercise in bedmaking. At a time when the human spirit was at its freest, she was enclosed on all

> sides. Art and thought and letters were reaching the highest development they were ever to know, but for her they hardly existed.

But whatever was the actual life of the Athenian lady, the Athenian ideal of womanhood was very high. In the wondrous temple that stood high above the city, looking down upon it and guarding it, was the figure that symbolized to the Athenians all that was good and beautiful and true, and it was the figure of a woman. It was always the figure of a woman that represented Victory, and nearly all the great Greek dramas deal with the fate of a woman, who was generally the wife or daughter of a king. The Sacred Mysteries of Eleusis, mysteries of such deep meaning that it was said that "partakers in them had better hopes concerning death and all eternity," centered around the story of the love and sorrow of a woman. A race that could produce such great figures as these must have thought nobly of womanhood.[7]

And so, in spite of her subordinate position in the background, the Athenian woman was of real influence in Athens. She reigned supreme in the household, and as her sons grew up, they recognized in her those qualities which every Greek, and especially the Athenian, was taught to value so highly: that quiet courage which by its very steadfastness overcomes all the little anxieties and annoyances of daily life; and that self-control and self-mastery which, putting self in the background, sets free the individual for service to others. The Athenian ideal of service was that the man should give it wholly to the state, and the woman wholly to her home; but narrow as was her horizon, limited as were her opportunities, the Athenian woman exercised an influence in Athens that helped to strengthen and preserve some of the noblest Athenian qualities.

---

[7] See Emily James Putnam: *The Lady.*

CHAPTER 16

The Athenian Schoolboy

The chief aim of Athenian education was the building of character. The Athenians were more concerned that their sons should grow up to be good citizens, loving what was beautiful and hating all that was ugly, than that they should know any great number of facts. The object of any education is to teach a child how to live, and a system of education is good or bad according as it fulfills this aim. As different states and countries, at different periods, have had different ideals as to what is meant by *living*, so they will all have had different kinds of education, each thought out in such a way as best to train the child for that conception of life believed in by his state or country. For example, the Spartan conception of life was that every citizen should be a good soldier, able to defend his country and to go out and fight her wars. Whether the Spartan ideal was a good one or not may be questioned, but it cannot be denied that Spartan education was an excellent preparation for such a life.

The Athenians had a much wider ideal than the Spartans. They, too, believed in the training of the body, and in making patriotic citizens who would count it a glory to die in defence of their city, but they also believed that it was a glory to *live* for their city, and to this end they trained the mind and the imagination as well as the body. To an Athenian a *good man* was a *good citizen*, one who, being physically perfect, would be able to defend his city in time of war, who, being able to think, would be capable of governing, and loving all that was beautiful would set high standards of taste in art, letters, and conduct. Praxiteles gave outward form to this ideal in his statue of Hermes, and though the Athenian ideal was not complete, Athenian education produced a warrior like Miltiades, statesmen like Themistocles and Pericles, a poet like Sophocles, artists like Pheidias and Praxiteles, philosophers like Socrates and Plato, and a historian like Thucydides.

The Athenians believed that training which aimed only at money-making, bodily strength, or mere cleverness apart from intelligence was mean and vulgar and did not deserve to be called education. True education, they held, made a child long to be a good citizen and taught him both how to rule and to obey. It must not be supposed that the Athenians despised wealth or the power of wealth. Only a wealthy state could have built the Parthenon or celebrated the great Panathenaic Festival, but the Athenians despised mere money-making, and they believed that a man's success was not to be measured by the amount of money he had made, but by the use to which he put it; and they believed that an education which taught a boy to be industrious and thrifty, to despise self-indulgence and luxury, to think straight and see clearly, would make him a better citizen than one which aimed only at making him a successful man of business. So they aimed at giving every boy a good education.

> First among things, [said one of their teachers], I reckon human education. For if you begin anything whatever in the right way, the end will probably be right also. The nature of the harvest depends upon the seeds you sow. If you plant good education in a young body, it bears leaves and fruit the whole life long, and no rain or drought can destroy it.[1]

---

[1] From *The Schools of Hellas*, by Kenneth J. Freeman.

The Athenian boy went to school when he was seven years old. At this age he was placed in the charge of a pedagogue, a trusted slave who accompanied him when he went to school, carried his books, and helped him, when necessary, with his lessons. The pedagogue was also expected to keep him in good order, teach him good manners, answer all his many questions, and punish him whenever he thought fit, which was probably very often.

Schools opened early, so early that Solon made a law forbidding schoolmasters to open their schools before sunrise and requiring them to be closed before sunset, so that the boys should not have to walk about the dark and empty streets. The Athenian boy, then, had to be early astir. "He gets up at dawn, washes the sleep from his eyes, and puts on his cloak. Then he goes out from his father's house with his eyes fixed upon the ground, not looking at anyone who meets him." (A modest and unassuming appearance in public was required of every boy.) "Behind him follow attendants and pedagogues, bearing in their hands the implements of virtue, writing-tablets or books containing the great deeds of old, or, if he is going to a music school, his well-tuned lyre."[2]

Arrived at the school, the pedagogue remained in an ante-room, where he waited with all the other pedagogues until morning school was over. The boy entered a larger room beyond, where he settled down to his lessons. The boys sat on low benches with their writing-tablets on their knees, and the master sat on a higher chair in front of them. Lyres and other musical instruments, a book-roll or two, or perhaps some drinking cups hung on the walls.

Athenian boys were taught three main subjects: letters, music, and gymnastics. The first thing connected with letters was to be able to read and write. The first writing lessons were given on

---

[2] Lucian, translated by Kenneth J. Freeman, in *The Schools of Hellas*.

wooden tablets covered with wax, and for a pen a stylus with a sharp metal point was used. With this stylus the letters were scratched on the wax. When a boy had learned to write better, he was allowed to write on papyrus with a reed dipped in a kind of sticky substance which took the place of ink.

> When the boy has learned his letters [we are told], and is beginning to understand what is written, as before he understood only what was spoken, they put into his hands the works of great poets, which he reads sitting on a bench at school; in these are contained many admonitions, and many tales, and praises of ancient famous men, which he is required to learn by heart, in order that he may imitate them and desire to become like them.[3]

Athenian boys had no books for children—they began by reading great poetry and literature. Much of the literature they learned by heart, standing in front of the master who recited it to them, and they learned it by repeating it after him line by line. In this way they mastered passages from the *Iliad* and the *Odyssey*, and though it must have been unusual, it was not an unknown feat for a boy to be able to recite the whole of those poems by heart. "My father," said one man speaking of his school days, "in his pains to make me a good man, compelled me to learn the whole of Homer's poems, and even now I can repeat the *Iliad* and the *Odyssey* by heart."[4] Reciting poetry in an Athenian school was by no means a dull affair, for the boys acted as they recited. The art of reciting poetry was held in high esteem not only in Athens, but all over Greece, and in all places where the Greek tongue was spoken and where Greek ideals prevailed. During the disastrous war that Athens waged

[3] Plato: *Protagoras*, translated by Jowett.

[4] Xenophon: *Banquet.*

against Sparta at the end of the fifth century B.C., an Athenian expedition was sent to Sicily. After a terrible fight in the harbor of Syracuse, the Athenians were utterly defeated, and all those who survived the battle were taken as prisoners and confined in the stone quarries near the city. They were exposed to the sun and the rain and almost starved to death. But any man who could recite a chorus or one of the scenes from a play of Euripides, the great Athenian poet, was given his freedom and allowed to return home.

A certain amount of arithmetic was also taught, for it was considered a good training for the mind.

> "No branch of education is considered so valuable a preparation for household management and politics, and all arts and crafts, sciences, and professions, as arithmetic; best of all by some divine art, it arouses the dull and sleepy brain, and makes it studious, mindful, and sharp,"

and it was said of arithmetic that "those who are born with a talent for it are quick at all learning, while even those who are slow at it have their general intelligence much increased by studying it."[5] But Athenian children, like others, sometimes found it difficult to learn, and "I am pretty sure," said an Athenian, "that you will not easily find many sciences that give the learner and student so much trouble and toil as arithmetic."[6]

Part of the day was given to the study of letters, and then the boys went to the music school, where they learned to play the lyre and sing. A song accompanied by the music of the lyre was a favorite part of the entertainment after a banquet, and every Athenian gentleman was expected to be able to sing and play whenever he was called upon. So much was it the mark of

[5] Plato: *Laws.*

[6] Plato: *Republic*, translated by Davies and Vaughan.

a gentleman that "he who doesn't know the way to play the lyre" became a proverbial expression for an uneducated person.

Very little is known about Greek music, but it was considered very necessary that the music taught should be of an ennobling and inspiring kind. The Lydian melodies were held to be altogether too soft and sentimental, and the Athenians preferred those known as Dorian because they were simpler and sterner and of a kind to inspire men to noble and manly deeds. Aristotle, who wrote so much about the ideal state, wrote also about the education an ideal state should give to its children. He held that "music is neither a necessary nor a useful accomplishment in the sense in which letters are useful, but it provides a noble and worthy means of occupying leisure time," and Aristotle, like all Athenians, believed that it was the part of a good education to teach not only how to work well, but also how to use leisure well. The Athenians thought music was a good medicine for all ills. One philosopher, when his temper had been ruffled and he felt irritated and tired, used to take up his harp and play, saying, "I am calming myself."

In the afternoon the boys were taken by their pedagogues to the *palaestra*, or wrestling-school, where they learned gymnastics. It was as important that the boy should have a well-trained, graceful body as that he should have a clear and well-furnished mind, and so he spent a good part of each day running, jumping, wrestling, and throwing the discus under a special master.

According to Plato, this education turned the Athenian boy from being "the most unmanageable of animals" into "the most amiable and divine of living beings." This change had not taken place without many a punishment of the boy, and it was a proverb that "he that is not flogged cannot be taught." Not long ago an old Greek papyrus was discovered which gives a vivid account of the discipline that was thought necessary by both parents and teachers for the schoolboy who preferred, as he probably often did, to play games instead of learning his lessons. A mother brought her truant boy, Cottalus, to his schoolmaster, Lampriscus, to receive a flogging for his misdeeds, and she said:

Mother Flog him, Lampriscus,
Across the shoulders, till his wicked soul
Is all but out of him. He's spent my all
In playing odd and even; knuckle bones
Are nothing to him. Why, he hardly knows
The door of the Letter School. And yet
the thirtieth
Comes round and I must pay—tears
no excuse
His writing tablet which I take the trouble
To wax anew each month lies unregarded
In the corner. If by chance he deigns to
touch it
He scowls like Hades, then puts
nothing right
But smears it out and out. He doesn't know
A letter till you scream it twenty times.
...
Yet he knows
The seventh and the twentieth of the month,
Whole holidays, as if he reads the stars,
He lies awake o' nights dreaming of them.
But, so may yonder Muses prosper you,
Give him in stripes no less than—
Lampriscus (briskly) Right you are.
Here, boys, hoist him
Upon your backs. I like your goings on,
My boy! I'll teach you manners!
Where's my strap,
With the stinging cow's tail?

Cottalus (in terror) By the Muses, sir—not with the stinger.
Lamp. Then you shouldn't be so naughty.
Cott. O how many will you give me?
Lamp. Your mother fixes that.
Cott. How many, Mother?
Mother As many as your wicked hide can bear.
(They proceed with the flogging.)
Cott. Stop!—That's enough! Stop!
Lamp. You should stop your ways.
Cott. I'll never do it more, I promise you.
Lamp. Don't talk so much, or else I'll bring a gag.
Cott. I won't talk—only do not kill me—please.
Lamp. (at length relenting) Let him down, boys.
Mother. No, leather him till sunset.
Lamp. Why, he's as mottled as a water snake.
Mother. Well, when he's done his reading, good or bad,
Give him a trifle more, say twenty strokes.[7]

Children were not always well behaved in other ways, it seems, and complaints were made by their parents that the children contradicted them and did not always rise when their elders came into the room, that they chattered too much before company, crossed their legs when they sat down, and completely tyrannized over their pedagogues.

But in spite of all his misdemeanors and punishments, in letters, music, and gymnastics, the Athenian boy was educated until he was eighteen years old. The stories of the ancient heroes who had fought at Troy, and those of more recent times who had defeated the Persians, filled him with enthusiasm for his race and a love of freedom for his city. Having to learn

[7] Herodas: *Mime*, III, translated by Kenneth J. Freeman in *The Schools of Hellas.*

many things without the aid of books, his mind grew quick, alert, and observant, and his music and gymnastics taught him the beauty of self-control and dignified restraint.

At eighteen, the Athenian youth left school. The state did not give him the full rights of a citizen until a few years later, and until then he was required to perform certain military duties; but he was no longer a boy, and he was considered old enough to understand the meaning of citizenship, and to know what were its duties and privileges. So it was then, at the time of leaving his boyhood behind, and entering upon the richer and fuller life before him, that the youth took the oath of the *ephebi*, or young men. He was given the shield and spear of the warrior, and then in the temple, before Zeus, the Lord of Heaven, and in the presence of the highest Athenian magistrates, he swore:

> "Never to disgrace his holy arms, never to forsake his comrade in the ranks, but to fight for the holy temples, alone or with others: to leave his country, not in a worse, but in a better state than he found it; to obey the magistrates and the laws, and defend them against attack; finally, to hold in honor the religion of his country."

CHAPTER 17

THE GREEK THEATER

THE GREEK DRAMA began as a religious observance in honor of Dionysus. To the Greeks this god personified both the spring and the vintage (the latter a very important time of year in a vine-growing country), and he was a symbol to them of that power there is in man of rising out of himself, of being impelled onwards by a joy within him that he cannot explain, but which makes him go forward, walking, as it were, on the wings of the wind, of the spirit that fills him with a deep sense of worship. We call this power *enthusiasm*, a Greek word which simply means *the god within us*.

From very early times, stories of Dionysus' life were recited at the religious festivals held in his honor, and then stories of the other gods and of the ancient heroes were told as well. It was from these beginnings that the drama came. Originally, the story was told in the form of a song, chanted at first by everyone taking part in the festival, and later by a chorus of about fifty performers, and at intervals in the song the leader would recite part of the story by himself. By degrees the recitation became of greater importance than the song; it grew longer, and after a time two people took part in it and then three; at the same time the chorus became smaller and of less importance in the action of the drama, until at last it could consist of only fifteen performers.

A Greek drama was in many ways much simpler than a modern drama. There were fewer characters, and usually only three speaking actors were allowed on the stage at once. There was only one story told and there was nothing to take the attention of the audience away from this. The Chorus, though it no longer told the story, was very important, for it set the atmosphere of the play, and lyrics of haunting loveliness hinted at the tragedy that could not be averted, because of terrible deeds done in the past, or if, indeed, there might be any help, the imagination was carried forward on wings of hope. The Chorus also served another purpose. In a modern drama, when the tragedy of a situation becomes almost too great for the audience to bear, relief is often found in some comic, or partly comic, episode which is introduced to slacken the tension. Shakespeare does this constantly. But comic episodes were felt to be out of place in a Greek drama, and therefore when a tragic scene had taken place, the Chorus followed it by a song of purest poetry. In one play of Euripides, a terrible scene of tragedy was followed by a song in which the Chorus prayed for escape from such sorrows on the wings of a bird to a land where all was peace and beauty. They sang:

Could I take me to some cavern for mine hiding,
 In the hilltops where the Sun scarce hath trod;
Or a cloud make the home of mine abiding,
 As a bird among the bird-droves of God.

And the song goes on to carry the imagination to a spot

Where a voice of living waters never ceaseth
 In God's quiet garden by the sea,
And Earth, the ancient life-giver, increaseth
 Joy among the meadows, like a tree.[1]

In the great Greek dramas, the Chorus is a constant reminder that, though they cannot understand or explain

[1] Euripides: *Hippolytus*, translated by Gilbert Murray.

them, there are other powers in the world than the wild passions of men.

The great dramatic festival in Athens was held in the spring in the theater of Dionysus, to the southeast of the Acropolis. The theater in Athens never became an everyday amusement, as it is today, but was always directly connected with the worship of Dionysus, and the performances were always preceded by a sacrifice. The festival was only held once a year, and while it lasted, the whole city kept holiday. Originally, admission to the theater was free, but the crowds became so great and there was such confusion and sometimes fighting in the rush for good seats, that the state decided to charge an admission fee and tickets had to be bought beforehand. But even then there were no reserved seats, except for certain officials who sat in the front row. In the time of Pericles, complaints were made that the poorer citizens could not afford to buy tickets, and so important was the drama then considered that it was ordered that tickets should be given free to all who applied for them.

An Athenian audience was very critical, and shouts and applause or groans and hisses showed its approval or disapproval of the play being acted. Several plays were given in one day, and a prize was awarded to the best, so the audience was obliged to start at dawn and would probably remain in the theater until sunset. Let us go with an Athenian audience and see a play which was first performed in the latter half of the fifth century B.C.

The theater is a great semi-circle on the slope of the Acropolis, with rows of stone seats on which about eighteen thousand spectators can sit. The front row consists of marble chairs, the only seats in the theater which have backs, and these are reserved for the priests of Dionysus and the chief magistrates. Beyond the front row is a circular space called the *orchestra,* where the Chorus sings, and in the center of which stands the altar of Dionysus. Behind the orchestra is the stage

Theater of Dionysos at Athens

on which the actors will act, at the back of which is a building painted to look like the front of a temple or a palace, to which the actors retire when they are not wanted on the stage or have to change their costumes. That is the whole theatre and all its stage scenery. Overhead is the deep blue sky, the Acropolis rises up behind, and the olive-laden hills are seen in the distance. Much will have to be left to the imagination, but the very simplicity of the outward surroundings will make the audience give all their attention to the play and the acting.

When the play begins, there will only be three actors on the stage at once. They will wear very elaborate costumes and a strange-looking wooden sole called a *cothurnus* or *buskin*, about six inches high, on their shoes to make them look taller and more impressive, and over their faces a curious mask with a wide mouth, so that everyone in that vast audience will hear them. There will be no curtain and the play is not divided into different acts. When there is a pause in the action, the Chorus will fill up the time with their song. If it is tragedy, we shall not see the final catastrophe on the stage, but a messenger will appear who will give us an account of what has happened. All this is very different from the way in which a modern play is given, but some of the greatest dramas the world possesses were written by Athenian dramatists and acted on this Athenian stage more than two thousand years ago.

On this occasion the play we are to see is "Iphigenia in Tauris," written by Euripides, one of the greatest of the Athenian dramatists.

The legends and traditions from which most of the Greek plays took their plots were, of course, well known to the Athenians. They were stories commemorating some great event, or explaining some religious observance, but naturally these legends were treated differently by different dramatists, each of whom brought out a different side of the story to enforce some particular lesson which he wished to bring home to the people; and this is especially true of the legends like that of Iphigenia, connected with the Fall of Troy.

In the opening speech of this play, Iphigenia very briefly tells her story up to the moment when the play begins. Just as the Greeks had been ready to sail for Troy, they were wind-bound at Aulis. The wise men were consulted as to the meaning of this, and how the gods who must in some way have been offended might be appeased, so that fair winds might send them on their way. Calchas, the seer, told them that Artemis demanded the sacrifice of lphigenia, daughter of Agamemnon, King of Argos, the great leader of the host, and her father sent for her accordingly. The maiden was at home with her mother, and the messenger who was sent to Argos to bring her was charged to say that her father desired to wed her to the hero Achilles. She came and the sacrifice was offered, but at the supreme moment, Artemis carried Iphigenia away and placed her in the land of the Tauri, a wild and barbarous tribe, as their priestess. These Tauri had an image of Artemis in a temple, to which they sacrificed all strangers who were

Theater masks (above)
Figurine of a tragic actor (below)

cast on their shores, and it was the duty of the priestess to consecrate each victim before he was slain. Here, performing this rite, had Iphigenia lived for more than ten years, but never yet had a Greek come to this wild land. She knew, of course, nothing of what had happened at Troy or afterwards; she did not know that on his return home, her father had been slain by Clytemnestra, his wife, or that Orestes, her brother, had avenged that death by slaughtering his own mother, after which deed he had wandered from place to place pursued by the relentless torment of the Furies. Bitter against the Greeks for having willed her sacrifice at Aulis, Iphigenia says of herself that she is "turned to stone, and has no pity left in her," and she half hopes that the day will come when a Greek shall be brought to her to be offered in his turn to the goddess.

In the meantime, Orestes, tormented beyond endurance by the Furies, had gone to the Oracle of Apollo to ask how he might be purified from his sin, and Apollo had told him to go to the land of the Tauri and bring back to Attica the image of Artemis his sister, so that it might no longer be stained by the blood of the human sacrifices. And so it comes about that Orestes is the first Greek who will be brought to Iphigenia for sacrifice to Artemis. It is at this moment that the play opens.[2]

Characters of the Play

Iphigenia
Orestes, her brother
Pylades, friend to Orestes
Thoas, King of Tauris
A Herdsman
A Messenger
Chorus of captive Greek women, handmaids to Iphigenia
The Goddess, Pallas Athena

[2] From the translation of *Iphigenia in Tauris* by Gilbert Murray.

The scene shows a great and barbaric temple on a desolate seacoast. An altar is visible, stained with blood. There are spoils of slain men hanging from the roof. Iphigenia, in the dress of a priestess, comes out of the temple, and in a speech that serves really as a prologue to the play, she tells her story. At the end of her speech, which is haunted throughout by a sense of exile and homesickness, she describes a strange dream she has just had, which she interprets as meaning that Orestes, her brother, is dead. She then goes into the temple.

Voice 1 Did someone cross the pathway? Guard thee well.
Voice 2 I am watching. Every side I turn my eye.

(Enter Orestes and Pylades. Their dress shows they are travelers. Orestes is shaken and distraught.)

Orestes How, brother? And is this the sanctuary
At last, for which we sailed from Argos?
Pylades For sure, Orestes. Seest thou not it is?
Orestes The altar, too, where Hellene blood is shed.
Pylades How like long hair those blood-stains, tawny red!
Orestes And spoils of slaughtered men—there by the thatch.
Pylades Aye, firstfruits of the harvest, when they catch
Their strangers!—'Tis a place to search with care.

(He searches while Orestes sits.)

During this search, Orestes, in a speech addressed to Apollo, explains why they are there and expresses hopelessness at their ever accomplishing the will of the god, and even suggests their turning back. But Pylades encourages him and bids him take courage, for, he says,

Danger gleams
Like sunshine to a brave man's eyes, and fear
Of what may be is no help anywhere.

Orestes Aye, we have never braved these leagues of way
To falter at the end. See, I obey Thy words.
They are ever wise. Let us go mark
Some cavern, to lie hid till fall of dark.
God will not suffer that bad things be stirred
To mar us now, and bring to naught the word
Himself hath spoke. Aye, and no peril brings
Pardon for turning back to sons of kings.
(They go out towards the shore.)

After they are gone, enter gradually the women of the Chorus. These are Greek women who have been taken captive in war by King Thoas, and so they are friendly to the exiled and lonely Iphigenia, for they are just as homesick as she is. They come now in obedience to a call from her to assist in mourning for Orestes, who, she is convinced by her dream, is dead.

Chorus

Peace! Peace upon all who dwell
By the Sister Rocks that clash in the swell
Of the Friendless Seas.
...
From Hellas that once was ours,
We come before thy gate,
From the land of the western seas,
The horses and the towers,
The wells and the garden trees,
And the seats where our fathers sat.

Leader

What tidings, ho? With what intent

Hast called me to thy shrine and thee,
O child of him who crossed the sea
To Troy with that great armament,
The thousand prows, the myriad swords?
I come, O child of Atreid Lords.
(Iphigenia, followed by attendants, comes from the temple.)

Iphigenia Alas! O maidens mine,
I am filled full of tears.
My heart filled with the beat
Of tears, as of dancing feet,
A lyreless joyless line,
And music meet for the dead.
For a whisper is in mine ears,
By visions borne on the breath
Of the night that now is fled,
Of a brother gone to death.
Oh sorrow and weeping sore,
For the house that no more is,
For the dead that were kings of yore
And the labor of Argolis!

Iphigenia and the Chorus then lament together over the ruin and loss that has befallen the House of Agamemnon. Suddenly the leader of the Chorus stops them.

Leader

Stay, yonder from some headland of the sea
There comes, methinks, a herdsman, seeking thee.
(Enter a herdsman. Iphigenia is still on her knees.)

Herdsman Daughter of Clytemnestra and her King,
Give ear! I bear news of a wondrous thing.

Iphigenia What news, that so should mar my obsequies?

Herdsman A ship hath passed the blue Symplegades,
And here upon our coast two men are thrown,
Young, bold, good slaughter for the altarstone
Of Artemis.
(She rises.)
Make all the speed ye may;
'Tis not too much. The blood-bowl and the spray!
Iphigenia Men of what nation? Doth their habit show?
Herdsman Hellenes for sure, but that is all we know.
Iphigenia No name? No other clue thine ear could seize?
Herdsman We heard one call his comrade "Pylades."
Iphigenia Yes. And the man who spoke—his name
was what?
Herdsman None of us heard. I think they spoke it not.
Iphigenia How did ye see them first, how make them fast?
Herdsman Down by the sea, just where the surge is cast—
Iphigenia The sea? What is the sea to thee and thine?
Herdsman We came to wash our cattle in the brine.
Iphigenia Go back, and tell how they were taken; show
The fashion of it, for I fain would know
All—'tis so long a time, and never yet,
Never, hath Greek blood made this altar wet.

The herdsman tells his tale of how the men were taken prisoners. Iphigenia hears in silence and at the end of it says:

'Tis well. Let thy hand bring them, and mine own
Shall falter not till here God's will be done.
(Exit herdsman.)

Iphigenia then gives way to her feelings. There are strangers to be sacrificed; to that she is accustomed, but these men are Greeks. Yet she herself suffered bitter things at the hands of the Greeks; should she not avenge these? By degrees, however, as she thinks of her youth, of her home, she melts, and at length withdraws into the temple, raging against the cruel deed that she must do, and not at all sure that she can nerve herself to do it.

The coming of these Greeks has brought Greece vividly back to the thoughts of the Chorus. All Greeks loved the sea and were seafarers, and the arrival of these two adventurous men reminds these exiled women of their home; and in their imagination they see the ship cross the sea, until it touches the friendless and cruel shore.

Chorus

But who be these, from where the rushes blow
On pale Eurotas, from pure Dirces,
    That turn not neither falter,
Seeking Her land, where no man breaketh bread,
Her without pity, round whose virgin head
Blood on the pillars rusts from long ago,
    Blood on the ancient altar.

A flash of the foam, a flash of the foam,
    A wave on the oar-blade welling,
And out they passed to the heart of the blue:
A chariot shell that the wild waves drew.
Is it for passion of gold they come,
    Or pride to make great their dwelling?
. . .
Through the Clashing Rocks they burst:
    They passed by the Cape unsleeping
Of Phineus' sons accurst:
They ran by the star-lit bay
    Upon magic surges sweeping,
Where folk on the waves astray
Have seen, through the gleaming gray,
Ring behind ring, men say,

The dance of the old Sea's daughters.
The guiding oar abaft
It rippled and it dinned,
And now the West wind laughed
And now the Southwest wind;
And the sail was full in flight,
And they passed by the Island White:
Birds, birds, everywhere,
White as the foam, light as the air;
And ghostly Achilles raceth there,
Far in the Friendless Waters.
A sail, a sail from Greece,
Fearless to cross the sea,
With ransom and with peace
To my sick captivity.
O home, to see thee still,
And the old walls on the hill.
Dreams, dreams, gather to me:
Bear me on wings over the sea;
O joy of the night, to slave and free,
One good thing that abideth!

Leader

But lo, the two whom Thoas sends,
Their arms in bondage grasped sore
Strange offering this, to lay before
The Goddess! Hold your peace, O friends.
Onward, still onward to this shrine
They lead the firstfruits of the Greek.
'Twas true, the tale he came to speak,
That watcher of the mountain kine.
O holy one, if it afford
Thee joy, what these men bring to thee,
Take thou their sacrifice, which we,
By law of Hellas, hold abhorred.

(Enter Orestes and Pylades, bound and guarded by Taurians. Re-enter Iphigenia.)

Iphigenia So be it.
My foremost care must be that nothing harms
The temple's holy rule—untie their arms.
That which is hallowed may no more be bound.
You, to the shrine within! Let all be found
As the law bids, and as we need this day.
(Orestes and Pylades are set free; some attendants go into the temple.)
Ah me!
What mother then was yours, O strangers say,
And father? And your sister, if you have
A sister: both at once, so young and brave
To leave her brotherless! Who knows when heaven
May send that fortune? For to none is given
To know the coming nor the end of woe;
So dark is God, and to great darkness go
His paths, by blind chance mazed from our ken.
Whence are ye come, O most unhappy men?
From some far home, methinks, ye have found this shore
And far shall stay from home forevermore.

Orestes asks Iphigenia not to make their fate worse by dwelling on it, nor to pity them. They know where they are and the cruel custom of the land.

Iphigenia Say first—which is it men call Pylades?
Orestes 'Tis this man's name, if that will give thee ease.
Iphigenia From what walled town of Hellas cometh he?
Orestes Enough!—How would the knowledge profit thee?

Iphigenia Are ye two brothers of one mother born?
Orestes No, not in blood. In love we are brothers sworn.
Iphigenia Thou also hast a name: tell me thereof.
Orestes Call me Unfortunate. 'Tis name enough.
Iphigenia I asked not that. Let that with Fortune lie.
Orestes Fools cannot laugh at them that nameless die.
Iphigenia Why grudge me this? Hast thou such mighty fame?
Orestes My body, if thou wilt, but not my name.
Iphigenia Nor yet the land of Greece where thou wast bred?
Orestes What gain to have told it thee, when I am dead?
Iphigenia Nay: why shouldst thou deny so small a grace?
Orestes Know then, great Argos was my native place.
Iphigenia Stranger! The truth!—From Argos art thou come?
Orestes Mycenae, once a rich land, was my home.
Iphigenia 'Tis banishment that brings thee here—or what?
Orestes A kind of banishment, half forced, half sought.
Iphigenia Wouldst thou but tell me all I need of thee!
Orestes 'Twere not much added to my misery.
Iphigenia From Argos!—Oh, how sweet to see thee here!
Orestes Enjoy it then. To me 'tis sorry cheer.
Iphigenia Thou knowest the name of Troy? Far doth it flit.
Orestes Would God I had not; nay, nor dreamed of it.
Iphigenia Men fable it is fallen beneath the sword?
Orestes Fallen it is. Thou hast heard no idle word.
Iphigenia Fallen! At last!—And Helen taken too?
Orestes Aye; on an evil day for one I knew.
Iphigenia Where is she? I, too, have some anger stored—
Orestes In Sparta! Once more happy with her lord!
Iphigenia Oh, hated of all Greece, not only me!
Orestes I, too, have tasted of her wizardry.

Iphigenia And came the armies home, as the tales run?
Orestes To answer that were many tales in one.
Iphigenia Oh, give me this hour full! Thou soon wilt die.
Orestes Ask, if such longing holds thee. I will try.
Iphigenia A seer called Calchas! Did he ever come?
Orestes Calchas is dead, as the news went at home.
Iphigenia Good news, ye gods!—Odysseus, what of him?
Orestes Not home yet, but still living, as men deem.
Iphigenia Curse him! And may he see his home no more.
Orestes Why curse him? All his house is stricken sore.
Iphigenia How hath the Nereid's son, Achilles, sped?
Orestes Small help his bridal brought him! He is dead.
Iphigenia A fierce bridal, so the sufferers tell!
Orestes Who art thou, questioning of Greece so well?
Iphigenia I was a Greek. Evil caught me long ago.
Orestes Small wonder, then, thou hast such wish to know.
Iphigenia That warlord, whom they call so high in bliss—
Orestes None such is known to me. What name was his?
Iphigenia They called him Agamemnon, Atreus' son.
Orestes I know not. Cease—my questioning is done.
Iphigenia 'Twill be such joy to me! How fares he? Tell!
Orestes Dead. And hath wrecked another's life as well.
Iphigenia Dead? By what dreadful fortune? Woe is me!
Orestes Why sighest thou? Had he any link with thee?
Iphigenia I did but think of his old joy and pride.
Orestes His own wife foully stabbed him, and he died.
Iphigenia O God! I pity her that slew—and him that slew.
Orestes Now cease thy questions. Add no word thereto.
Iphigenia But one word. Lives she still, that hapless wife?
Orestes No. Her own son, her firstborn, took her life.
Iphigenia O shipwrecked house! What thought was in his brain?
Orestes Justice on her, to avenge his father slain.
Iphigenia Alas! A bad false duty bravely hath he wrought.

Orestes Yet God, for all his duty, helps him not.
Iphigenia And not one branch of Atreus' tree lives on?
Orestes Electra lives, unmated and alone.
Iphigenia The child they slaughtered—is there word of her?
Orestes Why, no, save that she died in Aulis there.
Iphigenia Poor child! Poor father, too, who killed and lied.
Orestes For a bad woman's worthless sake she died.
Iphigenia The dead king's son, lives he in Argos still?
Orestes He lives, now here, now nowhere, bent with ill.
Iphigenia O dreams, light dreams, farewell! Ye, too, were lies.

Leader

We, too, have kinsmen dear, but, being low,
None heedeth, live they still or live they not.

Iphigenia *(with sudden impulse)*
Listen! For I am fallen upon a thought,
Strangers, of some good use to you and me.
...
Stranger, if I can save thee, wilt thou bear
To Argos and the friends who loved my youth
Some word? There is a tablet which, in ruth,
For me and mine ill works, a prisoner wrote,
Ta'en by the king in war. He knew 'twas not
My will that craved for blood, but
One on high Who holds it righteous her due prey shall die.
And since that day no Greek hath ever come
Whom I could save and send to Argos home
With prayer to any friend: but thou,
I think, dost loathe me not; and thou dost know

Mycenae and the names that fill my heart.
Help me! Be saved! Thou also hast thy part,
Thy life for one light letter—
(Orestes looks at Pylades.)
For thy friend, The law compelleth.
He must bear the end
By Artemis ordained, apart from thee.

Orestes Strange woman, as thou biddest let it be,
Save one thing. 'Twere for me a heavy weight
Should this man die. 'Tis I and mine own fate
That steer our goings. He but sails with me
Because I suffer much. It must not be
That by his ruin I should 'scape mine own,
And win thy grace withal. 'Tis simply done.
Give him the tablet. He with faithful will
Shall all thy hest in Argolis fulfill.
And I—who cares may kill me.
Vile is he who leaves a friend in peril and
goes free
Himself. And, as it chances, this is one
Right dear to me; his life is as my own.

Iphigenia O royal heart! Surely from some great seed
This branch is born, that can so love indeed.
God grant the one yet living of my race
Be such as thou! For not quite brotherless
Am even I save that I see him not,
Strangers—howbeit, thy pleasures shall
be wrought.
This man shall bear the message, and thou go
To death. So greatly thou wilt have it so.

Orestes then asks somewhat of the ritual by which Iphigenia will consecrate the victim, and where he will be buried. Iphigenia promises that he shall be duly buried according to the Greek customs, and then she goes into the temple to get the tablet. During her absence Orestes and Pylades have a long argument as to which shall bear the tablet to Argos, and which remain in the island to be sacrificed. It is finally decided that Pylades shall go back to Greece, and Orestes shall remain.

(Enter Iphigenia from the temple.)

Iphigenia Go ye within; and have all things of need
In order set for them that do the deed.
There wait my word.
(Attendants go in.)
Ye strangers, here I hold
The many-lettered tablet, fold on fold.
Yet—one thing still.

Iphigenia then tells Pylades that she is afraid that, once safe and free, he will forget the promise made when he was in danger of his life, and so she makes him swear in the name of Zeus that he will faithfully bear the message. She, on her side, in the name of Artemis swears that she will in very truth set him free. Pylades then reminds her that he might be shipwrecked and so lose the tablet, and asks that in that case he may be relieved from his vow. But Iphigenia, in her desperate longing for deliverance, refuses this, and instead says that she will tell him what is written in the tablet. If it should be lost, he must then bear the message by word of mouth.

Pylades For thy sake and for mine 'tis fairer so.
Now let me hear his name to whom I go
In Argolis, and how my words should run.
Iphigenia *(repeating the words by heart)*
Say: "To Orestes, Agamemnon's son,
She that was slain in Aulis, dead to Greece
Yet quick, Iphigenia sendeth peace."

Orestes Iphigenia! Where? Back from the dead?
Iphigenia 'Tis I. But speak not, lest thou break
my thread—
"Take me to Argos, brother, ere I die.
Back from the Friendless Peoples and the high
Altar of Her whose bloody rites I wreak."
Orestes *(aside)*
Where am I, Pylades? How shall I speak?
Iphigenia "Else one in grief forsaken shall, like shame,
haunt thee."
Pylades *(aside)*
Orestes!
Iphigenia *(overhearing him)*
Yes: that is the name.
Pylades Ye gods above!
Iphigenia Why callest thou on God
For words of mine?
Pylades 'Tis nothing. 'Twas a road
My thoughts had turned. Speak on—no need
for us
To question; we shall hear things marvelous.
Iphigenia Tell him that Artemis my soul did save,
I wot not how, and to the altar gave
A fawn instead; that which my father slew,
Not seeing, deeming that the sword he drew
Struck me. But she had borne me far away
And left me in this land—I charge thee, say
So much. It is all written on the scroll.
Pylades An easy charge thou layest on my soul,
A glad oath on thine own. I wait no more,
But here fulfill the service that I swore.
Orestes, take this tablet which I bear
To thine own hand, thy sister's messenger.
Orestes I take it, but I reck not of its scrip

Nor message. Too much joy is at my lip.
Sister! Beloved! Wildered though I be,
My arms believe not, yet they crave for thee.
Now, filled with wonder, give me my delight!
(He goes to embrace her. She stands speechless.)

Leader Stranger, forbear! No living man hath right
To touch that robe. The Goddess were defiled!

Orestes O sister mine, O my dead father's child,
Agamemnon's child; take me and have no fear,
Beyond all dreams 'tis I thy brother here.

Iphigenia My brother? Thou?—peace!
Mock at me no more.
Argos is bright with him and Nauplia's shore.

Orestes Unhappy one! Thou hast no brother there.

Iphigenia Orestes—thou? Whom Clytemnestra bare?

Orestes To Atreus' firstborn son, thy sire and mine.

Iphigenia Thou sayest it: oh, give me some proof,
some sign!

Old things of home are remembered between the two, and at length Iphigenia is convinced.

Iphigenia *(falling into his arms)*
Beloved! Oh, no other, for indeed
Beloved art thou! In mine arms at last,
Orestes far away.

Then follows a scene in which Iphigenia gives herself up to one emotion after another, and when Orestes reminds her that they are not yet safe, she suggests one wild plan after another.

Iphigenia And now, what end cometh?
Shall Chance yet comfort me,
Finding a way for thee

Back from the friendless Strand,
Back from the place of death—
Ere yet the slayers come
And thy blood sink in the sand—
Home unto Argos, home?
Hard heart so swift to slay,
Is there to life no way?
No ship!—And how by land?—
A rush of feet
Out to the waste alone.
Nay: 'twere to meet
Death, amid tribes unknown
And trackless ways of the waste—
Surely the sea were best.
Back by the narrow bar
To the Dark Blue Gate!
Ah God, too far, too far!
Desolate! Desolate!
What god or man, what unimagined flame,
Can cleave this road where no road is, and bring
To us last wrecks of Agamemnon's name
Peace from long suffering?

But Iphigenia has not yet learned all, and at length Orestes tells her why he is there. He repeats the words of Apollo:

"Go seek the Taurian citadel:
Seize there the carven Artemis that fell
From heaven, and establish it on Attic soil.
So comes thy freedom,"
And he continues:
"Sister, in this toil
Help us!—If once that image I may win
That day shall end my madness and my sin:

And thou, to Argos o'er the sundering foam
My many-oared barque shall bear thee home.
O sister, loved and lost, O pitying face,
Help my great peril; help our father's race.
For lost am I and perished all the powers
Of Pelops, save that heavenly thing be ours!"

This news somewhat sobers Iphigenia. She is confronted now with a very different thing from saving her brother's life. That had just now seemed almost impossible, but compared to this new demand, it seemed almost easy. This is an act of madness; it will be considered a most fearful act of sacrilege to steal the image of Artemis, yet Orestes asks for her help to do it. And then there is herself and her own hopes! She might perhaps succeed in saving his life and fleeing with him, but to steal the statue and then go with him is a task beyond any hope of accomplishment. What shall she do? She deliberately decides that she will save his life and give him the statue, and then she herself will confront the angry king and give her life for her brother.

Iphigenia I must wait then and be slain:
Thou shalt walk free in Argolis again,
And all life smile on thee—dearest, we need
Not shrink from that. I shall by mine own deed
Have saved thee. And a man gone from the earth
Is wept for. Women are but little worth.

But Orestes refuses to accept the sacrifice.

Orestes I stand with thee
One-hearted here, be it for life or death,
And either bear thee, if God favoreth,
With me to Greece and home, or else lie here

Dead at thy side.

...

Iphigenia To steal for thee the image, yet not die
Myself. 'Tis that we need.

They then begin to discuss every possible means of escape, and at last an idea comes to Iphigenia. She will tell the king that Orestes has come from Greece with his mother's blood upon him, and that therefore it would be a great offence to sacrifice him to the goddess. Before he is sacrificed, he must be cleansed in the waves of the sea. But his very presence has defiled the image of the goddess, and so that, too, must be taken to the shore and purified. Pylades shares in the guilt of his friend and will accompany him to the shore, and Iphigenia will go down with the image. The rest must be the work of Orestes, and he must arrange that they are taken on board his ship and so escape. It is a dangerous and a daring plan, but there is no hope anywhere else.

Iphigenia, Orestes, and Pylades will thus be saved, if saving be possible, but what of the Chorus, of these Greek women, companions of the exile and loneliness of Iphigenia? They are indeed "true of heart and faithful found," for with no hope of going home themselves, ignored even by Iphigenia in this tremendous moment of her own hope, they loyally promise secrecy about all that concerns the plot. Yet they, too, crave for home, and they give voice to their longings. They see in imagination the Greek land. Once again the misery of their capture and enslavement comes before them, but they rise above their sorrow as they sing of what it will mean to Iphigenia to cross the sea, to behold her home once again, and to reach the land of freedom.

Chorus

Bird of the sea rocks, of the bursting spray,
O halcyon bird,

That wheelest crying, crying on thy way;
Who knoweth grief can read the tale of thee:
One love long lost, one song forever heard
    And wings that sweep the sea.
Sister, I, too, beside the sea complain,
    A bird that hath no wing.
Oh, for a kind Greek marketplace again,
For Artemis that healeth woman's pain;
    Here I stand hungering.
Give me the little hill above the sea,
The palm of Delos fringed delicately,
The young sweet laurel and the olive tree
    Gray-leaved and glimmering.
...
Ah, the old tears, the old and blinding tears
    I gave God then,
When my town fell, and noise was in mine ears
Of crashing towers, and forth they guided me
Through spears and lifted oars and angry men
    Out to an unknown sea.
They bought my flesh with gold, and sore afraid
    I came to this dark East
To serve, in thrall to Agamemnon's maid.
This Huntress Artemis, to whom is paid
The blood of no slain beast;
Yet all is bloody where I dwell, Ah me!
Envying, envying that misery
That through all life hath endured changelessly.
    For hard things borne from birth
Make iron of man's heart, and hurt the less.
'Tis change that paineth; and the bitterness
Of life's decay when joy hath ceased to be
    That makes all dark the earth.
        Behold,

Two score and ten there be
Rowers that row for thee,
And a wild hill air, as if Pan were there,
Shall sound on the Argive sea,
Piping to set thee free.
Or is it the stricken string
Of Apollo's lyre doth sing
Joyously, as he guideth thee
To Athens, the land of spring;
While I wait wearying?
Oh, the wind and the oar,
When the great sail swells before,
With sheets astrain, like a horse on the rein;
And on through the race and roar,
She feels for the farther shore.
Ah me,
To rise upon wings and hold
Straight on up the steeps of gold
Where the joyous Sun in fire doth run,
Till the wings should faint and fold
O'er the house that was mine of old.
Or watch where the glade below
With a marriage dance doth glow,
And a child will glide from her mother's side
Out, out, where the dancers flow:
As I did, long ago.
Oh, battles of gold and rare
Raiment and starred hair,
And bright veils crossed amid tresses tossed
In a dusk of dancing air!
O Youth and the days that were!

(Enter King Thoas, with soldiers.)

Thoas Where is the warden of this sacred gate,
The Greek woman? Is her work ended yet

With these two strangers? Do their bodies lie
Aflame now in the rock-cleft sanctuary?

Leader Here is herself, O King, to give thee word.

(Enter, from the temple, Iphigenia, carrying the Image on high.)

Thoas How, child of Agamemnon! Hast thou stirred
From her eternal base, and to the sun
Bearest in thine own arms, the Holy One?

Iphigenia Back, Lord! No step beyond the pillared way.

Thoas But how? Some rule is broken?

Iphigenia I unsay that word. Be all unspoken and unwrought!

Thoas What means this greeting strange? Disclose thy thought.

Iphigenia Unclean the prey was that ye caught, O King.

Thoas Who showed thee so? Thine own imagining?

Iphigenia The Image stirred and shuddered from its seat.

Thoas Itself?—Some shock of earthquake loosened it.

Iphigenia Itself. And the eyes closed one breathing space.

Thoas But why? For those two men's blood-guiltiness?

Iphigenia That, nothing else. For, oh!—their guilt is sore.

Thoas They killed some of my herdsmen on the shore?

Iphigenia Their sin was brought from homes not gathered here.

Thoas What? I must know this—make thy story clear.

Iphigenia *(She puts down the Image and moves nearer to Thoas.)*
The men have slain their mother.

Thoas God! And these
Be Greeks!

Iphigenia They both are hunted out of Greece.

Thoas For this thou hast brought the Image to the sun?

Iphigenia The fire of heaven can cleanse all malison.

Thoas How didst thou first hear of their deed of shame?

Iphigenia When the image hid its eyes, I questioned them.
Thoas Good. Greece hath taught thee many a subtle art.
Iphigenia Ah, they too had sweet words to move my heart.
Thoas Sweet words? How, did they bring some news of Greece?
Iphigenia Orestes, my one brother, lives in peace.
Thoas Surely! Good news to make thee spare their lives—
Iphigenia My father, too, in Argos lives and thrives.
Thoas While thou didst think but of the goddess' laws!
Iphigenia Do I not hate all Greeks? Have I not cause?
Thoas Good cause. But now—what service should be paid?
Iphigenia The Law of long years needs must be obeyed.
Thoas To work then, with thy sword and hand-washing!
Iphigenia First I must shrive them with some cleansing thing.
Thoas What? Running water, or the sea's salt spray?
Iphigenia The sea doth wash all the world's ills away.
Thoas For sure. 'Twill make them cleaner for the knife.
Iphigenia And my hand, too, cleaner for all my life.
Thoas Well, the waves lap close by the temple floor.
Iphigenia We need a secret place. I must do more.
Thoas Some rite unseen? 'Tis well. Go where thou wilt.
Iphigenia. The Image likewise must be purged of guilt.
Thoas The stain hath touched it of that mother's blood?
Iphigenia I durst not move it else, from where it stood.
Thoas How good thy godliness and forethought! Aye,
Small wonder all our people holds thee high.
Iphigenia Dost know then what I fain would have?
Thoas. 'Tis thine to speak and it shall be.
Iphigenia Put bondage on the strangers both—
Thoas Why bondage? Whither can they flee?

Iphigenia Put not thy trust in any Greek.

Thoas *(to attendants)* Ho, men! Some thongs and fetters, go!

Iphigenia Stay: let them lead the strangers here, outside the shrine—

Thoas It shall be so.

Iphigenia And lay dark raiment on their heads—

Thoas To veil them, lest the Sun should see.

Iphigenia And lend me some of thine own spears.

Thoas This company shall go with thee.

Iphigenia Next, send through all the city street a herald—

Thoas Aye: and what to say?

Iphigenia That no man living stir abroad.

Thoas The stain of blood might cross their way.

Iphigenia Aye, sin like theirs doth spread contagion.

Thoas *(to an attendant)* Forth, and publish my command—

Iphigenia That none stir forth—nor look—

Thoas Nor look. How well thou carest for the land!

Iphigenia For one whom I am bound to love.

Thoas Indeed, I think thou hat'st me not.

Iphigenia And thou meanwhile, here at the temple, wait, O King, and—

Thoas Wait for what?

Iphigenia Purge all the shrine with fire.

Thoas 'Twill all be clean before you come again.

Iphigenia And while the strangers pass thee close, seeking the sea—

Thoas What wouldst thou then?

Iphigenia Put darkness on thine eyes.

Thoas Mine eyes might drink the evil of their crime?

Iphigenia And, should I seem to stay too long—

Thoas Too long? How shall I judge the time?

Iphigenia Be not dismayed.

Thoas Perform thy rite all duly. We have time to spare.
Iphigenia And God grant this cleansing end as I desire!
Thoas I join thy prayer.
Iphigenia The door doth open.
(She takes up the Image again.)
There passeth here a holy thing; begone,
I charge thee, from the road.
...
Begone and tremble from this road:
fly swiftly, lest ye be defiled.
O Queen and Virgin, Leto-born, have pity!
Let me cleanse this stain,
And pray to thee where pray I would: a
clean house shall be thine again,
And we at last win happiness. Behold, I
speak but as I dare;
The rest—oh, God is wise, and thou, my
Mistress, thou canst read my prayer.

(The procession passes out: Thoas and the bystanders veiled; attendants in front, then Iphigenia with the Image, then veiled soldiers, then Orestes and Pylades bound, the bonds held by other veiled soldiers following them. Thoas goes into the temple.)

Here follows a song from the Chorus which fills the interval during which the cleansing ceremonies are supposed to be taking place. At the end of the song there enters a messenger running.

Messenger Ho, watchers of the fane! Ho, altar-guard,
Where is King Thoas gone? Undo the barred
Portals, and call the King! The King I seek.
Leader What tidings—if unbidden I may speak?
Messenger The strangers both are gone, and we beguiled,

By some dark plot of Agamemnon's child:
Fled from the land! And on a barque of Greece
They bear the heaven-sent shape of Artemis.

Leader Thy tale is past belief—go swiftly on,
and find the King. He is but newly gone.

Messenger Where went he? He must know of what has passed!

Leader I know not where he went. But follow fast
And seek him. Thou wilt light on him ere long.

Messenger See there! The treason of a woman's tongue!
Ye are all in the plot, I warrant ye!

Leader Thy words are mad! What are the men to me?
Go to the palace, go!

Messenger *(Seeing the great knocker on the temple door.)*
I will not stir
Till word be come by this good messenger
If Thoas be within these gates or no—
(thundering at the door)
Ho, loose the portals! Ye within! What ho!
Open, and tell our master one doth stand
Without here, with strange evil in his hand.
(Enter Thoas from the temple.)

Thoas. Who dares before this portal consecrate
Make uproar and lewd battering of the gate?
Thy noise hath broke the Altar's ancient peace.

Messenger Ye gods! They swore to me—and bade me cease
My search—the King was gone. And all the while—

Thoas These women? How? What sought they by such guile?

Messenger Of them hereafter! Give me first thine ear
For greater things. The virgin minister
That served our altar, she hath fled from this
And stolen the dread Shape of Artemis,

With those two Greeks. The cleansing was a lie.
Thoas She fled? What wild hope whispered her to fly?
Messenger The hope to save Orestes. Wonder on!
Thoas Orestes—how? Not Clytemnestra's son!
Messenger And our pledged altar-offering. 'Tis the same.
Thoas. O marvel beyond marvel! By what name
More rich in wonder can I name thee right?
Messenger Give not thy mind to that. Let ear and sight
Be mine awhile; and when thou hast heard the whole
Devise how best to trap them ere the goal.
Thoas Aye, tell thy tale. Our Tauric seas stretch far,
Where no man may escape my wand of war.

The Messenger gives Thoas an excited account of what has happened, ending by saying that if he send out pursuers immediately, he may even yet seize the fugitives. Thoas gives his orders.

Thoas Ho, all ye dwellers of my savage town
Set saddle on your steeds, and gallop down
To watch the heads, and gather what is cast
Alive from this Greek wreck. We shall make fast,
By God's help, the blasphemers—send a corps
Out in good boats a furlong from the shore;
So we shall either snare them on the seas
Or ride them down by land, and at our ease
Fling them down gulfs of rock, or pale them high
On stakes in the sun, to feed our birds and die.
Women: you knew this plot. Each one of you
Shall know, before the work I have to do
Is done, what torment is—enough! A clear
Task is afoot. I must not linger here.

While Thoas is moving off, his men shouting and running before and behind him, there comes a sudden blasting light and thunder-roll, and Athena is seen in the air confronting them. This sudden appearance of a god to solve a problem at the end of a play is known as the *deus ex machina,* and there was actually some kind of machine by which the god appeared, as if suspended in the air.

Athena Ho, whither now, so hot upon the prey,
King Thoas? It is I that bid thee stay,
Athena, child of Zeus. Turn back this flood
Of wrathful men, and get thee temperate blood.
Apollo's word and Fate's ordained path
Have led Orestes here, to escape the wrath
Of Them that hate. To Argos he must bring
His sister's life, and guide that Holy Thing
Which fell from heaven, in mine own land
to dwell.
So shall his pain have rest, and all be well.
Thou hast heard my speech, O King. No death
from thee
May snare Orestes between rocks and sea:
Poseidon for my love doth make the sore
Waves gentle, and set free his laboring oar.

And thou, O far away—for, far or near
A goddess speakest and thy heart must hear—
Go on thy ways, Orestes, bearing home
The Image and thy sister. When ye come
To god-built Athens, lo, a land there is
Half hid on Attica's last boundaries,
A little land, hard by Karystus' Rock,
But sacred. It is called by Attic folk
Halae. Build there a temple, and bestow

Therein thine Image, that the world may know
The tale of Tauris and of thee, cast out
From pole to pole of Greece, a blood-hound rout
Of ill thoughts driving thee. So through
  the whole
Of time to Artemis the Tauropole
Shall men make hymns at Halae. And withal,
Give them this law. At each high festival,
A sword, in record of thy death undone,
Shall touch a man's throat, and the red
  blood run—
One drop, for old religion's sake. In this
Shall live that old red rite of Artemis.
And thou, Iphigenia, by the stair
Of Brauron in the rocks, the Key shall bear
Of Artemis. There shalt thou live and die,
And there have burial.

. . .

Ye last, O exiled women, true of heart
And faithful found, ye shall in peace depart,
Each to her home: behold Athena's will.
                Orestes,
Begone. Lead forth thy sister from this shore
In peace; and thou Thoas, be wroth no more.

Thoas Most high Athena, he who bows not low
His head to God's word spoken, I scarce know
How such a one doth live. Orestes hath
Fled with mine Image hence—I bear no wrath.
Nor yet against his sister. There is naught,
Methinks of honor in a battle fought
'Gainst gods. The strength is theirs. Let those
  two fare
Forth to thy land and plant mine Image there.
I wish them well.

These bondwomen no less
I will send free to Greece and happiness,
And stay my galleys' oars, and bid this brand
Be sheathed again, Goddess, at thy command.

Athena 'Tis well, O King. For that which needs must be
Holdeth the high gods as it holdeth thee.
Winds of the North, O winds that laugh and run,
Bear now to Athens Agamemnon's son:
Myself am with you, o'er long leagues of foam
Guiding my sister's hallowed Image home.
(She floats away.)

Chorus

Some women Go forth in bliss, O ye whose lot
God shieldeth, that ye perish not.

Others O great in our dull world of clay,
And great in heaven's undying gleam
Pallas, thy bidding we obey:
And bless thee, for mine ears have heard
The joy and wonder of a word
Beyond my dream, beyond my dream.

The play is over, and the sun is setting, so we, with the rest of the Athenians, must wend our way homewards. As we look up at the temples on the Acropolis, bathed in the golden evening light, we feel no surprise at the joy beyond their dreams of the lonely exiled Greek women, who had heard the joy and wonder of the word that bade them return to a land of such surpassing loveliness.

CHAPTER 18

THE TEMPLES OF ATHENS

I. Greek Temples

A GREEK TEMPLE was not a place where people met to worship, and it was never intended to hold a very large number of people. The religious ceremonies were carried on in the great spaces outside the temples, and sacrifices were offered on the altars which were always in the open air. The temple was the dwelling place of the god and the treasury where the gifts brought by the worshippers were kept.

Greek temples varied in size, but they were all built on the same general plan. The whole building was looked upon as the home of the god, and so the chamber in which the statue was placed was the central point, and all the other parts of the building were so constructed that they harmonized with the main purpose of the temple. Just as a Greek play had only one story in it, and no other episodes were allowed to distract the attention of the audience from the working out of the plot, so a Greek temple expressed one thought and nothing in the architecture was allowed to disturb it.

The earliest form of temple was the shrine, an oblong building with a portico, which had at first only two pillars in front, but which were later extended into a row of pillars across the whole front of the building. Then a portico was built at both ends of the temple, and lastly, in some temples

Greek columns:
Doric (top left)
Ionic (top right)
Corinthian (bottom)

a row of columns was built all around the building, with a double row in the portico at each end. Above the portico was a triangular gable called the *pediment,* which was usually filled with sculpture.

The Greeks used three kinds of columns in their buildings. The Doric column was the simplest; it had no base and tapered very slightly up to the capital which consisted of a thick slab of stone. The Doric was the type most often used by the Greeks, and in its simplicity and perfection of form it symbolized the finest Greek spirit. The Ionic column stood on a base; it was more slender than the Doric, and the capital consisted of two very graceful spirals. The Ionic was a lighter type of column than the Doric and was used a great deal by the Greeks in Asia Minor. A third type was introduced later, called the Corinthian. The capitals of this column were richly carved in the form of leaves, but the Greeks never liked it as much as the simpler and more graceful types, and it was not very much used until Roman times. All the columns were fluted.

The Greeks never used ornament for the sake of ornament. The column was used as a support, and ornament was felt to be entirely out of place on it, but the decoration on the capital served a purpose. As the eye followed the fluting upwards to where the vertical line met the horizontal, the simple decoration of the capital served to make the transition from one line to the other less abrupt. In Greek architecture no part of a building that bore any strain was ornamented, and wherever ornament was used it was always in harmony with the general purposes of the building.

These were the main characteristics of Greek temples. The greatest Athenian temples were on the Acropolis, the ancient citadel of Athens, which had been transformed by Pericles into a dwelling place for Athena.

II. The Acropolis in the Time of Pericles

> The fittest place for a temple or altar was some site visible from afar, and untrodden by foot of man, since it was a glad thing for the worshipper to lift up his eyes afar off and offer up his prayer.
>
> Socrates[1]

The Acropolis in ancient times

The Acropolis was approached by a flight of steps leading to the *Propylaea,* or Entrance Porch. Six great Doric columns stood at the entrance, and opening out to the right and left of the main hall were other porticoes, the walls of which were decorated with paintings showing the deeds of ancient heroes. The roof was of white marble, and standing at this entrance one could catch a glimpse of the sea in the distance. Tradition held that it was on this spot that Aegeus stood to watch for the ship that should bring back Theseus, and that it was from this high rock that he cast himself down in despair when he saw

[1] Xenophon: *Memorabilia.*

Views of the ancient Athenian Acropolis

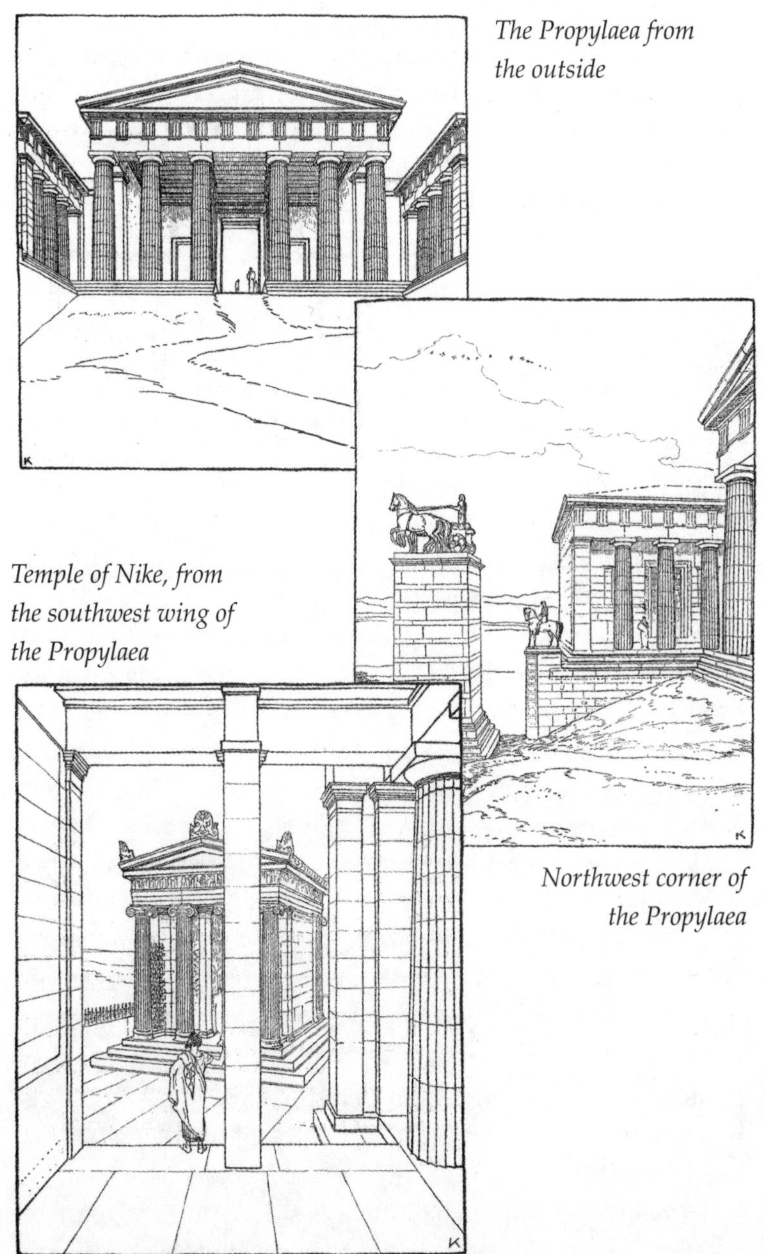

The Propylaea from the outside

Temple of Nike, from the southwest wing of the Propylaea

Northwest corner of the Propylaea

the ship returning with black sails, a sign, as he thought, that his son was dead.

To the right of the Propylaea, in the southwest corner of the Acropolis, was the little temple of Athena Nike, Athena of Victory. In this temple the goddess herself represented Victory, so she had no wings, which were always given by the Greeks to statues of Victory, and the temple came to be known as that of the Wingless Victory. A wonderful view is to be had from this temple, and the site for it was chosen because from where it stands, Salamis is in sight, and it was to be forever a thank-offering to Athena for the victory gained there over the barbarian foe.

Passing through the Propylaea, one came out upon the Acropolis, where rising up in majesty was the great bronze statue of Athena Promachos, Athena the Warrior Queen, Foremost in Fight, who went out to war with the armies of Athens and brought them home victorious. Pheidias, the great Athenian sculptor who had made the image of Zeus in the temple at Olympia, had made this statue, using for it the bronze which had been found amongst the Persian spoils after the battle of Marathon. The goddess stood upright, clad in armor and holding a spear in her hand. The tip of this spear was gilded, and it was said that sailors, as they drew near the land, could see it gleaming in the sunshine, and when they saw it they knew that home was near.

A little further, on the north side of the Acropolis, was the Erechtheum, called after the mythical king of Athens, Erechtheus. It was a very beautiful temple, and one of the porches has always been known as the Porch of the Maidens, because instead of being supported by columns, it is supported by the figures of six maidens. When the figure of a woman is used for this purpose, it is called in architecture a *caryatid.*

A temple to Athena had always stood on this spot since memory began, and it was hallowed by all kinds of associations.

Near the temple was the sacred olive tree of Athena, and within its walls was the old and most holy wooden statue of Athena, said to have dropped from heaven. It was in this temple that the goddess was worshipped in a more intimate way, for this was Athena Polias, the Guardian of the City and the Home. It was for this ancient wooden statue that specially chosen Athenian maidens wove the beautiful robe called the *peplos*, which was carried at the time of the festival held every four years to the temple and presented to the goddess.

But greater than all else on the Acropolis was the Parthenon, created by Ictinus the architect and Pheidias the sculptor. This most beautiful Greek temple in the world stood on the south side of the Acropolis. It was a Doric building surrounded by forty-six great pillars, and to the Athenian this building was the very soul of Athens. Elsewhere on the Acropolis it was Athena the goddess who was worshipped: Athena the Warrior, Athena the Guardian of the City, and in one place, though without a temple, Athena the Inspirer of all Arts and Crafts. But here in the Parthenon, Athena was more than the goddess; she symbolized Athens itself, all the achievements of Athens in war and peace, and the spirit that guided the Athenians.

The sculpture on the east pediment represented the birth of Athena. It was the old Homeric poem interpreted in stone.

> Her did Zeus the counselor himself beget from his holy head, all armed for war in shining golden mail, while in awe did the other gods behold it. Quickly did the goddess leap from the immortal head, and stood before Zeus, shaking her sharp spear, and high Olympus trembled in dread beneath the strength of the gray-eyed Maiden, while Earth rang terribly around, and the sea was boiling with dark waves, and suddenly brake forth the foam. Yes, and the glorious son of Hyperion checked for long his swift steeds, till the maiden took from her

Views of the ancient Athenian Acropolis

The Acropolis and Parthenon today

Erectheum from the northeast

Erectheum porch with caryatids

> immortal shoulders her divine armor, even Pallas Athena; and Zeus the counselor rejoiced.[2]

Zeus rejoiced not only because Athena was born, but because she symbolized the birth of Athens; as she sprang from the head of Zeus arrayed in all the symbols of power, so surely was it the will of the gods that Athens should be great and powerful.

The sculpture on the west pediment represented the contest of Athena with Poseidon for the possession of Athens. Poseidon represented material prosperity. His gift to Athens was the sea, over which sailed her ships, colonizing and trading and bringing wealth to the state. But Athens was not to be ruled by Poseidon; she was to account the things of the mind and spirit of greater value than those of material prosperity, and the victory was given to Athena.

The pediments symbolized the will of the gods for Athens. All around the building under the cornice were smaller groups of sculptures called *metopes*, and these represented in stone the way in which Athens had fulfilled the will of the gods for her. First, there were battles between gods and giants, the conflict between order and disorder, and in every case order had triumphed; then there followed battles between the ancient heroes of legend and tradition and all kinds of evil forces in nature, and in these battles Theseus, the hero-king, fought for Athens and prevailed.

The Parthenon was built after the Persians had been driven out of Greece. The Greeks called all who were not of Greek blood Barbarians, and they believed that it was the will of the gods that in every conflict between Greek and Barbarian, the Greek should in the end prevail. The Greek of the fifth century B.C. thought of all history as the working out of the great drama of the victory of the Greek spirit over that of the Barbarian; and the records of

---

[2] Homeric hymn to Athena.

Views of the ancient Athenian Acropolis

The Parthenon through the eastern portal, showing the statue of Athena

The Parthenon: west side

The Parthenon: northwest corner

this drama are seen in political history in the development of the Athenian Empire, in literature, in the history of Herodotus, and in art in the building of the Parthenon.

But the Parthenon symbolized more than the history of Athens—it was also the symbol of her religious life. On the outer wall, under the colonnade, was the great frieze symbolizing the Panathenaic procession, that great procession which every four years wound its way up to the Acropolis. This was the festival of Athena, and at the east end of the building was a group of gods and goddesses waiting for her coming. They were waiting for her in her own city, where she would take the foremost place. In the solemn procession, all classes of Athenians were represented: noble maidens, bearing baskets with offerings for the sacrifice; youths with offerings, and youths on horseback; chariots; grave elders and priests; and cattle for the sacrifice. Aliens, too, were there, for it was not only Athens that was symbolized, but the Athenian Empire, a symbol of what Athens hoped would be a united Greece. It is very difficult to distinguish between Athenian patriotism and religion: to the Athenian, the city was Athena, and Athena the city, and the Parthenon was the crown of both.

The Parthenon was entered by the eastern porch. The light inside was dim, but as the eye grew accustomed to the dimness, the statue of Athena slowly became clearly visible. There she stood, a great figure nearly forty feet high. She was clad in a sleeveless garment that reached to her feet, bracelets in the form of serpents were on her arms, and the aegis with the head of Medusa covered her breast. In her right hand the goddess bore an image of Victory, and her left hand rested on a shield, inside of which was coiled a snake. The statue was made of gold and ivory, and it was to the Athenians the symbol of all that was best in the Athenian ideals. Their passionate desire for freedom, their unfaltering search for truth, their great love of beauty were all personified for them in the calm and queenly figure of her whose battles were won, of Athena Parthenos. Having offered their sacrifices outside, they entered her temple with awe, believing that "he who enters the incense-filled temple must be holy; and holiness is to have a pure mind."[3]

III. Later History of the Acropolis

SUCH WAS THE ACROPOLIS of the fifth century B.C. But now the statues and the altars have disappeared, the columns are broken, and the temples stand in ruins. Is it just the lapse of time that has wrought such destruction on those matchless buildings? When Plutarch saw them, they had been standing for about five hundred years, and he said that there was still a bloom of newness upon them that seemed to preserve them from the touch of time, as if the hand that had wrought such buildings gave them the spirit of eternal youth.

At the beginning of the fifth century A.D., Alaric the Goth invaded Greece, but he left Athens undisturbed. The great statue of Athena Promachos was still standing, and the story was told later that as the Barbarian chieftain approached the Acropolis, the goddess Athena appeared before him, clad in mail, with her spear outstretched in defence of her city. He was so much awed by the vision that he withdrew and troubled Athens no more, and he sent messengers to the Roman rulers of the city and made peace with them.

Not long after, an edict was passed ordering all pagan temples in the Roman Empire, for Greece then formed part of it, to be closed or else converted into Christian churches, and from that time onwards nothing has been heard of the statue of Athena Parthenos, though a small copy of it was found later. The Parthenon itself was changed into a Christian church, dedicated to the Virgin Mary, and it remained so until Athens

[3] Author unknown: From *Select Epigrams from the Greek Anthology*, translated by J. W. Mackail.

was captured by the Turks in 1458. They changed the Christian church into a Turkish mosque and built a minaret at one corner. No further changes took place until the end of the seventeenth century, when during a war of the Turks with Venice, the Venetians were bombarding the Acropolis. The Venetians were told that powder was being stored in the Acropolis, and for several days they directed their fire against it. At first there was no result, even the guns, it was said, refusing to do such deadly work on so glorious a building. But at length a shell was thrown into it, the powder exploded, the roof crashed in, and a part of the walls collapsed.

The Parthenon was nothing but a ruin, and for more than a hundred years the sculptures of Pheidias lay neglected on the ground, broken and defaced. But at the beginning of the nineteenth century the attention of Lord Elgin, who was British Ambassador at Constantinople, was called to the danger that threatened them from the ignorance and indifference of the Turks and the unscrupulousness of travelers and visitors, who often defaced and carried off pieces of sculpture; and he made arrangements by which the British Government was allowed to buy the Parthenon sculptures and remove them to the British Museum.

Yet in spite of the ruin, the destruction, and the loss, what is still left of the ancient temples and statues is of such beauty that those who look upon it believe with the Greek poet that it will "live as a song for all who love music, living and yet to be, as long as earth or sun remain."

West front of the Parthenon in 1673

Destruction of the Parthenon

CHAPTER 19

THE DOWNFALL OF ATHENS

I. Rivalry Between Athens and Sparta and the Beginning of the Peloponnesian War

ATHENS IN THE MIDDLE of the fifth century B.C. was in very truth as Pericles had said, the "school of Hellas." For half a century after the Barbarian had been driven out of Greece, Athens went forward on the wings of youth, hope, and aspiration towards the fulfillment of her great ideal, that of the perfect citizen in the perfect state. Everything that was worthwhile in human life lay in that direction: Freedom, Order, and Progress; Truth and Beauty; Knowledge, Virtue, and Religion; and in the Greek world it was Athens who was the leader in all these things.[1]

And Athens realized this. The ideals set forth by Pericles in the Funeral Speech placed her in the position of a chosen people in the midst of a barbarian world, and it was to be her mission to save civilization for the world. Athens was a democracy, and her freedom, her thought, and her art were not the special possession of a small privileged group but of the whole body of citizens. Yet there was a flaw in the Athenian ideal of democracy; it was built upon slavery. The result of this was that in some things the Athenians were able to reach a point of perfection from which they could make

[1] See A. E. Zimmern: *The Greek Commonwealth.*

no further advance. Their greatest sculpture and architecture were flawless in their simplicity and beauty. They have been copied and imitated, but never surpassed. The Greek stage set certain limitations to the drama, but within these limitations the dramas of the great Athenian dramatists were well-nigh perfect. Other small nations in the history of the world have fought for their freedom just as passionately and with as much self-control, unbroken will, and self-sacrifice, and have obtained it; but it was Athens who first showed the world that right is stronger than might and will ultimately prevail. In their search for truth, the Athenian philosophers went as far as it was possible for them to go, but the very fact that they accepted the institution of slavery as a normal condition of life made any further advance in political thinking impossible. The history of the world shows that progress in political thought has always come from the struggle of an unprivileged class to obtain its just rights, and this could not take place in Athens, for the unprivileged were slaves, and slaves were slaves, and slaves they must always remain.

Athens fell, but her fall did not only or even chiefly come about because her democracy was founded upon slavery. In her great days Athens had been the Liberator of all the enslaved Greeks. Sparta had never been interested in the fate of the Greeks who were still under the Persian yoke, and it was Athens who had created the Delian League, and who had delivered the Ionians from their foreign rulers. But from being their Liberator, Athens gradually became their Mistress, and little by little she used her position in the League as a means to increase her own power. That which in the beginning had been organized by the statesman who was called by his fellow citizens the Just, that which had symbolized the Athenian ideal of freedom, became the instrument by which Athens became not only an Empire, but a Tyrant. And Pericles permitted it to be so.

Pericles had many opponents in Athens. Some disapproved of his imperial policy, and others accused him of extravagance in spending so much of the public money on temples. The most serious accusation brought against him was that in beautifying Athens he was spending not only money from the Athenian treasury, but also using that which belonged to the Delian League. This latter accusation was true, and the people called for an ostracism. But it resulted in the support of Pericles by the majority of the Athenians, and in the banishment of his opponent.

Pericles knew what he was doing when he used the money from the treasury of the Delian League. To Athens had been committed the trust of defending the allied islands and cities from Persian aggression and it was the money contributed by the allies for the cost of this defence that was kept in the treasury of the League. Pericles maintained that the beautifying of Athens was a symbol of her might and power, that the great buildings employed labor and encouraged commerce, both of which added to her prosperity, and that these outward signs of her wealth and might added to her ability to protect her allies. He had won for Athens the foremost position in Greece, and he was determined that she should keep it. To this end he argued that Athens was justified in using the money of the League, because the way in which it was being spent added not only to the glory but also to the security of all.

Pericles was also a great lover of all that was beautiful, and he was honestly desirous that the youth of Athens should grow up in a city that should be a joy forever, that would make them good and useful citizens, and inspire them with an abiding love for and pride in her. But there is a flaw in the character of a man who holds that the end, even if it is a great and glorious one, justifies any means.

Now Attica was very small, and in the days of her prosperity the population of Athens had increased so much that the state could no longer produce enough food to support the people. The far-seeing policy of Themistocles had made Athens stronger on sea than on land, and by the time of Pericles, the salvation of Athens lay in her navy. She was increasing her sea-power in all directions and establishing herself as mistress all over the Aegean and on the shores of the Euxine. This policy was not only dictated by the greed of power, but by the absolute necessity that if Athens were to live, she should control all the trade routes by which corn reached Greece. Without the corn from the shores of the Euxine, Athens would starve.

Sparta was a great land power, and at first this increasing sea-power of Athens did not touch her very closely, but it did affect Corinth, the next sea-power in Greece after Athens. As long as Athens confined her interests to the Aegean and the East, Corinth was not alarmed, but when the Athenians turned to the West and showed their intention of establishing their power there, the Corinthians became seriously alarmed, for this threatened their interests in Sicily and the South of Italy. Corinth had always been hostile to Athens, and she now appealed to Sparta, asking for help to crush Athens. Corinthian envoys went to Sparta, and in a powerful speech, one of them set forth the grievances of the Greek world against Athens, representing her power, and entreating the Spartans to lay aside their policy of inaction and to join with them in crushing the Tyrant state.

> "Time after time we have warned you of the mischief which the Athenians would do to us, but instead of taking our words to heart, you chose to suspect that we only spoke from interested motives. If the crimes which the Athenians are committing against Hellas were being done in a corner, then you might be ignorant, and we should have to inform you of them: but now,

what need of many words? Some of us, as you see, have been already enslaved; they are at this moment intriguing against others, notably against allies of ours; and long ago they had made all their preparations in expectation of war. ... And you have never considered what manner of men are these Athenians with whom you will have to fight, and how utterly unlike yourselves. They are revolutionary, equally quick in the conception and in the execution of every new plan; while you are conservative, careful only to keep what you have, originating nothing, and not acting even when action is most necessary. They are bold beyond their strength; they run risks which prudence would condemn; and in the midst of misfortune they are full of hope. Whereas it is your nature, though strong, to act feebly; when your plans are most prudent, to distrust them; and when calamities come upon you, to think that you will never be delivered from them. They are impetuous, and you are dilatory; they are always abroad, and you are always at home. For they hope to gain something by leaving their homes; but you are afraid that any new enterprise may imperil what you have already. When conquerors, they pursue their victory to the utmost; when defeated, they fall back the least. Their bodies they devote to their country as though they belonged to other men; their true self is their mind, which is most truly their own when employed in her service. When they do not carry out an intention which they have formed, they seem to have sustained a personal bereavement; when an enterprise succeeds, they have gained a mere installment of what is to come; but if they fail, they at once conceive new hopes and so fill up the void. With them alone to hope is to have, for they lose not a moment in the execution of an idea. This is the life-long task, full of danger and toil, which they are always imposing upon themselves. None enjoy their good things less, because they are always seeking for more. To do their duty is their only holiday, and they deem the quiet of inaction to be as disagreeable as the most tiresome business. If a man should say of them, in a word, that they were born neither to have peace themselves nor to allow peace to other men, he would simply speak the truth.

"In the face of such an enemy, Lacedaemonians, you persist in doing nothing. But let your procrastination end. Do not allow friends and kindred to fall into the hands of their worst enemies; or drive us in despair to seek the alliance of others; in taking such a course we should be doing nothing wrong either before the gods who are the witnesses of our oaths, or before men whose eyes are upon us. For the true breakers of treaties are not those who, when forsaken, turn to others, but those who forsake allies whom they have sworn to defend. We will remain your friends if you choose to bestir yourselves; for we should be guilty of an impiety if we deserted you without cause; and we shall not easily find allies equally congenial to us. Take heed then; you have inherited from your fathers the leadership of Peloponnesus; see that her greatness suffers no diminution at your hands."

Thus spake the Corinthians. Now there happened to be staying at Lacedaemon an Athenian embassy which had come on other business, and when the envoys had heard what the Corinthians had said, they felt bound to go before the Lacedaemonian assembly, not with the view of answering the accusations brought against them by the cities, but they wanted to put before the Lacedaemonians the whole question, and make them understand that they should take time to deliberate and not be rash. They also desired to set forth the greatness

> of their city, reminding the elder men of what they knew, and informing the younger of what lay beyond their experience. They thought that their words would sway the Lacedaemonians in the direction of peace. So they came and said that, if they might be allowed, they, too, would like to address the people.[2]

The Athenians were invited to speak, and they reminded the Spartans of how Athens had done more than any other state to save Greece from the Persian invader, and that Sparta herself owed her liberty to the undismayed courage of Athens.

> We maintain, [they said], that we rendered you a service at least as great as you rendered us. The cities from which you came to help us were still inhabited and you might hope to return to them; your concern was for yourselves and not for us; at any rate you remained at a distance while we had anything to lose. But we went forth from a city which was no more, and fought for one of which there was small hope; and yet we saved ourselves, and bore our part in saving you. If, in order to preserve our land, like other states, we had gone over to the Persians at first, or afterwards had not ventured to embark because our ruin was already complete, it would have been useless for you with your weak navy to fight at sea, but everything would have gone quietly just as the Persian desired.[3]

The Athenians then attempted to justify their imperial policy and to point out that, had the situation been reversed, and had it been the Lacedaemonians who had acquired an empire, they would have found it just as necessary as had

[2] Thucydides, I.

[3] Thucydides, I.

Athens to rule with a strong hand, and that they would have been even worse hated than was Athens. They concluded with a passionate appeal for peace:

> Do not then be hasty in deciding a question which is serious; and do not, by listening to the misrepresentations and complaints of others, bring trouble upon yourselves. Realize, while yet there is time, the inscrutable nature of war; and how when protracted it generally ends in becoming a mere matter of chance, over which neither of us can have any control, the event being equally unknown and equally hazardous to both. The misfortune is that in their hurry to go to war, men begin with blows, and when a reverse comes upon them, then have recourse to words. But neither you, nor we, have as yet committed this mistake; and therefore, while both of us can still choose the prudent part, we tell you not to break the peace or violate your oaths. Let our differences be determined by arbitration according to the treaty. If you refuse, we call to witness the gods, by whom you have sworn, that you are the authors of the war; and we will do our best to strike in return.[4]

The Spartans did not heed the plea for peace, and in 431 B.C. the long dreary war, known in history as the Peloponnesian War, began and dragged itself out for nearly thirty years. Compared to modern warfare, the actual fighting was not on a very large scale, and we seem to be reading of battles between what were, after all, only rather small states. But though the states were small, the statesmen who guided their policies and the men who fought for them were men of human passions like ours; and though the method of warfare

[4] Thucydides, I.

has changed, the effect of war on the minds and lives of men and women living at the time has changed very little. The future is hidden from the eyes of each generation of men, but the past lies open before them; and to those who read the past with understanding comes enlightenment when similar difficulties surround them, for the past shows not only the beginning and the middle, but also the end of the story.

When the Peloponnesian War broke out, almost fifty years had gone by since the Persian had been driven out of Greece, and the heroes of Marathon, of Thermopylae, and of Salamis had already passed into history. That war had been between the Greek and the Barbarian; this war was between Greek and Greek, and it rapidly spread over almost the whole Greek world. The real cause was the rivalry between Athens and Sparta, and it was fought to determine which should be supreme in Greece. Athens was a great sea-power, Sparta a great land-power; Athens was a freedom-loving democracy, Sparta was still governed by an oligarchy; Athens was dependent for her life on the corn that came from afar, Sparta was practically self-sufficient. When the war began, each side was confident and sure of victory. How was it to end?

II. Athens During the War

During the first part of the war, Athens was supreme at sea; and she strengthened her hold on all the trade routes. But she did not dare meet Sparta in a great open pitched battle on land, for the military power of the latter was no legend, but a most formidable fact.

Everything, however, did not go well with Athens during those first few years. Every year the Spartans had invaded Attica and burned and plundered the land surrounding Athens. This had driven all the country people into the city, where conditions became very congested and intolerable. And then it was that a scourge fell upon Athens, from which she never recovered. For two long summers and two long winters the Angel of Death stood over the city and darkened it with his wings and smote the inhabitants, so that one out of every four died. It was the Plague. The whole dreadful story can be read in the pages of Thucydides: how it began in the Peiraeus and then spread to Athens; of the sufferings of those who were seized with it, the rapidity with which it spread, and the impossibility of caring for the sick or burying the dead; of the lawlessness in the disorganized terror-stricken city; and of all the misery which came from seeing the inhabitants of the city dying in such numbers and from knowing that without the walls the country was being ravaged.

When the horror had passed and Athens once more lifted up her head, she was no longer the Athens of old. Her spirit was not only broken but changed. The war and the plague together lay heavy upon the Athenians, and they blamed Pericles because he had persuaded them to go to war, declaring that he was the author of all their troubles. Once again he made a great speech to them, reminding them that Athens had never yet yielded to misfortune, and that the greatest states and the greatest men are those who, when misfortunes come, are the least depressed in spirit and the most resolute in action. But Pericles did not live to guide Athens through the troubled waters which lay ahead of her. He had experienced the same misfortunes as his fellow citizens. His sister, his sons, and the friends who were nearest to him had died of the plague, and he himself was ill. As he lay dying, some of his friends who were still alive were sitting near him, and they spoke together of his greatness, his power, and the number of his victories. They did not think he was conscious, but he heard all that they said, and when they had finished, he asked them why they did not speak or make mention of that which was the most excellent and greatest thing of all. "For," said he, "no Athenian, through my means, ever wore mourning."[5]

Pericles had been a good general; he had added to the power of Athens both at home and abroad; and he had made her defences more secure by completing the Long Walls which had been begun by Themistocles. As a statesman, Pericles was an imperialist, and he believed that the Athenian Empire, which had grown naturally out of the position of Athens as Liberator of the Ionian Greeks, embodied the right relationship between Athens and her allies. Like Themistocles, he had a deep distrust of Sparta, and believing that sooner or later war with her was inevitable, he did all that lay in his power to make Athens ready when that day should come.

Though of noble birth, Pericles had always been on the side of the people in Athens, and during his rule the powers of the people were very much extended. Every office in the state was filled by popular election each year, so that there was constant change amongst those in authority, and Athens could never be sure of any settled policy in her affairs either at home or abroad. The supreme and final authority lay in the Assembly, but like all popular assemblies, it could be swayed and, at several critical moments in the history of Athens, was swayed, by sudden bursts of passion, or by the fiery eloquence of an unwise or an ambitious and self-seeking speaker. But as long as Pericles lived, the dangers of the democracy he had developed were not very apparent, for he was trusted absolutely, and he kept a wise, firm, and restraining hand on the passions of the people.

Pericles died in the year 429 B.C., and in the years following his death, the results of a long war began to be felt. Food became scarce and prices were high; it was difficult to get servants, for in the general disorganization of life that had come with the plague, slaves had escaped in large numbers;

[5] Plutarch: *Life of Pericles.*

the young men of Athens were no longer to be seen in the Agora and other public places, for all men capable of bearing arms were with the army.

Four years after the death of Pericles, Sparta made offers of peace, but feeling ran very high in Athens and it was believed that a peace then would not be lasting, so the offer was rejected and it was determined to carry on the war to the bitter end.

There is nothing that so well describes conditions in Athens during these war years as the comedies of Aristophanes. They carry us back to those exciting days, and it is amazing to see how much freedom of speech was allowed. The *Knights*, the *Clouds*, and the *Wasps* were all written in these years, and they are full of the excitement of the time, and often of outspoken criticism of those responsible for the carrying on of the war. But the war brought a lowering of ideals, and even where there was victory, there was also sorrow and loss and the ruin of homes. Euripides, one of the great dramatists of the time, in the *Trojan Women*, a play written during the war, stripped war of all its glamor and showed the misery that comes to the conquered:

And they whom Ares took,
Had never seen their children: no wife came
With gentle arms to shroud the limbs of them
For burial, in a strange and angry earth
Laid dead. And there, at home, the same long dearth
Women that lonely died, and aged men
Waiting for sons that ne'er should turn again,
Nor know their graves, nor pour drink-offerings,
To still the unslaked dust. These be the things
The conquering Greek hath won!
...
Would ye be wise, ye Cities, fly from war!
Yet if war come, there is a crown in death

For her that striveth well and perisheth
Unstained: to die in evil were the stain![6]

Pericles was dead, and Cleon, who had succeeded him as leader of the people, had no power to inspire the Athenians to be true to their highest ideals, and as conditions grew more and more difficult, Athens was forced at length to give herself up to a fight for her life. Anger, suspicion, and hatred took the place of the old ideals, and it seemed as

Euripides

Aristophanes

[6] Euripides: *The Trojan Women*, translated by Gilbert Murray.

if her strength had turned to weakness and despair. And then Athens sealed her own doom, for to save her own citizens from heavy taxation in order to carry on the war, without asking their consent, she doubled the amount of the tribute paid to her by her allies every year, and so she broke the charter once made in good faith between them.

But the end had not yet come. For a time, success lay with the Athenians, and they forced a Spartan garrison to surrender to them at Sphacteria on the west coast of the Peloponnesus, a victory which greatly encouraged them. But the years dragged on and the war continued and there seemed no end in sight. Then it was that Brasidas, a Spartan general, marched north from the Peloponnesus through Boeotia and Thessaly until he reached Amphipolis, an Athenian colony on the borders of Thrace and Macedonia, which he besieged. Cleon had gone to Amphipolis to help the Athenians, and he was expecting assistance from an Athenian general who was marching to the relief of the city. But he did not arrive in time, and Amphipolis was taken by the Spartans. Both Cleon and Brasidas were killed, and Athens exiled the general who had failed to arrive in time. He devoted the period of his exile to gathering materials for a history of the war, and though he may have been unsuccessful as a general, he became one of the greatest historians, not only of Greece, but of the world. His name was Thucydides.

The surrender of Amphipolis brought a lull in the war, and owing to the efforts of the Athenian general, Nicias, in 421 B.C. a peace was made, which was to last for fifty years.

III. Alcibiades

THE PEACE OF NICIAS did not last very long, however. Athens and Sparta were both too jealous of each other to really be reconciled, and neither kept to the terms of peace. There was a party in Athens which favored peace, but it was not so powerful nor so popular as the war party, and its leader, Nicias, did not possess the qualities of leadership which characterized the leader of the other side. This leader was Alcibiades, a young man who had recently risen to power and who was very popular. He was of noble birth, rich, very good-looking, and had great personal charm. He lisped when he spoke, but it was said that this "became him well and gave a grace and persuasiveness to his rapid speech." When he began to study, he obeyed all his other masters fairly well, but refused to learn to play the flute because he said it disfigured the face, and also because it was not possible to speak or sing while playing it. Alcibiades was a leader of fashion amongst the Athenian youths, and as soon as it became known that he despised the flute, playing on it went out of fashion and became generally neglected.

Alcibiades

Alcibiades was sought out by many people who liked to be in his company, chiefly because of his great personal beauty, but it is evident that at this time he must have shown many noble qualities and a good disposition, for Socrates, the great philosopher, showed much affection for him. Socrates saw that his wealth and position caused him to be flattered and made so much of by all kinds of people that he feared he would be corrupted by it, and he resolved, if possible, that his good qualities should be preserved. On his side, Alcibiades recognized the great worth of Socrates and listened willingly to his teaching.

Both Socrates and Alcibiades took part in one of the early campaigns of the Peloponnesian War. They shared the same tent and stood next to each other in battle, and in one sharp fight both behaved with special bravery. This was the occasion on which Alcibiades was wounded, but Socrates threw himself before him and protected him, and beyond any question saved his life.

Alcibiades had great advantages for entering public life; his noble birth, his riches, the personal courage he had shown in many battles, and the multitude of his friends and dependents threw open the doors for him. His popularity had also increased because of his success at the Olympic games. He had spent great sums of money on horses and chariots, and never did anyone else send so many as seven chariots to the Games. And they were so well equipped that in one race he carried off the first, second, and fourth prizes, which far outdid any distinction that ever was known or thought of in that kind.[7]

But Alcibiades did not follow the wise teaching of Socrates, and he grew luxurious, dissipated, and lawless in his way of living; he wore long purple robes like a woman, which dragged after him as he went through the marketplace; and he had a soft and luxurious bed prepared for him on his galley. All this made him disliked by a great number of Athenians and gradually raised up enemies for him; yet such was his personal charm, his eloquence, his courage, and his beauty that the Athenians made excuses for his excesses, indulged him in many things, and gave soft names to his faults, attributing them to his youth and good nature.[8]

Such was the man, unstable, ambitious, and unscrupulous, to whom was entrusted the guidance of affairs at Athens at this most critical hour of her fortunes.

[7] From Plutarch: *Life of Alcibiades.*

[8] From Plutarch: *Life of Alcibiades.*

Up to this time the relations of Athens with the Greeks beyond the sea had been chiefly confined to those in Ionia, but there were rich lands dwelled in by Greeks to the West, especially in Sicily and the South of Italy. Even in the lifetime of Pericles, the Athenians had cast a longing eye upon Sicily, but they did not attempt anything there until after his death. An opportunity for interference in Sicilian affairs was given them in 415 B.C. when the Peace of Nicias had brought a period of truce in the war with Sparta. The Greeks in one of the cities in Sicily appealed to Athens for help against Syracuse, which was oppressing them, and Alcibiades seized upon this as the first step in an Athenian conquest of Sicily. This was but the beginning of his ambitious plan, for he dreamed not only of the mastery of Sicily, but of nothing less than the conquest of Carthage and of Athenian rule over the whole Mediterranean world.

Alcibiades roused Athens to enthusiasm for an expedition to Sicily, and the young men, in particular, shared his hopes and ambitions. They listened to him when he talked of the wonders of the countries to which they were going, so that great numbers of them might be seen sitting in the wrestling grounds and public places, drawing on the ground maps of Sicily and the situation of Carthage. Nicias, conservative, experienced, and loyal, saw that it was not the welfare of Athens but his own personal ambition and love of glory that was moving Alcibiades, and Nicias did everything in his power to dissuade the people from following such a rash and ambitious policy. He told them that even if they conquered Sicily, they could not hope to keep it, and that the course they were in favor of pursuing would only add to the hatred already felt for them by Sparta, and could only end in disaster.

But the Athenians were deaf to the pleas of Nicias, and it was voted that the expedition should take place.

Then the preparations began. Lists for service were made up at home and orders given to the allies. The city had newly recovered from the plague and from the constant pressure of war; a new population had grown up; there had been time for the accumulation of money during the peace; so there was abundance of everything at command.

While they were in the midst of their preparations, the Hermae, or square stone figures carved after the ancient Athenian fashion and standing everywhere at the doorways both of temples and private houses, in one night throughout the city had nearly all of them their faces mutilated. The offenders were not known, but great rewards were publicly offered for their detection, and a decree was passed that anyone, whether citizen, stranger, or slave, might without fear of punishment disclose this or any other profanation of which he was cognizant. The Athenians took the matter greatly to heart; it seemed to them ominous of the fate of the expedition; and they ascribed it to conspirators who wanted to effect a revolution and to overthrow the democracy.

Certain metics and servants gave information, not indeed about the Hermae, but about the mutilation of other statues which had shortly before been perpetrated by some young men in a drunken frolic; and of this impiety they accused, among others, Alcibiades. A party who were jealous of his influence over the people took up and exaggerated the charges against him, clamorously insisting that he was at the bottom of the whole affair. In proof they alleged the excesses of his ordinary life, which were unbecoming in the citizen of a free state.

He strove then and there to clear himself of the charges, and also offered to be tried before he sailed (for all was now ready), in order that, if he were guilty, he might be punished, and if acquitted, might retain his command. But his enemies feared that if the trial took place at once, he would have the support of the army, and that the people would be lenient. They therefore exerted themselves to postpone the trial. To this end they proposed that he should sail now and not delay the expedition, but should return and stand his trial within a certain number of days. Their intention was that he should be recalled and tried when they had stirred up a stronger feeling against him, which they could better do in his absence. So it was decided that Alcibiades should sail.

About the middle of summer the expedition started for Sicily. Early in the morning of the day appointed for their departure, the Athenians and such of their allies as had already joined them went down to the Peiraeus and began to man the ships. The entire population of Athens accompanied them, citizens and strangers alike. The citizens came to take farewell, one of an acquaintance, another of a kinsman, another of a son; the crowd as they passed along was full of hope and full of tears—hope of conquering Sicily and tears because they doubted whether they would ever see their friends again, when they thought of the long voyage on which they were sending them. At the moment of parting the danger was nearer; and terrors which had never occurred to them when they were voting the expedition now entered into their souls. Nevertheless, their spirits revived at the sight of the armament in all its strength and of the abundant provisions which they had made. The strangers and the rest of the multitude came out of curiosity, desiring to witness an enterprise of which the greatness exceeded belief.

No armament so magnificent or costly had ever been sent out by any single Hellenic power. Never had a

> greater expedition been sent to a foreign land; never was there an enterprise in which the hope of future success seemed to be better justified by actual power.
>
> When the ships were manned and everything required for the voyage had been placed on board, silence was proclaimed by the sound of the trumpet, and before setting sail all with one voice offered up the customary prayers; these were recited, not in each ship, but by a single herald, the whole fleet accompanying him. On every deck both officers and men, mingling wine in bowls, made libations from vessels of gold and silver. The multitude of citizens and other well-wishers who were looking on from the land joined in the prayer. The crews raised the Paean and, when the libations were completed, put to sea.[9]

In due time they reached Sicily, where the generals in command held a conference as to the best way of beginning the attack.

In the meantime the enemies of Alcibiades in Athens took up the charges of impiety which had been made against him and did not rest until an order had been sent to Sicily ordering his return so that he might be brought to trial.

> From every quarter suspicion had gathered around Alcibiades, and the Athenian people were determined to have him tried and executed; so they sent a summons to him and to others against whom information had been given. He was ordered to follow the officers home and defend himself, but the latter were told not to arrest him; for the Athenians, having regard to their interests in Sicily, were anxious not to

[9] Thucydides, VI.

> cause excitement in their own camp, or to attract the attention of the enemy.[10]

So Alcibiades and those who were accused with him left Sicily. They sailed in their own ship, but were escorted by the Athenian galley sent for them. Before reaching Greece, both ships put in at a port in Italy, and here Alcibiades and his companions left their ship and disappeared, "fearing to return and stand their trial when the prejudice against them was so violent. They were sought for, but the crew of the galley could not find them and so they gave up the search and returned home."[11]

Before making plans for a further escape, Alcibiades lay concealed for a short time in Italy. It seemed strange to one who was with him that he had not enough faith in Athenian justice to return home and face a trial, but when asked if he did not trust his own native country, Alcibiades replied, "In everything else, yes; but in a matter that touches my life, I would not trust even my own mother, lest she might by mistake throw in the black ball instead of the white."[12] As Alcibiades did not appear in Athens to answer the charges against him, the Assembly convicted him and his companions of impiety, confiscated their property, sentenced them to death, and pronounced a solemn curse on their names. When this news reached him, all he said was, "I will make them feel that I am alive."

Alcibiades kept his word. He crossed to the Peloponnesus and went first to Argos. When he found there was no hope of his returning to Athens, he sent a message to Sparta, asking for a safe-conduct to that city, and assuring the Spartans that he would make them amends by his future services for all the mischief he had done them while he was their enemy. The Spartans gave him the security for which he asked, and he went to them eagerly, and was well received. In return

[10] Thucydides, VI.

[11] Thucydides, VI.

[12] Plutarch: *Life of Alcibiades.*

for this, he betrayed the weak points of his native city to her enemies and gave them valuable advice as to the best means of conquering Athens.

Now one characteristic of Alcibiades was the extraordinary ease with which he could adapt himself to his surroundings. Whenever he saw that it was to his own interest to adopt the habits and ways of those with whom he came in contact, he did so with no hesitation. At Sparta, he gave himself up to athletic exercises, he cut his hair short, bathed in cold water, and dined on black broth; in Ionia, he was luxurious, gay, and indolent; in Thrace, always drinking; in Thessaly, ever on horseback; and when later he lived with the Persian satrap, he exceeded the Persians themselves in magnificence and pomp.[13]

But though in Sparta Alcibiades lived as a Spartan and appeared devoted to their interests, he was, nevertheless, an Athenian, and the Spartans did not trust him. The Greeks never wholly trusted each other, and lack of sincerity in their political relations was one of the weak points in their character. When Alcibiades found that he was looked upon with suspicion in Sparta and that his life was actually in danger, he fled to Ionia and took refuge with the Persian satrap, with whom he soon became a great favorite. And, indeed, the charm of daily intercourse with this extraordinarily fascinating and dangerous man was more than anyone could resist. Even those who feared and envied him could not but take delight and feel a friendliness towards him when they saw him and were in his company. It was only in his absence that his real character was recognized.

And now followed a period of disloyal intrigue with the Persians. Alcibiades advised them to interfere in the war between Athens and Sparta, and sometimes to help one side and sometimes the other, until both should be so exhausted

[13] Plutarch: *Life of Alcibiades.*

that the Persian king could easily overcome them. Thus, not content with betraying Greek to Greek, Alcibiades descended to the shameful depths of betraying Greece to the Barbarian.

IV. The Downfall of Athens and the Supremacy of Sparta

ALCIBIADES HAD BEEN summoned back to Athens at the very beginning of the expedition to Sicily. It was in the summer of 415 B.C. that the Athenian fleet had set out with such magnificence and with such high hopes. Two years later, news was brought to Athens which at first the Athenians would not believe, so appalling was it. There had been a fearful battle in the harbor at Syracuse, the Athenians had been utterly vanquished, and great numbers had been imprisoned in the quarries which were deep and narrow.

> The sun by day was still scorching and suffocating, for they had no roof over their heads, while the autumn nights were cold. They were only allowed about half a pint of water and a pint of food a day. Every kind of misery which could befall man in such a place befell them. The Athenians had been utterly and at all points defeated. Fleet and army had perished from the face of the earth; nothing was saved, and of the many who went forth, few returned home.[14]

The Athenians were at first in utter despair.

> Whichever way they looked there was trouble; they were overwhelmed by their calamity, and they were in fear and consternation unutterable. The citizens

[14] Thucydides, VII.

> mourned and the city mourned; they had lost the flower of their youth, and there were none to replace them. And when they saw an insufficient number of ships in their docks, and no crews to man them, nor money in the treasury, they despaired of deliverance.
>
> During the following winter, all Hellas was stirred by the great overthrow of the Athenians in Sicily. The states which had been neutral determined that the time had come when, invited or not, they could no longer stand aloof from the war; they must of their own accord attack the Athenians. They considered, one and all, that if the Sicilian expedition had succeeded, they would sooner or later have been attacked by them. The war would not last long, and they might as well share in the glory of it. The Lacedaemonian allies, animated by a common feeling, were more eager than ever to make a speedy end of their protracted hardships. But none showed greater alacrity than the subjects of the Athenians, who were everywhere willing, even beyond their power, to revolt; for they judged by their excited feelings and would not admit a possibility that the Athenians could survive another summer.[15]

Athens was hated because from being the great deliverer of Greece, she had become a tyrant and an oppressor, and the small states who had been ruled by her were more than ready to transfer their allegiance to Sparta, who held out promises of freedom from oppression if they would join her. Yet Sparta was at this very time bargaining with the Persian king and promising that she would recognize his right to rule over all that the Great Kings had formerly ruled, even the Greeks who lived in Asia Minor, in return for money with which Sparta could pay her

[15] Thucydides, VII.

sailors. Never had Athens sunk so low as that. The end was not far off, but Athens, having recovered from her first overwhelming despair, regained some of her old courage. She economized in every way, so that new ships could be built, and she kept on the alert, lest she should be taken unawares by some surprise attack.

It was at this moment that Alcibiades began to intrigue and plot for a return to Athens. Gradually his friends gained the upper hand; the government of Athens had not been successful and it was overthrown. It had been said that the feeling of the Athenians towards Alcibiades was that "they love, they hate, but cannot do without him," and they proved the truth of the saying by recalling him. As of old, when once they came under the charm of his personality, the Athenians yielded to their enthusiasm for him.

> As soon as he was landed, the multitude who came out to meet him scarcely seemed so much as to see any of the other captains, but came in throngs about Alcibiades, and saluted him with loud acclamations, and followed him; those who could press near him crowned him with garlands, and they who could not come up so close yet stayed to behold him afar off, and the old men pointed him out, and showed him to the young ones.[16]

Yet there was bitterness mixed with this rejoicing, for the Athenians remembered that it was by following the advice of this man that some of their greatest disasters had fallen upon them.

The story of all that followed may be read in the pages of Thucydides and Xenophon. For a time Athens seemed to regain her old power, and she won so great a victory over the Spartans

---

[16] Plutarch: *Life of Alcibiades.*

that these proposed a peace, but it was to be a peace as between equals, and Athens would hear of no peace unless she herself should dictate it. So the war continued, until the ill-success of some ships in an engagement with the Spartans caused the people to turn once more against Alcibiades, and again he was exiled. After that the end came quickly. In 405 B.C. one last great battle was fought in which the Athenians were utterly defeated. The news of this disaster was taken to Athens, and it was night when the messenger arrived. When the tale was told

> a bitter wail of woe broke forth. From Piraeus, following the line of the Long Walls up to the heart of the city, it swept and swelled, as each man to his neighbor passed on the news. On that night no man slept. There was mourning and sorrow for those that were lost, but the lamentation was merged in even greater sorrow for themselves, as they pictured the evils they were about to suffer. On the following day the public assembly met, and, after debate, it was resolved to block up all the harbors save one, to put the walls in a state of defence, to post guards at various points, and to make all other necessary preparations for a siege.[17]

The Spartans came and closed in upon Athens. A hundred and fifty ships were moored off the Peiraeus, and a strict blockade was established against all merchant ships entering the harbor.

> The Athenians, finding themselves besieged by land and sea, were in sore perplexity what to do. Without ships, without allies, without provisions, the belief gained hold upon them that there was no way of

[17] Xenophon: *Hellenica* II.

> escape. They must now, in their turn, suffer what they had themselves inflicted upon others.[18]

At last, starved into submission, they surrendered, and terms were made with Sparta. They were bitter and humiliating terms:

> that the Long Walls and fortifications of Peiraeus should be destroyed; that the Athenian fleet, with the exception of twelve vessels, should be surrendered; that the exiles should be restored; and lastly, that the Athenians should acknowledge the headship of Sparta in peace and war, leaving to her the choice of friends and foes, and following her lead by land and sea.[19]

The Athenians themselves were made to help in the destruction of the walls, and as they did so, their enemies rejoiced to the music of the flute, believing that with the fall of Athens would dawn a day of liberty for Greece.

For over thirty years Sparta ruled in Greece. At the beginning of the Peloponnesian War, she had demanded of Athens that she should restore the liberties of all the Greeks who were her allies. Athens had refused, and now the Greek world waited anxiously to see what use Sparta would make of her great victory.

It soon became evident that the rule of Sparta was not to be a light one. Military governors were placed in every city of the old Delian League, and the citizens were forced to pay a heavy tribute to Sparta. Thirty men were set to rule in Athens, and for the eight months that these Thirty were in power, Athens endured cruelty, tyranny, and lawlessness. The Spartan domination soon became so unendurable that

---

[18] Xenophon: *Hellenica* II.

[19] Xenophon: *Hellenica* II.

one by one a number of Athenians fled from the city and took refuge in Thebes, which had hitherto been one of the bitterest enemies of Athens, but now realized that freedom and justice were not to be found in the Spartan ideal of empire, for it was nothing less than empire at which Sparta was aiming. At last a sufficient number of exiles had gathered at Thebes for them to make an attempt to drive out the Thirty from Athens. They were successful, and the old Athenian form of government was restored.

But there was no real peace, and for a few years fighting went on in different places. Sometimes Sparta was successful, sometimes Athens, but nothing decisive happened. At last Sparta began to intrigue with Persia, and in 386 B.C. Artaxerxes the King interfered in the affairs of Greece, and proposed terms of peace, known as the King's Peace, which were accepted. The Greek cities in Asia Minor were to belong once more to the Persians, and all the other Greek city-states were to be independent, and the treaty concluded with the words: "Should any refuse to accept this peace, I, Artaxerxes, will make war upon them, with the help of those who are of my mind, both by land and sea, with ships and with money."

It was a betrayal of Greece to the ancient foe. The Greek states had never been able to unite for long at a time. Had they been able to hold together, and especially had Athens and Sparta done so, they could have prevailed against the Persian in Asia Minor and maintained the independence of their kinsmen in Ionia. But their jealous fears of anything that might limit their freedom as independent states made any permanent alliance impossible, and the long years of the Peloponnesian War, of all wars in history one of the most humiliating, because so unnecessary and unjustifiable, had bred hatreds and suspicion, greed and jealousy, from which Greece never recovered. But though politically her power was gone, her work for the world was not finished.

V. The March of the Ten Thousand[20]

Artaxerxes, the King of Persia, had a younger brother, Cyrus, who was accused of plotting against his life. He had Cyrus seized and would have put him to death, but his mother made intercession for him and so his life was spared. This set Cyrus to thinking, not only how he might avoid ever again being in his brother's power, but how, if possible, he might become king in his stead. Now Cyrus was a man who was much beloved. He was honorable, upright, and chivalrous, and marvelously skilled in horsemanship. He understood, not only how to make friends, but also how to keep them, and any man who did him willing service was sure to win his reward. For this reason, Cyrus was always able to command men who were willing to follow him in any undertaking, no matter how dangerous it might be.

In order to possess himself of the throne of his brother, it was necessary for Cyrus to raise an army, and he sent trusted agents to various places to collect as many men as would be willing to follow him on a hazardous expedition. Amongst other men who joined his army were a great many Greeks. Though the King's Peace was not made for some years after this, the great battles of the Peloponnesian War were over, and there were large numbers of men who had spent so many years in fighting that they were restless and unwilling to return to their old settled life. About ten thousand Greeks joined the army of Cyrus, and in 401 B.C. they set out. These Greeks had not been told the real object of the expedition; they thought they were to fight against some hill-tribes in Asia Minor, and they joined the rest of the army in Sardis, not knowing the long march they were about to begin.

At first all seemed to be going well, but when they had gone for some distance, the Greeks began to suspect that they

---

[20] Based on Xenophon: *The Anabasis.*

were going further than they had expected, and some of them wanted to turn back. But Cyrus promised to give them more pay, and they continued their march. On they went, until they reached the Euphrates. They crossed the river, and for some days they continued their march along the opposite bank until they reached Cunaxa, not far from Babylon. Here at length Cyrus met the Persian army, which came against him under the king, his brother. A fierce battle followed, in which the Greeks were victorious, but Cyrus was killed, and so the victory availed them nothing. The Persians entrapped the Greek generals and murdered them, and there was nothing left for the Greeks to do but return to Greece in some way or other. But Greece was more than a thousand miles off, and they did not know the way; they had no leaders, they were in a strange land and surrounded by enemies, and they had no means of procuring supplies by the way. Nevertheless, they decided, in spite of all these difficulties, to choose new generals and to start.

Chief of the new generals was a young Athenian called Xenophon, and he advised the Greeks (there were ten thousand of them) to burn all the baggage that they did not need and to set out and find their way back to Greece as best they could. They followed his advice, and Xenophon himself has given us the account of that March of the Ten Thousand back to Greece. He called his story the *Anabasis* or *The March Up Country,* and he tells us how they went through strange and unknown lands, and how they suffered from enemies, from the cold, and from hunger. They followed the Tigris for a time and passed the ruins of Nineveh, but so complete had been the destruction of that proud city that the retreating Greeks did not know that they were treading her beneath their feet.

Winter came on, and the cold was terrible. In one place they marched through deep snow, with the North wind blowing

Xenophon

in their teeth, benumbing the men. They suffered from snow-blindness and frostbite, and some of them in despair refused to go on. But in spite of all these hardships, the greater number went on, until at length they reached a city where they were given a friendly reception. The governor of the city gave them a guide, who promised that within five days he would lead them to a place from which they would see the sea. "And," he added, "if I fail of my word, you are free to take my life." He kept his promise, and on the fifth day they reached a mountain which the men in front immediately climbed. From the top they caught sight of the sea, a symbol to the Greeks of home and safety. A great cry arose, and the shout grew louder and louder, so that Xenophon feared that something extraordinary had happened, and he mounted his horse and galloped to the rescue. But as he drew nearer, he heard the soldiers shouting and passing on to each other the joyful cry: "Thalatta! Thalatta!" ("The Sea! The Sea!") When all had reached the summit, they fell to embracing one another, generals and officers and all, and the tears flowed down their cheeks.

The sea was the Euxine, and without very great difficulty the Greeks found ships which took them home. But before they left the spot whence they had first seen the sea, they erected a great pile of stones, on which they laid all that was left to them of their scanty possessions: some skins, wicker shields, and staves, and these they dedicated to the gods of Greece for having granted them so great a deliverance.

CHAPTER 20

The Great Days of Thebes

I. Legends and Early History of Thebes

Up to the end of the Peloponnesian War, the history of Greece had been chiefly the history of Athens and Sparta. The end of the war left Sparta supreme, but she did not know how to use her power. She was stern and harsh, cared little for literature, and disliked changes. She had not the imagination to put herself in the place of Athens and to understand how she should rule such independent, sea-faring, intellectually alert, and artistic people. The short period of her supremacy ended in failure, and then she was, in her turn, overthrown by another Greek state. This state was Thebes, a state which had not hitherto played a very honorable part in Greek history. Always jealous of Athens, Thebes had taken every opportunity to side against her. She had treated the sturdy, independent little city of Plataea with great cruelty; she had sided with the Barbarian invader during the Persian Wars, and with Sparta during the Peloponnesian War, and it was only when the Spartan rule became intolerable to friends and enemies alike that she offered a refuge to the Athenian exiles.

The city of Thebes lay in the rich plains of Boeotia, where meat and corn and wine were to be had abundantly. The nearby hills provided excellent hunting, and the Thebans were a people known to their neighbors as loving pleasure and all the good things of the world, as being good fighters, but men

Pindar

who were intellectually dull. There were some exceptions, however, for Thebes produced two men of genius: Pindar, the poet, and Epaminondas, the mighty general.

Pindar was born in the sixth century B.C., but he lived to be an old man, and the Persians had been driven out of Greece before he died. He was a noble, and his poems are the last lyrics that sing of an order of society that was about to give way to the rule of the people. Many of Pindar's lyrics were written in honor of the winners at the Olympic Games, and in reading them one can almost see the chariot racing along the course, hear the people shouting, and feel the joy of the victor as he receives his prize. Pindar was very conservative; he belonged to a generation which had not yet begun to question the existence of the gods, and all his poems are filled with unquestioning faith in them and in their righteousness. Especially did he delight to honor Apollo, and long after his death it was believed that he was particularly dear to the god, for it was said that every night at Delphi he was honored by the summons: "Let Pindar the poet come in to the supper of the god."

But if Thebes had had no honored past in history, she was rich in legend and story. Thebes had been founded by Cadmus in obedience to the word of Apollo. On the spot where the city was to be built, he had slain a fearful dragon, and taking the dragon's teeth, he had sown them in the ground as a sower sows his seed, and immediately a host of armed men had sprung up from the ground, who became the first citizens of the new city. With their help, Cadmus built a citadel which was known through all the days of Theban history as the Cadmeia.

Thebes was surrounded by strong walls and the city was entered by seven gates. Another story told how the foundations of these walls and gateways had been laid by Amphion, who then took his lyre and played such divine music on it that the walls rose by magic as he played, until they stood in such strength that they completely protected the city, and later were able to endure a great siege.

But the gods had not always smiled upon Thebes. Pindar tells us that "for every good a mortal receives from the gods, he must likewise receive two evils," and this seemed to be true of the royal house of Thebes. Dark and tragic are the tales of the fate of these ancient rulers. It was Oedipus, who having first guessed the answer to the riddle of the Sphinx, then in ignorance killed his own father and became king, only to learn in later years of what he had done, and to be driven forth from his kingdom, blind and helpless. Other legends tell of Antigone, the faithful daughter of Oedipus, who accompanied him in his wanderings and tended him until his death.

II. Epaminondas

Epaminondas was born in Thebes late in the fifth century B.C. He belonged to a very old family, one of the few which claimed to be descended from the dragon's teeth sown by Cadmus. Though of an ancient family, he was poor, but he was among the best educated among the Thebans; he had been taught to play the harp and to sing to its accompaniment, to play the flute, and to dance. A wise philosopher was his instructor, to whom he was so attached that, young as he was, he preferred the society of the grave and stern old man to that of companions of his own age. After he grew up and began to practice gymnastics, he studied not so much to increase the strength as the agility of his body; for he thought that strength suited the purposes of wrestlers, but that agility made a man a better soldier, so he spent most of his time in warlike exercises.

Epaminondas, we are told, was

> modest, prudent, grave, wisely availing himself of opportunities, skilled in war, brave in action, and of remarkable courage. He was so great a lover of truth that he would not tell a falsehood, even in jest; he was also master of his passions, and gentle in disposition. He was a remarkable keeper of secrets, a quality no less serviceable sometimes than ability to speak eloquently.[1]

Amongst the statesmen who helped to make Greece great, none were more honorable or of greater integrity than Epaminondas. It was not possible to corrupt or bribe him, and he was entirely free from covetousness. This was shown when the envoy of King Artaxerxes the Persian came to Thebes to bribe Epaminondas with a large sum of gold (to get the Thebans to help the king), but Epaminondas said to him:

> There is no need for money in this matter; for if the king desires what is for the good of the Thebans, I am ready to do it for nothing; if otherwise, he has not sufficient silver or gold to move me, for I would not exchange the riches of the whole world for my love for my country. I do not wonder that you have tried me thus as you did not know me, seeing that you thought me like yourself, and I forgive you; but get you away immediately lest you corrupt others, though unable to corrupt me.[2]

---

[1] Cornelius Nepos: *Life of Epaminondas.*

[2] Cornelius Nepos: *Life of Epaminondas.*

Under Epaminondas, Thebes became the ruling power in Greece, but only for a very short time. The Thebans were good soldiers only as long as they had inspiring leaders; without a great leader they were unable to hold what they had gained. One of the characteristics of a great man is that he knows how to use his opportunities, and Epaminondas had this gift. The story of his life is the story of a great general. At his side was his friend Pelopidas, a man of extraordinary courage, great enthusiasm, and utter devotion to his leader.

Epaminondas made the Theban army a very formidable fighting force, and with this powerful army he set himself to break the power of Sparta and to put that of Thebes in its place. In 371 B.C. the Spartans were defeated by the Thebans under Epaminondas in a great battle at Leuctra, not far from Thebes, and this victory made Thebes for the time the chief military power in Greece. For nine years she kept her power, though fighting continued. Epaminondas wanted to capture Sparta itself, and he marched four times down into the Peloponnesus. In spite of the long marches his men were obliged to make, they were in splendid condition. They had implicit faith in their general and would follow him anywhere. "There was no labor which they would shrink from, either by night or by day; there was no danger they would flinch from; and with the scantiest provisions, their discipline never failed them."[3]

The Thebans had marched for the fourth time to the Peloponnesus, and they were at Mantinea, and here in 362 B.C. Epaminondas fought his last great battle against Sparta. Thebes was victorious, but she bought her victory dearly, for Epaminondas was mortally wounded. As he was carried from the field, he asked for the two captains who stood nearest to him and would take his place. But he was told that both had been killed. "Then make peace with the enemy," he

[3] Xenophon: *Hellenica*, VII.

murmured, and drawing out the spear which had wounded him, he fell back dead.

Epaminondas was dead, and there was no one to take his place. He had broken the power of Sparta, and the Peloponnesus was now divided into a number of camps, each at war with the other, and confusion reigned everywhere in Greece. Thebes had been no more able to unite Greece than Sparta had been, but under Epaminondas the art of war had been so developed and changed that in the hands of a commander of genius, an army had become a more formidable weapon than had ever before been deemed possible.

Six years before the battle of Mantinea, a half-barbarian boy of fifteen had been brought from Macedonia to Thebes as a hostage. This boy was Philip of Macedon, and he spent three years in Thebes learning all that the greatest military state then in Greece could teach him. He was destined himself to be a great commander, and the father of one yet greater. There was now no Greek state powerful enough to uphold Greek freedom. As a statesman, Epaminondas had failed, for he left nothing but confusion behind him, but as a general of genius, he was the teacher of Philip and Alexander of Macedon, whose growing power was now to menace the freedom not only of Greece, but of the world.

CHAPTER 21

Alexander the Great

I. Philip of Macedon

History is the story of the way in which man has learned how to live, and in learning this, man has come, from time to time, to periods of great change: periods when the old order of things has changed, passing into the new. These times are always very difficult for those who live in them, for so much of the old seems to be undergoing destruction that the building of the new is not noticed, for those who destroy generally make more noise than those who build.

Greece was living through one of these periods of change when Philip became king of Macedon. Not very much is known about the early Macedonians. They were partly barbarian, partly Greek, and, when they first appear in history, very disunited. In the plains dwelled a number of tribes who were said to be of Greek origin. They were closely bound to the king, and the chief of them were known as his Companions. Scattered about the hills were numerous tribes, more barbarian than Greek, who looked on the king of Macedonia as their overlord, but who were a constant source of danger to him, as they were frequently struggling for independence. When a weak king ruled, the story of Macedonia became that of petty warfare with these hill-tribes, but strong kings were always trying to unite these warring elements into a nation.

In 359 B.C. Philip became king of Macedonia. He had spent three years in Thebes, where he had seen the transformation that the military genius of Epaminondas had effected in the Theban army, and now at the age of twenty-four, he found himself ruler of Macedonia. But his inheritance was one that might have daunted the stoutest heart. He had no allies and no money; enemies surrounded him on all sides, and there was no unity in his kingdom. But he had youth, a few faithful friends, unbounded ambition, and a body fit to endure any hardships. Philip never asked anything of his soldiers that he was not ready to do himself, yet he was not a man whom they loved, and he inspired fear rather than affection.

Philip had three definite aims in his policy: to create a standing army, one that would be ready to march and fight at all times, in winter as well as summer; to unite all Macedonia into a real kingdom, and then to unite all Greece under his rule. Having done that, he intended to march into Asia against the Persian king.

Philip created his army, he subdued and united Macedonia, and then he was ready to turn to Greece. Athens, Sparta, and Thebes were now all weak. The power of the city-state was passing away and was to yield in time to the new idea of national unity, but it was not to yield without a conflict. The struggle between Philip and the Greek states was more than a struggle between a strong state and several weak ones; it was a conflict of ideas. On the one side was Athens and the states who sided with her, the last representatives of the independent city-state who still jealously guarded their political freedom; on the other side was Philip, who represented this new idea of national unity. He determined to subdue most of Greece by force, but he would have liked Athens to yield to him of her own free will. The power of her fleet and her armies had been broken, but her thought, her art, and her culture remained. Could Philip have been received by Athens with goodwill, and been recognized by her as the leader of all Greece, he would have held it of greater importance than any military victory. He wrote letters to Athens' statesmen, sent special envoys to Athens to plead his cause, he tried to prove to her that her fears of him were groundless, and he treated the very soil of Attica as if it were sacred. It is a striking picture: Philip, the warrior, at the head of a powerful army, lowering his sword before the politically weak little state, because of the might of her spirit. And that spirit was not dead. One more flash of the old Athenian independence flamed out in the defiance she hurled at Philip.

Philip advanced. He seized and held Thermopylae, the gateway into Greece; he upheld the rights of Delphi against a neighboring state and was recognized by the Oracle as the defender of Apollo. Then he marched into Boeotia, where Athens and Thebes made a last tremendous stand against him. In 338 B.C. one of the decisive battles of the world was fought at Chaeronea. On one side was an army of the last representatives of the old city-state, a confused array of men, some of them citizen-soldiers serving without pay, some of them hired mercenaries; and on the other side, the first great army of one united nation. The battle was fought on a hot summer's day, and it was fierce and long, but at length the Greeks gave way and Philip was victorious. He had little mercy for Thebes, and she drank the cup of bitterness to the dregs. Some of her leaders were banished, others were put to death, a Macedonian garrison was placed in the city, and all Theban lands were confiscated.

Athens was treated with greater mercy. On the day of the victory over her, Philip

> did not laugh at table, or mix any amusements with the entertainments; he had no chaplets or perfumes; and as far as was in his power, he conquered in such a way that nobody might think of him as a conqueror. And neither did he call himself the king, but the

> general of Greece. To the Athenians, who had been his bitterest enemies, he sent back their prisoners without ransom, and restored the bodies of those that were slain in battle for burial, and he sent Alexander his son to make peace and an alliance with them.[1]

Underlying all his ambition, all his reliance on military power, was yet the feeling (partly unconscious, yet there) that, after all, the things of the spirit were greater than those of pomp and power, and he longed for recognition from Athens. But Athens, though forced to recognize his supremacy, never accepted him willingly.

Philip's next move was to organize an expedition into Asia, in order to crush the power of Persia, and as such an expedition would take Philip out of Greece, most of the Greek states agreed to join it. But first he returned to Macedonia, where enemies were always to be found stirring up hostility to him. A royal marriage gave a good excuse for a great public festivity, and a procession was planned, in which Philip, robed in white, was to walk in state. It must have been a moment of great triumph. His ambitions were fulfilled. The Macedonian army was the greatest in the world, he had united the hostile elements in his kingdom and made of them a nation, he had conquered Greece and been recognized as the chief general of all the Greek armies, and now he was about to set forth to conquer Persia. He was still young, and there seemed nothing to prevent the fulfillment of every further ambition. But suddenly, as the stately procession moved forward, a man darted out from the crowd of spectators, buried his dagger deep in the heart of the king, and Philip fell dead.

He was succeeded by his son Alexander, who in a speech to the Macedonians summed up the achievements of his father. He said to them:

---

[1] From Justin.

My father found you, vagabond and poor, most of you clad only in skins, tending a few sheep on the mountainsides, and to protect them you had to fight against the border tribes, often with small success. Instead of the skins, my father gave you cloaks to wear, and he led you down from the hills into the plains and made you the equal in battle of the neighboring barbarians, so that your safety depended no longer on the inaccessibility of your mountain strongholds, but on your own valor. He taught you to live in cities, and he gave you good laws and customs, and instead of being the slaves and subjects of those barbarians by whom you and your possessions had long been harried, he made you lords over them. He also added the greater part of Thrace to Macedonia, and by seizing the most conveniently situated places on the seacoast, he threw open your country to commerce. He made it possible for you to work your mines in safety. He made you rulers over the Thessalonians, of whom you had formerly been in mortal fear, and by humbling the Phocians he gave you, instead of a narrow and difficult road into Greece, a broad and easy one. To such a degree did he humble the Athenians and Thebans, who had ever been ready to fall upon Macedonia, that instead of your paying tribute to the former and being vassals to the latter, both states turned to us for protection. He marched into the Peloponnesus, and after setting affairs there in order, he was publicly declared commander-in-chief of the whole of Greece in the expedition against the Persian. And he considered this great distinction not as personal honor to himself, but as a glory for Macedonia.[2]

---

[2] Arrian: *Anabasis of Alexander.*

The new king was only twenty years old. It seemed as if his father had been cut off at the height of his career, and that his death could mean nothing but disaster to the power of Macedonia. But what seems like a tragedy and the failure of human hopes is sometimes the door through which an individual or a nation passes to greater things. Philip had done his work. He was a great soldier and had made great conquests, but he inspired no love and he lacked the imagination which would have made him see with the eyes of the conquered, and so rule them that they would have become real parts of a mighty whole. Philip's son was young, but he had this gift, and so the tragedy of Alexander's father's death was the beginning of new and greater opportunities for him, and the door through which Greece was to pass from the old order into the new.

II. Demosthenes

Demosthenes

Though forced to acknowledge the political supremacy of Philip, Athens had never given him the real homage he so greatly desired, that of the spirit. And that she persisted in her refusal was largely due to the orator Demosthenes.

Politically, Athens was now weak, and her constant wars were a great strain on all her resources. But at this time, most of her fighting was done at a distance from Athens and by hired mercenaries. A great change had come over her since the days of Marathon and Salamis. No longer was it the pride of the Athenians that her citizens themselves defended her, and though the young men liked to boast that their forefathers had fought at Marathon, they preferred a more pleasure-loving life than was possible in a camp, and so they paid other men to go out and fight for them.

Demosthenes fought against this spirit, and when Philip made advances to Athens and tried to conclude an alliance with her, Demosthenes made speech after speech against such a policy, imploring the people not to make terms with the stranger, but to make ready for war, and to give their own lives on the battlefield instead of paying others to die for them.

Demosthenes had been a delicate child, very shy and with a stammer in his speech. He grew up, however, with a passion for oratory, and he would go to hear the noted orators of his time and listen to every word they said, going home afterwards to practice the art of speaking himself. The first time he spoke in public, he met with discouragement, for his style was awkward, his voice weak, and he stammered. He determined, however, that he would overcome all these obstacles, and

> he built himself a place to study underground, and hither he would come constantly every day to form his action, and to exercise his voice; and here he would continue, oftentimes without intermission, two or three months together, shaving one half of his head, that so for shame he might not go abroad, though he desired it ever so much.[3]

It was known that Demosthenes worked very hard over his speeches, and that he never spoke in the Assembly unless he had thought over the subject and prepared what he intended to say. It became a matter of joke in Athens that instead of depending on inspiration, his speeches "smelt of the lamp." In

[3] Plutarch: *Life of Demosthenes.*

his old age, Demosthenes told some of his friends how he had overcome his defects of speech.

> His inarticulate and stammering pronunciation he overcame and rendered more distinct by speaking with pebbles in his mouth; his voice he disciplined by declaiming and reciting speeches or verses when he was out of breath, while running or going up steep places; and that in his house he had a large looking-glass, before which he would stand and go through his exercises.[4]

To cure a habit he had of raising his left shoulder while speaking, he suspended a naked sword over it whenever he practiced, and he would stand on the seashore during a storm to declaim, so that he might accustom himself to the uproar in a public assembly.

Demosthenes has been called the greatest of orators. Opinions have differed since, as to whether his policy was the wisest for Athens to follow at that moment, but every word he uttered was inspired by a passionate love for Athens, and he at all times entreated the Athenians to be true to their own great spirit and their ancient patriotism.

> Never to this day, [he said on one occasion], has this People been eager for the acquisition of money; but for honor it has been eager as for nothing else in the world. It is a sign of this that when Athens had money in greater abundance than any other Hellenic people, she spent it all in the cause of honor; her citizens contributed from their private resources, and she never shrank from danger when glory was to be won. Therefore she has

[4] Plutarch: *Life of Demosthenes.*

> those eternal and abiding possessions, the memory of her actions, and the beauty of the offerings dedicated in honor of them, the Porticoes which you see, the Parthenon, the Colonnades, the Dockyards.

The speeches of Demosthenes against the policy of making friends with Philip are known as the *Philippics*, a word which has become part of later language, and in the greatest of these, he shows the Athenians how their lowered ideals have permitted political corruption and were leading them to destruction.

> What is the cause of these things, [he asked], for as it was not without reason that the Hellenes in old days were so prompt for freedom, so it is not without reason or cause that they are now so prompt to be slaves. There was a spirit, men of Athens, a spirit in the mind of the People in those days which is absent today, the spirit which vanquished the wealth of Persia, which led Hellas in the path of freedom, and never gave way in face of battle by sea or land; a spirit whose extinction today has brought universal ruin and turned Hellas upside down. What was this spirit? It was nothing subtle or clever. It meant that those who took money from those who aimed at dominion or at the ruin of Hellas were execrated by all. Where are such sentiments now? They have been sold in the market and are gone.[5]

In burning words Demosthenes pleaded with the Athenians to fight themselves with their old spirit for their freedom.

> I wonder that you, men of Athens, who once raised your hand against Sparta in defence of the rights of

[5] Third Philippic.

> the Hellenes ... who spent your own fortunes in war contributions and always bore the brunt of the dangers of the campaign, that you, I say, are now shrinking from marching, and hesitating to make any contribution to save your own possessions. ... This is our own personal and immediate duty; and I say that you must contribute funds, you must go on service in person with a good will. ... You must get rid of all excuses and all deficiencies on your own part; you cannot examine mercilessly the actions of others, unless you yourselves have done all that your duty requires.[6]

Demosthenes possessed the power of appealing to both the reason and the emotions of his hearers, and in the end Athens followed his advice. But it resulted in disaster. Those who had opposed Demosthenes, especially the statesman Aeschines, turned upon him in anger, and accused him of sacrificing the lives of the young men, and of spending their treasure for nothing. Athens had followed his advice and had been beaten, and now Philip was her master. As Aeschines and his opponents had been laying such stress on the consequences of his policy, Demosthenes defended himself in what was, perhaps, the greatest of his speeches. In one part of it he warned the Athenians that what he had to say might startle them, but

> let no one, [he said], in the name of Heaven, be amazed at the length to which I go, but give a kindly consideration to what I say. Even if what was to come was plain to all beforehand; even if all foreknew it; even if you, Aeschines, had been crying with a loud voice in warning and protestation, you who uttered

[6] Second Olynthia Oration.

not so much as a sound; even then, I say, it was not right for the city to abandon her course, if she had any regard for her fame, or for our forefathers, or for the ages to come. As it is, she is thought, no doubt, to have failed to secure her object, as happens to all alike, whenever God wills it: but then, by abandoning in favor of Philip her claim to take the lead of others, she must have incurred the blame of having betrayed them all. Had she surrendered without a struggle those claims in defence of which our forefathers faced every imaginable peril, who would not have cast scorn upon you, Aeschines—upon you, I say; not, I trust, upon Athens nor upon me? In God's name, with what faces should we have looked upon those who came to visit the city, if events had come round to the same conclusion as they now have, if Philip had been chosen as commander and lord of all, and we had stood apart, while others carried on the struggle to prevent these things; and that, although the city had never yet in time past preferred an inglorious security to the hazardous vindication of a noble cause? What Hellene, what foreigner, does not know that the Thebans, and the Spartans who were powerful still earlier, and the Persian king would all gratefully and gladly have allowed Athens to take and keep all that was her own, if she would do the bidding of another, and let another take the first place in Hellas? But this was not, it appears, the tradition of the Athenians; it was not tolerable; it was not in their nature. From the beginning of time no one had ever yet succeeded in persuading the city to throw in her lot with those who were strong, but unrighteous in their dealings, and to enjoy the security of servitude. Throughout all time she has maintained her perilous struggle for preeminence, honor, and glory. And this policy you look upon as so lofty, so proper to your own national character that, of your forefathers also, it is those who have acted thus that you praise most highly. And naturally, for who would not admire the courage of those men, who did not fear to leave their land and their city, and embark upon their ships that they might not do the bidding of another; who chose for their general Themistocles (who had counseled them thus), and stoned Cyrsilus to death when he gave his voice for submission to a master's orders—and not him alone, for your wives stoned his wife also to death. For the Athenians of that day did not look for an orator or a general who would enable them to live in happy servitude; they cared not to live at all, unless they might live in freedom. For every one of them felt that he had come into being, not for his father and his mother alone, but also for his country. And wherein lies the difference? He who thinks he was born for his parents alone awaits the death which destiny assigns him in the course of nature; but he who thinks that he was born for his country also will be willing to die, that he may not see her in bondage, and will look upon the outrages and the indignities that he must needs bear in a city that is in bondage as more to be dreaded than death.

Now were I attempting to argue that *I* had induced you to show a spirit worthy of your forefathers, there is not a man who might not rebuke me with good reason. But, in fact, I am declaring that such principles as these are your own; I am showing that *before* my time the city displayed this spirit, though I claim that I, too, have had some share, as your servant, in carrying out your policy in detail. But in denouncing the policy as a whole, in bidding you be harsh with me, as one who has brought terrors and dangers upon the city, the prosecutor, in his eagerness to deprive me of my distinction at the present moment, is trying to rob you of praises that will last throughout all time. For if you condemn the defendant on the grounds that my policy was not for the best, men will think that your own judgment has been wrong, and that it was not through the unkindness of fortune that you suffered what befell you. But it cannot, it cannot be that you were wrong, men of Athens, when you took upon you the struggle for freedom and deliverance. No! by those who at Marathon bore the brunt of the peril—our forefathers. No! by those who at Plataea drew up their battleline, by those at Salamis, by those who off Artemisium fought the fight at sea, by the many who lie in the sepulchers where the People laid them, brave men, all alike deemed worthy by their country, Aeschines, of the same honor and the same obsequies—not the successful or the victorious alone! And she acted justly. For all these have done that which it was the duty of brave men to do; but their fortune has been that which Heaven assigned to each.[7]

III. Alexander the Great

At the age of twenty, Alexander succeeded to Philip's throne. He is one of the personalities in history who have most appealed to the imagination, not only of his contemporaries, but of all ages. He had the beauty of a young Greek god, a brilliant mind, and personal charm which endeared him to his companions. From his father he had inherited great military genius, extraordinary powers of organization, tireless

[7] On the Crown.

Alexander

energy, and inordinate ambition; and from his mother, a wild half-barbarian princess, a passionate nature, given to outbursts of fierce and uncontrolled anger, and a romantic imagination.

During the boyhood of Alexander, his father was constantly away at war, but he saw to it that his son was well educated. His first teachers accustomed him to a Spartan discipline, and so trained his body that in later years he was able to undergo fatigue and endure hardships that astonished all who were with him.

When Alexander was twelve years old, an episode occurred which convinced his father that he needed the best guidance that could be found for him. A horse, Bucephalus by name, was offered to Philip for the sum of thirteen talents, and the king, with the prince and many others,

> went into the field to try him. But they found him so very vicious and unmanageable that he reared up when they endeavored to mount him, and would not so much as endure the voice of any of Philip's attendants. Upon which, as they were leading him away as wholly useless and untractable, Alexander, who stood by, said, "What an excellent horse do they lose for want of address and boldness to manage him!" Philip at first took no notice of what he said; but when he heard him repeat the same thing several times, and saw he was much vexed to see the horse sent away,

> "Do you reproach," said he to Alexander, "those who are older than yourself, as if you knew more, and were better able to manage him than they?" "I could manage this horse," said Alexander, "better than others do." "And if you do not," said Philip, "what will you forfeit for your rashness?" "I will pay," answered Alexander, "the whole price of the horse." At this the whole company fell to laughing; and as soon as the wager was settled amongst them, he immediately ran to the horse and, taking hold of the bridle, turned him directly towards the sun, having, it seems, observed that he was disturbed at and afraid of the motion of his own shadow; then letting him go forward a little, still keeping the reins in his hands and stroking him gently, when he found him begin to grow eager and fiery, with one nimble leap Alexander securely mounted him; and when he was seated, by little and little he drew in the bridle, and curbed him without either striking or spurring him. Presently, when he found him free from all rebelliousness, Alexander let the horse go at full speed. Philip and his friends looked on at first in silence and anxiety for the result; till seeing him turn and come back rejoicing and triumphing for what he had performed, they all burst out into acclamations of applause; and his father, shedding tears, it is said, for joy, kissed him as he came down from his horse, and in his transport said, "O my son, look thee out a kingdom equal to and worthy of thyself, for Macedonia is too little for thee!"[8]

It was evident that Alexander would not submit to be controlled in what he did, but that a steady guiding hand

[8] Plutarch: *Life of Alexander.*

was needed to develop his best nature, and so Philip sent for the philosopher Aristotle, who was his tutor for four years. Aristotle taught him the best that Greece could offer in literature, philosophy, and natural science. Alexander had no small opinion of his own powers, and considered himself quite the equal, if not the superior, of the best minds of his time, and he wanted to be recognized as such. Later, when Aristotle had published some of his writings, Alexander wrote to him: "You have not done well to publish your books of oral doctrine; for what is there now that we excel others in, if those things which we have been particularly instructed in be laid open to all?"[9] Alexander had been born with a love for study, and his education gave him a real appreciation of all that was best in Greek thought. He used to sleep with a copy of Homer under his pillow, and he told Aristotle that he would "rather excel others in the knowledge of what is excellent than in the extent of his power and dominion."[10] Alexander grew to love his tutor greatly, and in later years he would say that as from his father he had received life, so from Aristotle he had learned to lead a good life.

Aristotle

[9] Plutarch: *Life of Alexander.*

[10] Plutarch: *Life of Alexander.*

Such a personality soon made Alexander the idol of Macedonia, but, as in the case of his father, that was not enough; Macedonian, and therefore in the eyes of Greece a half-barbarian, he wanted to be accepted by the Greeks as a Greek and to receive their hero-worship. Like Philip, he was determined to march into Asia, subdue the Persian king, and become a world ruler, but it was necessary that he should subdue Greece first. He did this very quickly, and in 335 B.C., one year after he became king, he marched against Thebes, which had organized a revolt against him. He came upon the city with almost magical swiftness, for in thirteen days he had transported his army two hundred and fifty miles. A rumor had spread in Greece that he was dead, but suddenly, there he was before the walls of Thebes. In two days all was over. The city was razed to the ground, and the inhabitants either slain or sold into slavery. Yet in the midst of all the horror, Alexander gave an order which seized upon the Greek imagination: the house of Pindar was to be left untouched, for no war was being waged against Greek civilization.

Alexander went to Corinth, where he was elected general of the army that was to invade Persia. He was surrounded by men who praised and flattered him, but one man refused to take any notice of him whatever. This was the cynical philosopher Diogenes.

> Alexander found him in a cask by the roadside. When he saw so much company near him, he raised himself a little, and vouchsafed to look upon Alexander; and when Alexander kindly asked whether he wanted anything, "Yes," said he, "I would have you stand from between me and the sun." Alexander was so struck at this answer, and surprised at the greatness of the man who had taken so little notice of him, that as he went away he told his followers, who were laughing at the

> moroseness of the philosopher, that if he were not Alexander, he would choose to be Diogenes.[11]

The time had now come when at the head of a mighty army, Alexander could start for Asia. This army was made up of Macedonians and of men from all the most warlike states of Greece. It had been thoroughly trained and disciplined, and it served under a general only twenty-two years of age, it is true, but who had already shown himself a military genius and who was adored by every soldier, from the highest to the lowest. It was an army that was never to know defeat.

Alexander did not hide his purpose from the Persian king, for he sent him word that he considered himself lord of Asia: "I, Alexander, consider the whole of thy treasure, and the whole of thy land to be mine." To the Greeks this did not represent any overweening pride, for Alexander was but expressing the belief that was held by Aristotle, the greatest Greek thinker of the age, that Greeks were justified in enslaving the Barbarian.

No story of conquest is more romantic than that of Alexander. On first reaching Asia Minor, he went to Ilium, where he dedicated his armor to Athena, and took in its place some weapons which tradition said had been used in the Trojan War, and he laid a wreath on the tomb of Achilles. Then he started on his march. He came, while passing through Asia Minor, to Gordium, where he saw the celebrated Gordian knot, by which the yoke was fastened to the pole of an ancient chariot. An old prophecy had been made that the man who untied this knot would rule the world. Alexander tried to loosen it, but losing patience, he took his sword and cut it. He meant to rule the world, and he knew that his empire would only be won by the sword.

[11] Plutarch: *Life of Alexander.*

Alexander marched through Syria into Egypt, and when he was in Egypt, he made a journey through the desert of Libya to consult the oracle, Zeus Ammon.

> Few men would have started upon so long and dangerous a journey without misgivings, for there was likely to be scarcity of water, and violent winds that would blow about the poisonous sand of the desert and cause the death of those who inhaled it. But Alexander was not to be turned from anything he was bent upon; for hitherto fortune had helped him in all his plans, and the boldness of his temper gave him a passion for overcoming difficulties. In this journey the gods seemed to favor him as usual, for plentiful rains fell, which not only relieved the soldiers from fear of dying of thirst, but made the sand moist and firm to travel on and purified the air. Besides, some ravens kept up with them in their march, flying before them and waiting for them if they fell behind; but the greatest miracle of all was that if any of the company went astray in the night, the ravens never ceased croaking until they were guided to the right path again.
>
> Having passed through the wilderness, they came to the place where the high priest of Ammon bade Alexander welcome in the name of the god, and called him son of Zeus. And being asked by the king whether any of his father's murderers had escaped punishment, the priest charged him to speak with more respect, since his was not a mortal father. Then Alexander desired to know of the oracle if any of those who murdered Philip were yet unpunished, and further concerning dominion, whether the empire of the world should be his? This, the god answered, he should obtain, and that Philip's death was fully revenged, which gave him so much

> satisfaction that he made splendid offerings to Zeus, and gave the priests very rich presents.[12]

Before leaving Egypt, Alexander founded the city of Alexandria,

> which takes its name from him. The position seemed to him a very fine one in which to found a city, and he thought it would become a prosperous one. Therefore, he was seized by an ardent desire to undertake the enterprise, and he marked out the boundaries of the city himself, pointing out where the marketplace was to be constructed, where the temples were to be built, stating how many there were to be, and to what Greek gods they were to be dedicated—and specially marking a spot for a temple to the Egyptian Isis. He also pointed out where the wall was to be carried out. The soothsayers (pondering upon certain lucky omens) told Alexander that the city would become prosperous in every respect, but especially in regard to the fruits of the earth.[13]

Before his death, Alexander founded many cities called by his name, but the Alexandria of Egypt was the greatest, and the one that was to survive even to the present day. For more than two thousand years it has held its position as one of the chief ports in the Eastern part of the Mediterranean. Alexander did not intend that it should become the capital of Egypt, but he did intend that it should take the place of Tyre, so that the trade coming from the East should be in the hands of Greeks and not of Phoenicians.

---

[12] Plutarch: *Life of Alexander.*

[13] Arrian: *Anabasis of Alexander.*

The army worshipped Alexander, and he knew how to appeal to the imagination of his followers and to gain their devotion. He was once detained by a serious illness, caused by bathing in an ice-cold river. One of his physicians had prepared medicine for him, but before he had taken it, one of his commanders sent the king a letter bidding him beware of Philip (the physician) who, he said, had been bribed by Darius to poison him. Having read the letter, Alexander

> put it under his pillow without showing it to anybody, and when Philip came in with the potion, he took it with great cheerfulness and assurance, giving him the letter to read. It was well worth being present to see Alexander take the draught and Philip read the letter at the same time.[14]

On one occasion

> he had made a long and painful march of eleven days, during which his soldiers suffered so much from want of water that they were ready to give up. While they were in this distress, it happened that some Macedonians who had fetched water in skins upon their mules from a river they had found out came about noon to the place where Alexander was, and seeing him almost choked with thirst, presently filled a helmet and offered it to him. He asked them to whom they were carrying the water; they told him to their children, adding that if his life were but saved, it was no matter for them though they all perished. Then he took the helmet into his hands, and, looking round about, when he saw all

[14] Plutarch: *Life of Alexander.*

> those who were with him stretching their heads out and looking earnestly after the drink, he returned it again with thanks without taking a drop of it. "For," said he, "if I alone should drink, the rest will be out of heart." When the soldiers heard him speak in this way, they one and all cried out to him to lead them forward boldly, and began whipping on their horses. For while they had such a king they said they defied both weariness and thirst, and looked upon themselves to be little less than immortal.[15]

On another occasion the hardships endured by the army were so great that the men were almost ready to refuse to follow Alexander any further. But he called them together, and spoke to them, reminding them that he asked no one to suffer what he himself did not suffer.

> I often sit up at night to watch for you, [he said], that you may be able to sleep. Who is there of you who knows that he has endured greater toil for me than I have for him? I have been wounded with the sword in close fight; I have been shot with arrows; and though I have suffered these things for the sake of your lives, your glory, and your wealth, I am still leading you as conquerors over all the land and sea, all rivers, mountains, and plains.[16]

And the magic of his personality silenced all their murmuring and banished all their discontent.

Followed by this devoted army, Alexander started on a marvelous campaign which led him to the uttermost limit of the then known world, even beyond the Indus into India.

---

[15] Plutarch: *Life of Alexander.*

[16] Arrian: *Anabasis of Alexander.*

In battle after battle he met those who opposed his path and conquered them. Alexander did not know the meaning of the word *impossible*. He was told once that a certain mountain pass was impracticable. For other men, it would have been, but Alexander gave orders that his spearmen should cut steps in the steep rock, and where before only the surest-footed goats had climbed, Alexander and his men passed in safety. His men followed him over snowy mountains in winter, and across thirsty deserts in summer, up and down the lower ranges of the Himalaya Mountains, where the best European armies of today can only go with difficulty. They crossed the plains of India in the rainy season, and even went through that country so unfit for human habitation that Mohammedan conquerors of a later age declared it was a place fit only to be dwelled in by the souls of the lost.

Nothing stopped Alexander—not the mountain barrier, nor the deep river, nor the burning sands. On he went, until he reached what he believed to be the River Ocean that girdled the earth.

Everywhere Alexander had been victorious, until even the Great King of Persia himself was utterly defeated and Alexander was seated upon his throne. He burned the Persian palace at Persepolis in order "to take vengeance on the Persians for their deeds in the invasion of Greece, when they razed Athens to the ground and burned down the temples. He also desired to punish the Persians for all the other injuries they had done the Greeks."[17]

When the news of the victories of Alexander over the Persians reached Greece, great was the amazement. For centuries, the name of the Great King had stood for all that was powerful and invincible. Though he had been driven out of Greece, he was still believed to be omnipotent in Asia. The

---

[17] Arrian: *Anabasis of Alexander.*

general feeling was voiced by one of the orators, speaking of what was happening in the Athenian Assembly:

> What is there strange and unexpected that has not happened in our time? We have not lived the life of ordinary men, and the things we have seen will become a tale of wonder to posterity. Is not the King of the Persians, he who channeled Athos, he who bridged the Hellespont, he who demanded earth and water of the Greeks, he who dared to write in his letters that he was lord of all men from the rising of the sun unto its setting, is he not struggling now, no longer for lordship over others, but already for his life?

Alexander had conquered the Great King and seated himself on the royal throne of Persia under the canopy of gold. But now that he had reached the summit of his ambition and was master of the greatest empire in the world, a change came over him, and he began to indulge his passions and to give himself up to all kinds of dissipation. He dressed like a Persian, which deeply offended the Greeks, who became jealous of the increasing favor the king showed to the Barbarian.

Slowly the leaders of Alexander's army began to realize the change that was taking place in their general, and though he gained in popularity with the Persians, he began to lose some of the devotion hitherto felt for him by the Greeks and Macedonians, and he was becoming estranged from his old followers. At length they realized that it was not a Greek conquest that would enslave Asia of which he dreamed, but of a world empire, in which the Barbarian would live on equal terms with the Greek. Alexander was far-seeing beyond his age, and he had learned that men whose customs are alien to those in which he had been brought up were not always to be despised, and that if he dreamed of holding the world empire he had conquered, he could only do so by treating all parts of it alike, and by encouraging intercourse between the different races which composed it. However wise this may have been, it is not difficult to understand the feeling of the older Greeks, who had been educated to feel a gulf between them and the Barbarian that nothing could ever bridge. The climax of the estrangement between Alexander and his old companions came in a tragic scene at a banquet. Alexander and his friends had been drinking fast and furiously, then songs had been sung, some of which ridiculed the Macedonian officers who had recently been unfortunate in a skirmish. The older men present were offended, but Alexander laughed and had the song repeated. Clitus, who had been an old and trusted friend of the king, said angrily, "It is not well to make a jest of Macedonians among their enemies, for, though they have met with misfortunes, they are better men than those who laugh at them." Angry words passed between him and the king, until, unable to control his rage, Alexander snatched a spear from one of his guards and ran it through the body of Clitus, who fell dead to the ground. Dead silence followed this mad deed, and Alexander was sobered by the sight of the man he had loved lying dead at his feet, slain by his own hand. He drew the spear out of the body and would have killed himself with it, had the guards not interfered and led him by force to his chamber. All that night and the next day he wept bitterly and would speak to no one. At length one of his friends entered the room where he lay and said to him in a loud voice:

> Is this the Alexander whom the whole world looks to, lying here weeping like a slave for fear of what men will say? It is Alexander himself who, by the right of his conquests, should be the law to decide what is right and wrong. Do you not know, Alexander, that Zeus is represented with Justice and

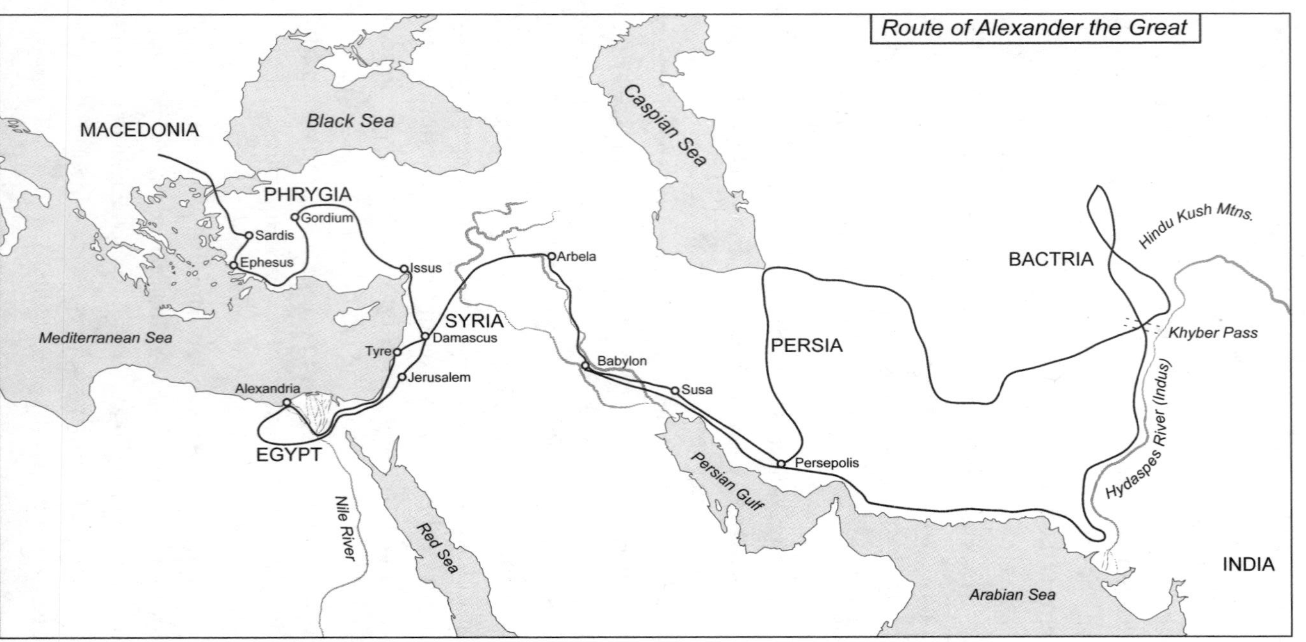

The route of Alexander's conquests, from Macedonia through Asia Minor, Phoenicia, Egypt, Persia, India, and back to Babylon where he died

> Law on either side of him, to show that all the deeds of a conqueror are lawful and just?[18]

The king was soothed by these words, for he was only too ready to believe, as his friend had said, that whatever he might choose to do was right. But he was spoiled by such flattery which only increased his arrogance and made him yield more to his passions than before.

Having conquered and established an empire which extended from Greece and Macedonia in Europe across Asia to India, and which included Egypt and Libya, Alexander prepared to set out on yet another expedition to the West and to enter Arabia. He was in Babylon, and spent a long day attending to military duties. Towards evening, he left his chair of state to take a little relaxation. During his absence, a half-crazy man appeared, who, without any warning, sat himself down on the king's seat. The attendants looked on in horror at such an act, which seemed to them great impiety, but they did not dare turn him out, for suddenly superstitious fears took hold of them, and in frightened voices they whispered to each other that this could foretell nothing but some great calamity.

It was in the early summer of 323 B.C. that Alexander was ready to start on his march, but the night before he was to leave Babylon, he became ill of a fever. For a few days he was still able to attend to some business from his bed, but he grew rapidly worse. Suddenly the army realized that he was dying, and his old friends, forgetting whatever estrangement had come between them, entreated to be allowed to see him once more. They were admitted to the chamber where he lay, and passed in silence before him. He was so weak that he "could not speak, and only touched the right hand of each, and raised his head a little, and signed with his eyes."

---

[18] From Plutarch: *Life of Alexander.*

The next day Alexander was dead. Deep and awe-struck silence fell upon the city and camp for four days, and then, his generals having found amongst his papers plans for the western campaign, they endeavored to carry them out. But they were not successful, and never again did the great army fight under one leader. Having lost the almost magical inspiration of Alexander's leadership, his successors were unable to keep the empire which he had conquered.

Almost from the moment of his death, Alexander was worshipped as a god. He was the great hero of his age, and even in his lifetime, it was believed that he was half-divine. Dying so young (he was only thirty-three), possessed of great strength and godlike beauty, capable of rare generosity, brave almost to recklessness, planning conquests so far-reaching that they appealed to the imagination of everyone, given to outbursts of savage anger and vindictive rage—all these characteristics were looked upon as more than human. For more than two thousand years, the name of Alexander has been immortal in the East. There is hardly an ancient city from Babylon almost to the borders of China that does not claim Alexander as its founder; his name still clings to old traditions and legends; to this very day the Parsees curse him for having caused the destruction of the ancient sacred Persian writings when he captured Persepolis and burned it. Later generations of men have differed as to the lasting value of some of his work, but the name of Alexander, and the story of his hero-deeds, have become a permanent possession of the imagination of mankind.

The idealized portrait of Alexander usually showed him gazing off into the distance, toward future conquests.

This realistic portrait of Alexander copies a statue by Lyssipus, the only sculptor for whom Alexander actually sat.

CHAPTER 22

THE GIFTS OF GREECE TO THE WORLD

I. The Greek Spirit

WHAT MAN ACHIEVES is, in regard to its permanent value, of less importance than the spirit in which he achieves it; *what* one learns is of less importance than *how* one learns; learning facts is of less importance than developing certain qualities of mind. It is not possible, and were it possible it would not be desirable, to reproduce in modern life the conditions of a past age, but certain qualities of the mind and spirit are undying, and some of the greatest of these qualities have come to us from the Greeks.

> History is the story of the way in which man has learned, and is still learning, how to live: of how through long centuries he has sought to satisfy the practical needs of his body, the questioning of his mind, and the searching of his spirit.[1]

Mankind is still engaged upon the high adventure for this threefold quest, and not yet has any one civilization succeeded in bringing into perfect accord the demands of the body, of the mind, and of the spirit. If in the beginning of this story in the ancient world, the Hebrews stand supreme amongst the

[1] *The Book of the Ancient World.*

teachers of those who have sought to satisfy the searching of the spirit, so are the Greeks the great teachers of those who have sought to satisfy the questioning of the mind. The Greeks gave to the mind of man three definite qualities: the love of Freedom, the love of Truth, and the love of Beauty. These are practical qualities which show themselves quite definitely in what the Greeks did, in what they thought, and in what they built, or in other words, in their political history, their literature, and their art.

It must not be thought that the Greeks perfectly fulfilled their great ideals—Greek history shows quite clearly that they did not. If the story of the Greeks as it has been told in this book has emphasized their ideals rather than their failure always to attain these, it is because their ideals are the imperishable gifts they have given to the world. But the Greeks were not dreamers; they were practical men, keen and interested in all the practical affairs of everyday life. Their history shows how they failed in perfectly carrying out their ideals because of certain weaknesses of character, and of certain conditions and limitations in their life from which the men of today can learn many useful lessons. The greatness of the Greeks lies not in what they did not do or did imperfectly, but in their spirit, that spirit which in their political history, their literature, and their art sought for Freedom, Truth, and Beauty.

The Greeks showed the world the way to Freedom. They won their own national freedom against almost overwhelming odds, for never before had a small country maintained her independence in the face of a great empire and been victorious. They also maintained a political freedom, which they carried too far, for the inability of Greek states to form alliances and to unite was one of the sources of weakness which finally led to their downfall. Nevertheless, the spirit of sturdy independence is one that has endured. The Greeks carried their vision of freedom further than the political independence of each state, and one of their chief characteristics was their personal freedom. In a speech to the Athenian army before the battle in the harbor at Syracuse, Nicias "reminded them that they were the inhabitants of the freest country in the world, and how in Athens there was no interference with the daily life of any man."[2] Modern times are apt to pride themselves on the freedom of speech allowed to all, but no modern state permits greater liberty of speech (and some would not tolerate as much) than was allowed in Athens in the fifth century B.C., when Aristophanes wrote his satirical comedies.

The Greeks loved Truth. By this is not meant *truthfulness*, for the Greeks were insincere and never trusted even one another, but the spirit which desired to see all things straight, "with an unclouded clearness of mind"—the spirit which could distinguish clearly between right and wrong, which could judge without prejudice or passion, above all the spirit which knew its own limitations and which acknowledged what it did not know. Perhaps the greatest Greek searcher for truth was Socrates, and some knowledge of his life and teaching will show us what is our debt to Greece in the story of how the mind of man has gained freedom in its search for truth.

II. Socrates

DURING THE LAST YEARS of the Peloponnesian War, a strange figure might have been seen in Athens: a short, ugly, odd-looking man, poorly-clad and utterly indifferent to criticism of his habits or appearance, but a man to whom everyone listened when he began to speak. This was Socrates, the Greek philosopher.

His father was a stone-cutter and a poor man, but he seems to have given to his son the best education that was to be had in Athens, for Socrates often quoted from Greek literature,

[2] Thucydides, VII.

Socrates

especially from Homer, and he spoke of having studied with his friends "the treasures which the wise men of old have left us in their books."

Very little is known of the early life of Socrates, but he passed his youth and early manhood during the greatest years of Athenian history. He was born ten years after the Persian had been defeated at Plataea and driven out of Greece; as a boy, he had seen the Long Walls being built; he had grown up in the Athens of Pericles, a contemporary of Sophocles, Euripides, Pheidias, and Thucydides. When the clouds gathered over Athens and war came, Socrates served in the army as a common soldier; he had lived through the short-lived triumphs and the tragic disasters which befell the city; he had been hungry when food was scarce; he had seen Athens besieged and taken; he had watched the Long Walls destroyed, and he had lived through the terror when the Thirty ruled Athens. It was a life lived in very stirring times, and Socrates had taken his share in the happenings. During the war, he served in one of the Northern campaigns, and he amazed everyone by his extraordinary power of enduring hunger and thirst, and all the hardships of a cold Thracian winter. One of his friends says of this time that

> his fortitude in enduring cold was surprising. There was a severe frost, for the winter in that region is really tremendous, and everybody else either remained

> indoors, or if they went out had on an amazing quantity of clothes, and were well-shod, and had their feet swathed in felt and fleeces. In the midst of this, Socrates with his bare feet on the ice and in his ordinary dress marched better than the other soldiers who had shoes, and they looked daggers at him because he seemed to despise them. Another tale of what he did on this expedition is worth hearing. One morning, he was thinking about something which he could not resolve; he would not give it up, but continued thinking from early dawn until noon—there he stood fixed in thought; and at noon attention was drawn to him, and the remark ran through the wondering crowd that Socrates had been standing and thinking about something ever since the break of day. At last in the evening after supper, some Ionians, out of curiosity (I should explain that this was not in winter but in summer), brought out their mats and slept in the open air that they might watch him and see whether he would stand all night. There he stood until the following morning, and with the return of light he offered up a prayer to the Sun and went his way.[3]

At the close of the war, Socrates was in Athens, a man now of over sixty years of age. He held one or two offices of state, when he was known for his fearless refusal to do what he thought was wrong. On one occasion he refused to obey orders that were given him, because he believed that obedience would involve him in doing what he thought to be wrong. "I showed," he said, "not by mere words but by my actions, that I did not care a straw for death: but that I did care very much indeed about doing wrong."

---

[3] Plato: *Symposium*, translated by Jowett.

Socrates was very poor, and as he would take no money for his teaching, his means of livelihood were very scanty. He went about barefoot and had only one cloak, which he wore until it was so old that it became a matter of joke amongst his friends. He not only had no luxuries of any kind, but hardly the bare necessities of life, yet he was quite content and used to say, "How many things there are which I do not want." Socrates married Xanthippe, a woman of a most violent temper. He used to say that one ought to live with a restive woman, just as horsemen manage violent-tempered horses; and "as they," said he, "when they have once mastered them, are easily able to manage all others; so I, after managing Xanthippe, can easily live with anyone else whatever."[4]

The Athenians had always been intellectually very alert and had tried to solve all kinds of problems. They asked how it was that things came into being, how they continued to exist, of what they were made, and similar questions. But when Athens had become an empire and ruled over many men and states, the questions began to change. People were less interested in how things originated than in questions arising from their daily experience. They asked, what is a state, what is a citizen, what is justice, what is temperance, courage, cowardice, and so on. In order to answer these questions, a body of teachers had arisen in Athens who were called Sophists, or *Wise Men*. They taught every kind of subject and established a number of schools. The older Greek teachers did not like these Sophists, partly because they took money for their teaching, and hitherto, though Athenian philosophers had accepted presents, they had never charged definite fees; partly because they taught so many subjects that it was thought they could teach nothing thoroughly; partly because they seemed to aim at teaching young men to argue in order to get the better of their opponents

[4] Diogenes Laertius.

rather than to seek for Truth; and above all, because they were often skeptical as to the existence of the gods. There were some very good teachers amongst the Sophists, and they opened up a great many new fields of thought to the Athenians, but a weak side to their teaching was that they only stated general principles, and often asserted as absolute facts things that never had been definitely proved one way or the other. They used words carelessly without stopping to think of their real meaning, and they never suggested that there was anything they did not know.

Socrates saw that though the teaching of the Sophists might increase *information,* it was fatal to real *thinking,* and he began to teach in Athens in order to show what real thinking was. He taught in no school, had no classes, and took no pay. He was willing to talk to any and everyone who would listen to him. He ever

> lived in the public eye; at early morning he was to be seen betaking himself to one of the promenades or wrestling grounds; at noon he would appear with the gathering crowds in the marketplace; and as day declined, wherever the largest throng might be encountered, there was he to be found, talking for the most part, while anyone who chose might stop and listen.[5]

Socrates talked to and questioned everyone, and tried to show people what real knowledge was. He was filled with a passionate belief in the importance of truth above all things. He said that to make inaccurate statements and to use words with a wrong or careless meaning was "not only a fault in itself, it also created an evil in the soul." He showed those

[5] Xenophon: *Memorabilia.*

who listened to him the evil that came from pretending to know what one did not know, and the first step in his teaching was to make them realize their ignorance. To this end he questioned and cross-examined them, until they contradicted themselves, or found no answer and generally ended in hopeless difficulties, simply because they would not acknowledge at the beginning that they did not know what he had asked. One of his friends once said, "Indeed, Socrates, I no longer believe in my answers; everything seems to me to be different from what it used to seem," and another speaking of him said, "Socrates makes me acknowledge my own worthlessness. I had best be silent for it seems that I know nothing at all."

Socrates believed that Virtue was Knowledge, that if a man knew a thing was wrong, he would not do it, and that those who knew what was right would always do it. In this Socrates was not wholly right; he only saw a part of the truth, but his greatness lies in that he was the first to teach the importance of having a reason for what we believe, of learning accurate habits of mind, and that the search for knowledge is one rich in imagination and beauty.

Socrates was always arguing, talking, questioning, but he was never rude or discourteous to those who disagreed with him, he never brought his own personal feelings into his arguments, and he never descended to expressions of wounded pride or irritation.

The teaching of Socrates opened the minds of those who listened to him to the possibilities to which knowing the truth might lead them, and he had great influence over numbers of young Athenians. It was all new to them; they had never heard anything like it before. "Mere fragments of you and your words," said one of them, "even at second-hand, and however imperfectly repeated, amaze and possess the soul of anyone who hears them," and he went on to say,

> I have heard Pericles and other great orators, and I thought that they spoke well, but I never had any similar feeling; my soul was not stirred by them, nor was I angry at the thought of my own slavish state. But this Socrates has often brought me to such a pass that I have felt as if I could hardly endure the life I am leading. For he makes me confess that I ought not to live as I do, neglecting the wants of my own soul. And he is the only person who ever made me ashamed, and there is no one else who does the same.[6]

But if Socrates gained friends, his method of exposing the ignorance of others also gained him enemies. No one before had ever thought such thoughts, and to ordinary Athenians his questioning was wicked. But Xenophon, one of his friends, tells us that "no one ever heard him say or saw him do anything impious or irreverent, and he was so piously and devoutly religious that he would take no step apart from the will of heaven." Yet his enemies maintained that he disbelieved in the gods. His teaching was all the more disturbing because Athens, having been defeated by Sparta, had just lived through the terrible months of the rule of the Thirty, and though these had been driven out (this was in the year 399 B.C.), Athens was in a state of unrest, fear, and suspicion. Anyone who taught anything new was looked upon as a possible enemy to the state, and the enemies of Socrates seized this opportunity to bring definite accusations against him. They said: "Socrates is guilty, inasmuch as he does not believe in the gods whom the city worships, but introduces other strange deities; he is also guilty inasmuch as he corrupts the young men, and the punishment he has incurred is death."[7]

---

[6] Plato: *Symposium*, translated by Jowett.

[7] Diogenes Laertius.

A trial followed. In an Athenian trial, first the accusers made their speeches, and then the accused was allowed to defend himself. Plato, the great pupil of Socrates, has given us the speech made by his master at his trial, a speech known as the *Apology of Socrates*. In it the philosopher, now an old man of over seventy, set forth the principles which had guided him in his teaching.

He began by saying that he had never taught men to disbelieve in the gods, and that the accusation of impiety against him was false, but he did say that it was fair to ask him just what he had been trying to do which had given rise to these reports. He then told them the story of how a friend of his had gone to Delphi, and had asked the Oracle if there were any man wiser than he, and that the Oracle had answered that there was no man.

> Now see why I tell you this. I am going to explain to you the origin of my unpopularity. When I heard of the Oracle I began to reflect. What can God mean by this dark saying? I know very well that I am not wise, even in the smallest degree. Then what can he mean by saying that I am the wisest of men? It cannot be that he is speaking falsely, for he is a god and cannot lie. And for a long time I was at a loss to understand his meaning. Then, very reluctantly, I turned to seek for it in this manner. I went to a man who was reputed to be wise, thinking that there, if anywhere, I should prove the answer wrong, and meaning to point out to the Oracle its mistake, and to say, "You said that I was the wisest of men, but this man is wiser than I am."

But Socrates went on to say that after talking to this man, who was a politician, he found that he was not wise because he thought he knew things that he did not know, and because he would not acknowledge his ignorance. He tried to prove to him that he was not wise, but only succeeded in making him his enemy.

> Next, [said Socrates], I went to another who was reputed to be still wiser than the last, with exactly the same result. And there again I made him, and many other men, my enemies.
>
> By reason of this examination, Athenians, I have made many enemies of a very fierce and bitter kind, who have spread abroad a great number of calumnies about me, and people say that I am a "wise man." For the bystanders always think that I am wise myself in any matter wherein I convict another man of ignorance. But, my friends, I believe that only God is really wise: and that by this oracle he meant that men's wisdom is worth little or nothing. I do not think that he meant that Socrates was wise. He only made use of my name, and took me as an example, as though he would say to men, "He among you is the wisest, who, like Socrates, knows that in very truth his wisdom is worth nothing at all." And therefore I still go about testing and examining every man whom I think wise, whether he be a citizen or a stranger, as God has commanded me; and whenever I find that he is not wise, I point out to him on the part of God that he is not wise. And I am so busy in this pursuit that I have never had leisure to take any part worth mentioning in public matters, or to look after my private affairs. I am in very great poverty by reason of my service to God.[8]

Socrates then went on to prove that nothing in his teaching could corrupt the young men, as his enemies declared he was

[8] Plato: *Apology*, translated by F. J. Church.

doing, and to prove his belief in the gods. He knew that he was on trial for his life, but no fear of death stopped him from speaking that which he believed to be the truth.

> My friends, [he said], if you think that a man of any worth at all ought to reckon the chances of life and death when he acts, or that he ought to think of anything but whether he is acting rightly or wrongly, and as a good or bad man would act, you are grievously mistaken. It would be very strange conduct on my part if I were to desert my post now from fear of death or of any other thing, when God has commanded me, as I am persuaded that he has done, to spend my life in searching for wisdom, and in examining myself and others. That would indeed be a very strange thing; and then certainly I might with justice be brought to trial for not believing in the gods; for I should be disobeying the Oracle, and fearing death, and thinking myself wise when I was not wise. For to fear death, my friends, is only to think ourselves wise, without being wise, for it is to think that we know what we do not know. For, anything that man can tell, death may be the greatest good that can happen to them: but they fear it as if they knew quite well that it was the greatest of evils. And what is this but that shameful ignorance of thinking that we know what we do not know?
>
> Athenians, if you put me to death, you will not easily find another man to fill my place. God has sent me to attack the city, as if it were a great and noble horse, to use a quaint simile, which was rather sluggish for its size, and which needed to be roused by a gadfly; and I think that I am that gadfly that God has sent to the city to attack it, for I never cease from settling upon you as

> it were at every point, and rousing and exhorting, and reproaching each man of you all day long.[9]

Socrates then referred to the custom in Athens that when a man was on trial for his life, his wife and children sometimes appeared in court in order to appeal to the pity of the judges and so obtain a favorable sentence, but he refused to do that for knowing that the judge had taken an oath to administer justice justly, he believed that such an act on his part would be an attempt to make them break their oaths.

> Were I to be successful and to prevail on you by my prayers to break your oaths, I should be clearly teaching you to believe that there are no gods: and I should be simply accusing myself by my defence of not believing in them. But, Athenians, that is very far from the truth. I do believe in the gods as no one of my accusers believes in them: and to you and to God I commit my cause to be decided as is best for you and for me.

Socrates was found guilty by 281 votes to 220, and the penalty to be indicted was death. He had the right under Athenian law to suggest an alternative penalty.

> What counter-penalty shall I propose to you Athenians? What I deserve, of course, must I not? What is a suitable reward to be given to a poor benefactor who requires leisure to exhort you? There is no reward, Athenians, so suitable for him as a public maintenance in the Prytaneum. It is a much more suitable reward for him than for any of you who has won a victory at the Olympic Games with his horse or his chariots. So if I am

[9] Plato: *Apology*, translated by F. J. Church.

> to propose the penalty which I really deserve, I propose this—a public maintenance in the Prytaneum.
>
> Or shall I propose imprisonment? And why should I pass the rest of my days in prison, the slave of successive officials? Or shall I propose a fine, with imprisonment until it is paid? I have told you why I will not do that. I should have to continue in prison, for I have no money to pay a fine with. Shall I then propose exile? Perhaps you would agree to that. Life would indeed be very dear to me if I were unreasonable enough to expect that strangers would cheerfully tolerate my discussions and reasonings, when you who are my fellow citizens cannot endure them, and have found them so burdensome and odious to you that you are seeking now to be released from them. No indeed, Athenians, that is not likely. A fine life I should lead for an old man, if I were to withdraw from Athens, and pass the rest of my days in wandering from city to city, and continually being expelled.[10]

The alternatives were not accepted, as indeed Socrates knew they would not be, and he was condemned to die. He accepted the sentence calmly, "and with infinite gentleness and manliness. No one within the memory of man, it is said, ever bowed his head to death more nobly."[11] But death offered no terrors to Socrates.

> If death [he said to his judges] is a journey to another place, and the common belief be true, that there are all who have died, what good could be greater than this? Would a journey not be worth taking, at the end of

[10] Plato: *Apology*, translated by F. J. Church.

[11] Xenophon: *Memorabilia*.

> which, in the other world, we should be released from the self-styled judges who are here, and should find the true judges who are said to sit in judgment below? Or what would you not give to converse with Orpheus and Homer? I am willing to die many times if this be true. And above all, I could spend my time in examining those who are there, as I examine men here, and in finding out which of them thinks himself wise, when he is not wise. What would we not give, my judges, to be able to examine the great leader of the expedition against Troy, or Odysseus, or countless other men and women whom we could name? It would be an infinite happiness to converse with them, and to live with them, and to examine them. Assuredly there they do not put men to death for doing that. For besides the other ways in which they are happier than we are, they are immortal, at least if the common belief be true.
>
> But now the time has come, and we must go hence; I to die, and you to live. Whether life or death is better is known to God, and to God only.[12]

Socrates was taken to prison where he spent a month before his sentence was carried out. The delay was caused by the voyage of the sacred ship, said to be that of Theseus, which had only just set out on its annual voyage to Delos, and no Athenian could be put to death during its absence. He spent this month talking to his friends, especially to Crito, who was very devoted to him, and who entreated him to escape from prison, an escape for which he could very easily have arranged. But the brave old man, loyal to his principles to the end, refused, and he reminded Crito how all his life he had taught that the greatest misfortune that could befall a man

[12] Plato: *Apology*, translated by F. J. Church.

was to do wrong, and the greatest crime a man could commit against his state was to break her laws.

The last day arrived. The story of that day has been told by one who was present:

> I will try to relate the whole story to you from the beginning. On the previous days I and the others had always met in the morning at the court where the trial was held, which was close to the prison: and then we had gone in to Socrates. We used to wait each morning until the prison was opened, conversing, for it was not opened early. When it was opened, we used to go in to Socrates, and we generally spent the whole day with him. But on that morning we met earlier than usual; for the evening before we had learned, on leaving the prison, that the ship had arrived from Delos. So we arranged to be at the usual place as early as possible. When we reached the prison, the porter, who generally let us in, came out to us and bade us wait a little, and not to go in until he summoned us himself; "for the Eleven," he said, "are releasing Socrates from his fetters, and giving directions for his death today." In no great while he returned and bade us enter. So we went in and found Socrates just released, and Xanthippe, you know her, sitting by him, holding his child in her arms. When Xanthippe saw us, she wailed aloud and cried, in her woman's way, "This is the last time, Socrates, that you will talk with your friends, or they with you." And Socrates glanced at Crito and said, "Crito, let her be taken home." So some of Crito's servants led her away, weeping bitterly and beating her breast.[13]

[13] Plato: *Phaedo*, translated by F. J. Church.

Once more Socrates and his friends conversed, and once more he expressed his joy at "going to the place where he hoped to gain the wisdom that he had passionately longed for all his life." They talked together until later in the day, and then he rose and went into another room to bathe himself:

> Crito went with him and told us to wait. So we waited, talking of him and dwelling on the greatness of the calamity which had fallen upon us: it seemed as if we were going to lose a father, and to be orphans for the rest of our life. When he had bathed, and his children had been brought to him (he had two sons quite little, and one grown up), and the women of his family were come, he spoke with them in Crito's presence and gave them his last commands; then he sent the women and children away, and returned to us. By that time it was near the hour of sunset, for he had been a long while within. When he came back to us he sat down, but not much was said after that.

Presently the gaoler came in and told him that the hour had come for him to die:

> I have found you, [he said], the noblest and best man that has ever come here; and now I am sure that you will not be angry with me, but with those who you know are to blame. And so, farewell, and try to bear what must be as lightly as you can; you know why I have come.

With that he turned away weeping and went out.

> Then Crito made a sign to his slave who was standing by, and the slave went out, and after some

delay returned with the man who was to give the poison, carrying it prepared in a cup. When Socrates saw him, he asked, "You understand these things, my good sir, what have I to do?"

"You have only to drink this," he replied, "and to walk about until your legs feel heavy, and then lie down; and it will act of itself." With that he handed the cup to Socrates, who took it quite cheerfully, without trembling, and without any change of color or of feature, and looked up at the man with that fixed glance of his, and asked, "What say you to making a libation of this draught? May I, or not?" "We only prepare so much as we think sufficient, Socrates," he answered. "I understand," said Socrates. "But I suppose that I may, and must, pray to the gods that my journey hence may be prosperous: that is my prayer; be it so." With these words he put the cup to his lips and drank the poison quite calmly and cheerfully. Till then most of us had been able to control our grief fairly well; but when we saw him drinking, and then the poison finished, we could do so no longer. My tears came fast in spite of myself; it was not for him, but at my own misfortune in losing such a friend. Even before that, Crito had been unable to restrain his tears, and had gone away, and Apollodorus, who had never once ceased weeping the whole time, burst into a loud cry, and made us one and all break down by his sobbing and grief, except only Socrates himself. "What are you doing, my friends?" he exclaimed. "I sent away the women chiefly in order that they might not offend in this way; for I have heard that a man should die in silence. So calm yourselves and bear up." When we heard that we were ashamed, and we ceased from weeping.[14]

---

[14] Plato: *Phaedo*, translated by F. J. Church.

Socrates then walked about a little, but soon lay down on the couch, and slowly the numbness crept over him. He knew that when it reached his heart, he would die. Once more he spoke. "Crito," he said, "I owe a cock to Aesculapius; do not forget to pay it." These were his last words, for in a few minutes he was dead.

> Such was the end [said the friend who was with him to the last] of a man who, I think, was the wisest and justest, and the best man that I have ever known. But I did not pity him, for he seemed to me happy, both in his bearing and in his words, so fearlessly and nobly did he die. I could not help thinking that the gods would watch over him still on his journey to the other world, and that when he arrived there it would be well with him, if it was ever well with any man.[15]

III. Greek Literature: the Philosophers

THE WORD *philosophy* means the love of wisdom, and to the Greeks this wisdom was the serious effort made to understand both the world and man. To us *philosophy* generally means a wise understanding of the right way of living, but with the Greeks it included a great deal of what we today call *science*. Greek philosophy was concerned with finding out the origins of things, and from that knowledge to build up a right way of life. We do not today go to the Greeks to learn science: their answers to the questions asked were, some of them, wrong, and some of them inadequate. But modern science has been made possible by the qualities of mind which the Greeks brought to their inquiries: their passionate desire to know the truth about things, their power of going behind old

[15] Plato, *Phaedo*, translated by F. J. Church.

superstitions, and of seeing things as they really are, their open-mindedness and willingness to accept new truths, and their powers of patient study, observation, and of reaching the unknown from the known.

The earliest Greek philosophers lived in Ionia in the sixth century B.C., and the greatest of them were Thales of Miletus and Pythagoras of Samos. Something has already been said about Thales. He went further than the Egyptians and Babylonians had done, not so much because of the new discoveries he made, but because he brought to those discoveries not only the desire to know that they were facts, but the desire to go behind the facts and find out the reason for their existence.

Thales lived to be an old man, but neither age nor infirmities lessened his zeal for learning, and

> it is said that once he was led out of his house by an old woman for the purpose of observing the stars, and he fell into a ditch and bewailed himself, on which the old woman said to him, "Do you, O Thales, who cannot see what is under your feet, think that you shall understand what is in heaven?"[16]

Pythagoras of Samos lived later in the sixth century than Thales. He was a great traveler and seems to have visited not only the mainland of Greece, but also Egypt and Crete, where he had many rare experiences going into the innermost parts of temples, where, as a rule, no strangers were admitted. He also went to Italy, where he founded a school and gathered about three hundred pupils around him.

Though it was not believed by the world at large until nearly two thousand years later, Pythagoras taught that

[16] Diogenes Laertius.

the world was round, and, as far as is known, he was the first thinker who made this discovery. It was Pythagoras who laid the foundations for later mathematical knowledge, especially in geometry and arithmetic, and who taught that there was a science of numbers apart from their use as a practical means of calculation.

In the fifth century B.C., Athens had become an empire and the "school of Hellas," and the center of Greek learning was found there and no longer in Ionia. The story of Socrates has already been told. This great teacher did not write anything himself because he believed that it was a greater thing for a man to live well than to write well, and that his particular way of teaching and constant intercourse with his fellow men was the best way of teaching those truths in which he believed. The account of Socrates' life and teaching, however, was written down and given to the world by his pupil Plato, who carried on his master's work. Plato was about twenty-eight years old when Socrates was put to death, and for twelve years after that time he traveled. Then he returned to Athens, bought a house and garden (unlike Socrates, he was well-off), and spent the next forty years of his life teaching in the Academy. Plato was an idealist, and in addition to his writings about Socrates, he has left us the *Republic*, the picture of what he thought an ideal state should be, and some other works in which he discusses at great length

Plato

what things it is most worthwhile that men should pursue in life, and why they should pursue them. He taught that goodness was worth being sought after for its own sake and not for any material reward that comes from pursuing it. In all his teaching he emphasizes the fact that the greatest things in life and those which are eternal are not always the things that can be seen, and that the soul of man does not live on material things but on wisdom, beauty, truth, and love.

As a young man, Plato had seen in Athens, under the rule of the Thirty, the lawlessness and confusion that arose from a tyrannously ordered state, and the *Republic* was an attempt to show what he thought life in an ideal state might be. His vision was not a very practical one, but Plato was not a practical statesman. The great value of the *Republic* to the world today is that just because its ideals could never be wholly carried out, the questions which all statesmen in all ages have had to settle could be and were fearlessly discussed, unhampered by the compromises and conventions which beset modern politics.

Plato could write of other things besides politics and ideals. He had a gift for poetry which comes out in many a fairy tale that he introduces here and there into his writings, knowing that sometimes a great truth can be more easily driven home in such a form. Socrates and a friend were once walking by the stream Ilissus. It was a hot summer's day, and as they were barefoot, they cooled their feet in the water and then sat down under the shade of a plane tree to rest and talk. And as they rested, Socrates told his friend the legend of the grasshoppers. They were said to have been

> human beings in an age before the Muses. And when the Muses came and song appeared, they were ravished with delight and, singing always, never thought of eating and drinking, until at last in their forgetfulness they died. And now they live again in

> the grasshoppers; and this is the return which the Muses make to them: they neither hunger nor thirst, but from the hour of their birth they are always singing, and never eating or drinking; and when they die they go and inform the Muses in heaven, who honor them on earth.[17]

When Philip of Macedon wanted the best Greek teacher known as a tutor for his son Alexander, he sent for Aristotle. We know very little about the life of Aristotle. He had been a pupil of Plato at the Academy for twenty years and had learned the best of all that great philosopher could teach him. On his return from Macedonia, he founded a school of his own at Athens, the Lyceum, where he spent the rest of his life teaching and studying. He died in 322 B.C., one year after his pupil Alexander. But if little is known of the details of his life, we know something of his character from things that Alexander said about him, and the esteem in which he held him, and something of the kindliness of his nature from his will, which has been preserved. He made provision for all who had faithfully served him and gave many of his slaves their freedom. He had been twice married, and his second wife, "who behaved so well towards me," was so provided for that she could marry again, and he made arrangements for the marriage of his daughter. In reading of the life of the Athenian man and the Athenian woman, their ways seem to lie far apart and the wife to have had very little share in the interests of her husband. In his will Aristotle gives us a glimpse of the place which the wife, sometimes, at least, held. He left directions that the bones of his first wife, the wife of his youth, were to be taken from their resting place and buried with his, and this was to be done "as she herself charged."

---

[17] Plato: *Phaedrus*, translated by Jowett.

The work of Aristotle is amazing, for he not only wrote on every conceivable subject, but wrote as a master. For more than a thousand years after his death, the books he wrote were studied in schools and universities, and formed the foundation of all education. He wrote on astronomy, mathematics, biology, botany, and many other subjects, and he has not only been called the "*Father of Natural Science,*" but his writings remained the standard authority on many scientific subjects for centuries after his death. Aristotle was more practical than Plato, though less inspiring as a writer. As we have already seen, he, too, wrote about an ideal state in his *Politics.* Aristotle believed that the life of a state was like that of an individual; that the aim of both should be noble living, and that peace and justice between states was just as important as between individuals. But he did more than describe an ideal state; he described the education which such a state should give to its youth, the result of which should be not that a man should boast that his state was great and glorious, but that, being the citizen of such a state, in all that he did he should strive to be worthy of her.

Greek philosophy and science had begun in Ionia and then passed to Athens. To the thinkers of the fourth century B.C., the fall of Athens must have seemed a great disaster, but in reality it was of the utmost service to the world. The Greek spirit was one of those imperishable things that cannot die, and it was to go out from Athens and spread over a wider world than it had hitherto known. It spread first to Alexandria, where, in the Hellenistic Age, the next great group of philosophers and men of science were to be found.

IV. Greek Literature: the Historians

THE GREEKS WERE NOT THE first people in the world who wrote history, but they wrote it as it had never been written before, and some of the greatest history in the world is that which was written by Greeks. These writers were not content with merely narrating events that had taken place, they made what the word *history* means in Greek, an *inquiry*. They possessed the imagination not only to describe events and scenes vividly, but to feel as the people about whom they were writing felt, and to understand the passions that moved them at great crises of their history. They were the first historians who took the trouble to find out why nations and individuals acted as they did, and to sift their evidence, finding out what was true and what was false.

The oldest of the Greek historians was Herodotus, the "*Father of History*," an Ionian born in Halicarnassus in 484 B.C. He spent a good part of his life traveling, during which time he collected materials which he afterwards used in his history. He was a man who was intensely interested in everything he saw, a very credulous traveler, for he seems to have believed almost everything that was told him: old traditions, all kinds of miraculous occurrences, and many things that it is evident could never have happened. Though he undoubtedly believed a great deal that was not true, he did not swallow all that was told him, for after narrating some marvel he would say, "I am bound to report all that is said, but I am not bound to believe it."

Herodotus

Herodotus was a deeply religious man, and he lived before the disturbing days when men began to question the existence of the gods. To him history was a great drama, the plot of which was the triumph of the Greek over the Barbarian, which he saw as the will of the gods, and to him, as to all devout Greeks of his day, all wrong-doing, all disobedience to the will of the gods brought its own punishment, its retribution—what the Greeks called its Nemesis.

As a storyteller, Herodotus is unrivaled. He wrote his history in order that "the great and wonderful deeds done by the Greeks and Persians should not lack renown," and the earlier books which give an account of all he had learned in his travels in the East, of Egypt and Babylonia, of Lydia and Persia, lead up to the great climax, the invasion of Greece by the Persians. In the pages of Herodotus we live again, as we live nowhere else, through all the excitement and thrill of the days when Greece fought the Barbarian and drove him out of the land.

Thucydides

The greatest of the Greek historians was Thucydides, great not only among the Greek writers, but among the historians of the world. He was born about 471 B.C., and he wrote the history of the Peloponnesian War. Thucydides was an Athenian, a man of wealth and good position, and was one of the few who had the plague and recovered from it. As the war went on, he was anxious to fight and help bring it to a victorious close, but a far greater career was in store for him. He was elected a general and sent at the head of an army to relieve Amphipolis and prevent its surrender to the Spartans. But he arrived too late, the city had been taken, and he was exiled in consequence. To this exile we owe his history.

Thucydides is one of the most accurate and impartial of historians. He was filled with an abiding love for Athens, but, unlike some Athenians, he felt no bitterness towards her for exiling him. The only remark he made about his banishment was that it gave him the opportunity to write his history. He was scrupulously fair to both sides, and he told us himself of the care he took to be accurate and to accept nothing on the evidence of mere tradition.

> Men do not discriminate, [he said], and are too ready to receive ancient traditions about their own as well as about other countries; and so little trouble do they take in the search after truth; so readily do they accept whatever comes first to hand. Of the events of the war I have not ventured to speak from any chance information, nor according to any notion of my own; I have described nothing but what I either saw myself, or learned from others of whom I made the most careful and particular inquiry. The task was a laborious one, because eye-witnesses of the same occurrences gave different accounts of them, as they remembered or were interested in the actions of one side or the other. If he who desires to have before his eyes a true picture of the events which have happened, and of the like events which may be expected to happen hereafter in the order of human things, shall pronounce what I have written to be useful, then I shall be satisfied. My history is an everlasting possession, not a prize composition which is heard and forgotten.[18]

[18] Thucydides, I.

Unlike Herodotus, Thucydides did not trace events to the will of the gods, but he held that the deeds of men and the use or misuse they made of their opportunities were responsible for them. He never moralizes, but in the clear and reasoned order in which he narrates events, the story is carried down from the beginning to its inevitable conclusion.

Thucydides has preserved for all time the memory of what Athens was in her greatest days, and the ideals of one of her great statesmen. But the claim of his book to be an "everlasting possession" is justified not because of the actual history he recorded, but because of the critical and scientific way in which he made his inquiry, which has become a model for all later historians.

Thucydides left the story of the Peloponnesian War unfinished; he never even finished the last sentence. The story was completed by Xenophon. Xenophon was not a great historian like his predecessors, but he has left us valuable information about the later events of the war in the *Hellenica*, the romantic tale of adventure which tells how a band of ten thousand Greeks found their way home from the heart of Mesopotamia[19], and the *Economist*, a delightful picture of a Greek household.[20]

There is one other Greek writer who, though he did not write history, has left us much valuable historical information. This was Plutarch (A.D. 46-120), who lived long after the great days of Greece had passed. He was a Greek from Boeotia, a well-educated man who had many friends with whom he was wont to discuss all kinds of subjects: philosophy, history, literature, or politics, and he was also a writer. The great work for which his name is remembered is the *Parallel Lives of the Greeks and Romans*. These are the biographies, arranged in pairs, of a Greek and a Roman, each pair followed by a

[19] See Chapter XVI, v, *The March of the Ten Thousand.*

[20] See Chapter XII, ii, *The Athenian Lady.*

comparison between the two. Plutarch never imagined that he was writing history, and in these *Lives* there is no wide view over a whole period, but in each life there is a vivid picture of a personality and a character. Plutarch knew how to choose picturesque details and anecdotes, and he was attracted by simple, upright, honorable, patriotic characters, which makes his book a storehouse of stories about such men. Few biographies in the world have been read so widely or have achieved such immortality as have the *Lives* of Plutarch, and probably none have done more to encourage manliness and the spirit of good sportsmanship.

V. Greek Literature: the Dramatists

A CLASSIC IS A WORK of art or of literature that never dies, a book that will be read forever, no matter when or by whom it was written. We have said that when the history of a nation is recorded in language we call it literature, but by such literature is meant not only historical writing, but whatever takes the form of letters. The history of a nation is an inquiry into how that nation *thinks* as well as into what it *does*, and its philosophers, historians, and dramatists are as much a part of its history as its statesmen and men of action. The great Greek dramatists were men living the life of their time, and it was a time when stirring things were happening. The dramas of Aeschylus, Sophocles, and Euripides were written during the period which began with the repulse of the Persians, which included the golden days of Pericles, and which saw the tragic changes which came over Athens during the long-drawn-out misery of the Peloponnesian War.

Now the great Greek dramas are among the classics of the world. There are various reasons for this, but one, and not the least, is that they are the outward expression of that love of beauty and of self-control that is one of the priceless gifts of Greece to the world. To the Greek, beauty meant perfection in all that he did, the association of beautiful words and forms with beautiful deeds and scenes. To him *beauty* was the same as *goodness*, and ugliness was evil. And beauty meant self-control, the absence of all excess and exaggeration. The Greek dramatists had no models to guide them, yet they produced works that almost perfectly attained this Greek ideal of Beauty.

The oldest of these dramatists was Aeschylus. He took an active part in the Persian Wars, and he thought this of so much greater importance than any literary success he had achieved that his epitaph, said to have been written by himself, saying nothing about his poetry, states only that he fought the Persians. His name and birthplace were inscribed and then that "the grove of Marathon can bear witness to his good soldierhood, and the long-haired Mede who felt it." One of the few Greek plays of which the plot was not taken from ancient Greek legend was the *Persians* of Aeschylus, interesting because it is the first historical play written by a poet who took part himself in the events of which it tells.

The greatest work of Aeschylus was a Trilogy (i.e., three consecutive plays bearing on the same subject): the *Agamemnon*, the greatest of all his plays; the *Libation-Bearers*, and the *Furies*. These tell the tale, so often told in the Greek drama, of the murder by his wife of Agamemnon on his return from Troy, of Orestes who avenged his father's death, of the Furies who followed him as a result of his deed, and of how in the end he found release. These plays are haunted throughout by the belief that over certain families hangs a curse, that the sins of their fathers are visited on their children, and that from this punishment there is no escape. Aeschylus was filled with the realization of the power of the great unseen forces that move the world, but he believed that if on one side there were the Furies demanding blood for blood, on the other were Apollo and Athena, symbols of the self-control that could overcome the heritage of anger and of passion.

Sophocles lived through the great years of Athens. Only sixteen years old when the battle of Salamis was fought, he must have been filled with all the enthusiasm of youth over the victory. It was said of Sophocles that he had "such charm of character that he was loved by everybody wherever he went." Life seems to have been happy and prosperous for him from the beginning. He won the first prize at the festival with his first play, and when he was only twenty-eight he won a prize over Aeschylus, who was then nearly sixty.

The greatest plays of Sophocles are those which tell of the ancient legends of Thebes: of Oedipus as King, and then as Outcast, and of *Antigone,* who in one play—*Oedipus at Colonus*—goes forth with her exiled father, and in another, the great play that bears her name, was faced with the terrible problem of having to break either the laws of God or those of the state, and of deciding which she would do. By all who understand the real greatness of the Greek drama, Sophocles is accounted the greatest of the dramatists. He represents in literature the spirit that Athena Parthenos represented on the Acropolis: a spirit of reverence, of the serenity that comes when the conflict is over and the victory won, and of triumphant belief in all that is good and beautiful and true.

Very different from either Aeschylus or Sophocles was Euripides. According to tradition, he was born in the island of Salamis on the very day of the battle. As he grew up, he became a friend of Socrates, but for the most part he lived a solitary life, not very much liked, and taking as little part in public life as he could. He was essentially a student, and was one of the first Athenians to collect a library. Euripides lived in Athens during the Peloponnesian War, a period of restless questioning, of breaking away from old traditions and beliefs, of lowering of the old ideals. The war had brought a new spirit and Euripides represented it. He criticized customs and beliefs which he thought were unworthy of the best spirit in Athens, he questioned belief in the gods, and in one great play, the *Trojan Women*, he showed the misery brought by war. He was the first poet to strip war of its glamor and to show it as it affected the conquered. In the *Electra* and in *Iphigenia in Tauris*, Euripides deals with the familiar tragedy of Orestes, pursued by the Furies after the murder of his mother, and in the *Alcestis* he tells the old tale of how a noble woman was willing to sacrifice her life for that of a selfish husband, and of how she was brought back from the gates of Hades by Heracles.

The strength of Euripides lies in his wonderful portrayal of character. He judges his characters by the standards of the men and women of his own day and not by those of the gods and heroes, and he is a merciless critic. This makes his dramas most extraordinarily vivid and human, but it also accounts for some of the criticism and dislike he met with in his own day.

Aristophanes wrote comedies. His plays are based on the daily life of his time, and to understand them one must know what were the political questions of his day, who were the leaders, who were the writers, the gossip of the Agora and the barber's shop, and the likes and dislikes of the men amongst whom he lived. But to those who know enough of these things to follow his allusions, the plays of Aristophanes are full of interest, and we learn a great deal about life in Athens from them.

Aristophanes was younger than Euripides, but, unlike the older man, he was very conservative, and he disliked the new ways by which the Sophists were teaching the youths, for he believed that the new methods would make them irreverent, good at idle talk but at nothing else, shallow, and effeminate. He constantly compared the young men of his own day with those of the generation that had fought at Marathon, and in comparing them he found them wanting, for to him the heroes of the age of Marathon represented all that was best in Athenian manhood.

VI. Greek Art

The Greeks loved Beauty, especially the Athenians of the fifth century B.C., but they did not spend all their time in a conscious search for it. They were very busy about and interested in a great many other things: the administration of the city, relations with other states, often fighting, trading and traveling, building ships, and sending out colonies. We have already seen what the Greeks meant by Beauty, and an appreciation of it touched all these things.

Now a great mistake has been made in modern times, in that art has too often been looked upon as a luxury, as something that the rich can have but not the poor, something that has not very much to do with practical everyday life. But to believe that is to misunderstand altogether what art is, for art is something that is *done,* not something that is merely *looked at*. All men have within them a vision of what kind of world they would make, if it was left to them to order, and in its widest meaning, art is the outward and concrete expression of that vision. To confine art to architecture, sculpture, and painting is to rob it of half its meaning. The forms of art are as many and varied as are the interests of everyday life, and this belief is one of the great gifts of Greece to the world. It was not given to every Greek to be a great artist. Not everyone could be an Aeschylus and write the *Agamemnon,* a Sophocles and write the *Antigone,* a Pheidias and create the *Parthenon,* or a Praxiteles and model the *Hermes,* but everyone could work in the spirit of which these great works are the supreme examples.

The history of a nation is an inquiry into how that nation expresses itself in stone and marble, as well as into what it thinks and does; and its architects, artists, and sculptors stand beside its historians, philosophers, dramatists, and statesmen as the men who have made its history.

In its narrower, modern sense, art is the outward sign of the spirit of a nation as it is expressed in painting and in stone and marble. Except for the vase paintings, Greek painting has almost entirely disappeared, but the achievements of the Greeks in architecture and sculpture are among the greatest that the world has ever seen. Something has already been said about Greek architecture; the same spirit expressed itself in Greek sculpture. To know the Greeks and the real worth of what they have given to the world, it is not enough to read *about* them; one must learn to know them first-hand. To do that one must read what they wrote (if not in Greek, then in translations), and look at what they built and at their sculpture (if not at the originals, then by means of casts and photographs), and when one does that, one begins to know a little of what the spirit was that produced such things. The Greeks considered that the human form was the most fitting subject for representation in sculpture, yet they were not great portrait makers; that was left for a later race to achieve. What they aimed at doing was to give outward expression to those qualities of the mind and spirit which they, as a people, prized so highly: Beauty, Self-control, Harmony, Restraint. The greatest Greek sculpture was, as it were, the answer, wrought in marble, to the prayer of Socrates to Pan: "Beloved Pan, and all ye other gods who haunt this place, give me beauty in the inward soul; and may the outward and the inward man be at one."

The Greeks lived at a time when so much was being done for the first time, and to all their art they brought a spirit of youth and of joy in creation, yet also a spirit of patience in achieving results, for they were never in a hurry, and they knew that there were no shortcuts to the perfection which was to them so important a part of beauty. Their statues are very idealistic, but their idealism was practical, and though, as we know, they did not always fulfil their ideals, they knew that fulfillment was possible. Though the sculpture of the Greeks represented man, not as he always was, but as they believed he might be, did he but follow where his best instincts led, it did sometimes result in something that to them was not only an ideal, but something so real and lifelike that they could say of a sculptured figure of a Sleeping Ariadne:

> Strangers, touch not the marble Ariadne, lest she even start up on the quest of Theseus.[21]

[21] Author unknown: From *Select Epigrams from the Greek Anthology*, translated by J. W. Mackail.

CHAPTER 23

THE HELLENISTIC AGE

I. The Extent of Greek Influence

ALEXANDER WAS A GREAT CONQUEROR and he won for himself a mighty empire. But that empire did not last, for his successors were unable to hold it together. It would almost seem as if he had crowded into his short reign of barely thirteen years hero-deeds and marvelous exploits, which, however much they may have done to enrich tradition and to appeal to the imagination, were hardly of any great permanent value. Alexander, however, did more than create a passing empire; he did more than any other one man to spread the knowledge of Greek civilization over the world. Wherever he passed with his conquering army, he founded cities where he established colonies of Greeks: men who spoke the Greek tongue, worshipped the Greek gods, read and loved Greek literature, and lived according to Greek ideals. Such cities were founded in Egypt, in Asia Minor, in Syria, in Babylonia, in Persia, and even in the distant lands until then unknown, further to the mysterious East.

But Alexander did yet more to spread Greek civilization than by the founding of cities. All the great ports of the Eastern Mediterranean were in his hands, which meant that Greek merchants were established there, and that the whole commerce of that region was in the hands of Greeks.

The history of Greek civilization may be divided into two periods. The first lasted until the days of Alexander; it included the early experiments made by Greek states in the art of governing themselves, the repulse of the Barbarian, the great days of Athens, the disastrous Peloponnesian War. Through all this period Greece was learning how to do things. She was in the making and was creating what was to live as long as men should love what was great, but she was living for herself. This period is called the *Hellenic Period*.

Beginning with Alexander, Greek civilization stepped out into a new age. Greece was no longer living for herself, she was living for the world. Greek civilization had been far-flung over Asia; the Barbarian was adopting Greek customs, Greece was the teacher of the world in science, in art, and in all that was meant by civilized living. This period lasted from the time of Alexander until Greece became part of the Roman Empire in 146 B.C., and is known as the *Hellenistic Age*. The center of Greek civilization was now no longer in Athens, but in Alexandria, the city in Egypt founded by Alexander, and which from its situation was the natural link between the East and the West.

II. Alexandria

ALEXANDRIA HAD NOT been founded for very many years before she was the rival of Carthage—that powerful commercial city founded by Phoenicia, mistress of the Mediterranean—and she held undisputed sway in the Eastern Mediterranean, known as the Levant. From that time to the present day, Alexandria has been the door through which the commerce of the East and the West has passed.

In the Hellenistic Age, Alexandria developed into a very beautiful city. Temples and all kinds of public buildings, great palaces, gardens, docks, and warehouses were built. At the entrance to the harbor stood a great lighthouse, called the Pharos, from the island on which it stood, and which was considered so great a marvel that it was numbered among the Seven Wonders of the ancient World.

This period was in many ways like a more modern one. Greek civilization had stepped out into a new world. The conquering armies of Alexander, going out to the ends of the earth, had made communication possible between places that had hitherto hardly known of each other's existence. Science had made such remarkable strides that man's power over nature had been enormously increased, and the increase of scientific knowledge was affecting the old religious beliefs in the gods. Nothing seemed to be quite the same as it had hitherto been, and then, as at all such times, the minds of men were affected by the changes. Some became more conservative than before and wanted nothing changed because to them the old was necessarily the best, and there was only evil in what was new. Others went to the other extreme and wanted everything changed, because to them the new must necessarily be better than the old. But quietly in between these two extremes were the thinkers, those who were keeping alive that Greek spirit which knew that the vision of the whole truth had not yet been given to any man, and that the way to progress was not by destroying the old, but by building upon it in order to go on from a firm foundation to a fuller knowledge of the truth. Not to Thales, Socrates, nor to Aristotle, nor yet to the men of the twentieth century has the complete vision of the truth of all things been vouchsafed, but to those who follow the quest in the spirit of the Greeks of old is granted to add a little to the progress of human knowledge.

It was in the Museum at Alexandria that the thinkers worked. This Museum was founded by Ptolemy Soter, one of the rulers of Egypt after the break-up of Alexander's empire, and very much developed by his son, Ptolemy Philadelphus. This Museum, the Temple of the Muses, was what today would be called a university. It had lecture halls where mathematicians, astronomers, poets, and philosophers taught; courts and porches where men walked and talked; houses where the men of learning lived. Above all, it had a library, which contained several thousand books. This library was cataloged by Callimachus, the first librarian of whom there is any record, and there were a hundred and twenty books of his catalog. *Book*, however, is the wrong word to use for the collection in the Alexandrian Library, for there were no *books* then, as we know them. Rolls took the place of books, and Callimachus soon found that the big rolls were very inconvenient. It is said that he complained that "a big book is a big nuisance," and that it was when he was librarian that the plan of dividing the large rolls into a number of smaller ones was thought of. These were easier to handle, but one work required a great many of the smaller rolls—thirty-six were required for the *Iliad* and the *Odyssey*.

As the fame of the library spread, students from all over the Greek world came to Alexandria, and there was a great demand for additional copies of the works in the library. For more than three centuries, Alexandria was the great book-producing mart in the world. The Museum possessed a good collection of the best known copies of the works of the classic writers, and Ptolemy Philadelphus very much enlarged this collection. He bought every copy of all existing Greek works he could, and, as he paid very high prices for them, there was a steady flow of books to Alexandria from all over the civilized world. It is said that he refused to send food to the Athenians at a time of famine unless they agreed to give him certain copies they still possessed of the works of Aeschylus, Sophocles, and Euripides. He paid liberally for them, not only in the promised shipment of corn, but also in silver.

As more and more copies of the classic writers were wanted, a regular publishing trade arose in Alexandria. Callimachus was not only the librarian of the library, but a publisher of the works of classic writers. Large numbers of copyists were employed whose business it was to make careful and accurate copies of the works required. This accounts for the fact that in certain works of ancient literature it is sometimes difficult to know what really is the original form of certain lines or passages, because in spite of their care, the copyists made mistakes, and unfortunately many original copies of the classics were lost in the great fire which destroyed the library in the last century B.C. The Alexandrian school of copyists was a very famous one, and Alexandrian Editions of the classics were considered the very best to be had.

III. Science in the Hellenistic Age

GREEK SCIENCE HAD BEEN born in Ionia, and during the Hellenic Period of Greek civilization, it had gone hand in hand with philosophy. The earliest days of pure science came in the Hellenistic Age, and its home was in Alexandria. Among the many names of men of this time who contributed something of value to science, there are two which must be remembered—those of Euclid and Archimedes.

Euclid lived in Alexandria. He was a mathematician and wrote a great work on geometry. No scientific work in the world has lived in quite the same way as has this book of Euclid, for since the time that Euclid's *Elements* was written, it was used as a school textbook without interruption until a very few years ago.

Archimedes was probably the greatest of the Greek scientific thinkers of the third century B.C. He did not live in Alexandria; he was a native of Syracuse in Sicily, but he was in close touch with all the scientific work that was being done there. He was a great scientific investigator, the inventor of many practical and ingenious devices, and discovered the principle of moving heavy objects by means of pulleys and levers. An extraordinarily large ship was made for the king of Syracuse, a ship of marvel to that age. It contained a gymnasium, gardens of most wonderful beauty and full of rich plants, a temple to Aphrodite, a drawing room with its walls and doors of boxwood, having a bookcase in it, a bathroom with three brazen vessels for holding hot water, and a fish pond. All the furnishings were of the most exquisite craftsmanship, and all the rooms had floors of mosaic, in which the whole story of the *Iliad* was depicted in a most marvelous manner. There were doors of ivory, beautiful couches, and it was full of pictures, statues, goblets, and vases of every form and shape imaginable. But the ship was so large that no one could move it. Archimedes, however, we are told, launched it by himself with the aid of only a few people. For, having prepared a *helix* (probably some mechanical contrivance with pulleys), he drew this vessel, enormous as it was, down to the sea. And it was said that Archimedes was the first person who ever invented this helix.[1]

Archimedes believed it possible to move greater objects even than the ship, and he is said to have boasted, "Give me a place to stand on, and I will move the earth."

This great inventor did other things which struck the imagination of the men among whom he lived, for of some of them they had never seen the like before. During the siege of Syracuse by the Romans in 212 B.C., Archimedes invented marvelous war engines: strange grappling hooks which, it was said, could seize an enemy's ship and overturn it in the sea; and he showed the Syracusans how to set up a water pump in their ships, so that should water get into the hold, it could be pumped out and the ship saved from sinking. He is also said to have made some arrangement of mirrors and burning glass by means of which the Roman ships were set on fire. But in spite of all these inventions, the Romans took the city, and Archimedes was killed. He had been found by a Roman

[1] From *Athenaeus.*

soldier, sitting in his house and paying no heed to any danger, but intent on drawing mathematical diagrams on the ground. Looking up and seeing the enemy, all he had said was, "Stand away, fellow, from my diagram." The soldier, not knowing who he was, killed him.

IV. The End of Greek Independence and the Power From the West

It is said that on his deathbed, Alexander bequeathed his empire "to the strongest," but there was no one general able enough or strong enough to succeed him, and for about fifty years after his death, his empire was torn by strife and bloodshed. At last some kind of peace and order was restored, but the one great empire of Alexander had disappeared, and the civilized world was broken up into a number of independent states, of which the most important were the kingdoms of Syria, Egypt, and Macedonia. During the long wars which had preceded this settlement, many battles had been fought on Greek soil. The Greeks were not strong enough to prevent this, and neither were they able to maintain their independence when Macedonia became a kingdom. She was too powerful and strong a neighbor, and Greece fell under her rule. Tyrants were established in the Greek cities, a deep humiliation to the freedom-loving Greeks.

But once more the old Greek spirit flared up and the tyrants were driven out. From time to time in the history of Greece, states had joined together in various leagues and alliances, but the inability of the Greeks to combine for long, even when their very life demanded it, had prevented such leagues from lasting any great length of time. But in 281 B.C., when once again the independence of Greece was threatened, one of these old leagues was revived, the Achaean League. It lasted for nearly a century and is of the greatest interest to modern times, for until the union of the American states, about two thousand years later, there was nothing in the history of the world like it again.

The Achaean League was not an alliance, but a real federation of states, with one central government. Each separate state kept its own sovereign rights over all its domestic affairs, but questions of war and peace, the support of the army, and all relations with foreign states were controlled by the federal government. It was the only experiment in ancient times of real federal government.

The head of the League was called the general, and it was under the general Aratus that it became very powerful. Almost all the more important of the Greek states entered the League, with the exception of Athens and Sparta. Neither by persuasion, nor by force, unless she might be recognized as head of the League, would Sparta consent to become a member, and so powerful was she in the Peloponnesus that Aratus begged the aid of Macedonia to subdue her. Sparta was conquered, but Macedonia regained her supremacy in Greece, and the power of the Achaean League was broken.

The old Greece of history no longer existed. Greek civilization had spread over the Mediterranean world, but the free and independent city-state had disappeared, and nothing lasting had taken its place. Alexander himself, and still more his successors, had failed to create an empire which gave to those who belonged to it any sense of citizenship in it. The Hellenistic world was a Greek civilization, but it failed to arouse in men of Greek birth that patriotism which the city-state had inspired.

The creation of a world state of which men were to be proud to call themselves citizens, and for which they would gladly die, was to be the work of another great power, which, even as the old Greece was passing, was growing strong in the West. Rome was steadily conquering the civilized world. Already she ruled over Italy and was extending her power over the Eastern Mediterranean. She conquered Macedonia, and one by one the old free states of Greece and those of the Achaean League lost their independence, until in 146 B.C., Corinth, rich, commercial, gay Corinth, was taken by Rome, and Greece became a Roman province. The citizens of this great state, which was to include not only Greece and the Levant, but the whole Mediterranean and lands far beyond its shores, were to be proud of the name of Roman. Yet Rome, destined to be the Mistress of the World, and in political power an empire, succeeding where Greece had failed, owed all that was most worthwhile in the things of the higher intellectual life of the mind to Greece. The Greek spirit was never to die.